Reconstructing Religious, Spiritual and Moral Education

Clive Erricker and Jane Erricker

Foreword by Jack Priestley

ROUTLEDGE/FALMER
Taylor & Francis Group

First published 2000 by RoutledgeFalmer
11 New Fetter Lane, London EC4P 4EE

Simultaneously published in the USA and Canada
by RoutledgeFalmer
29 West 35th Street, New York, NY 10001

RoutledgeFalmer is an imprint of the Taylor & Francis Group

Typeset in Goudy by
Keyword Publishing Services Ltd
Printed and bound in Great Britain by
TJ International Ltd, Padstow, Cornwall

British Library Cataloguing in Publication Data
A catalogue record for this book is available from the
British Library

Library of Congress Cataloging in Publication Data
Erricker, Clive.
   Reconstructing religious, spiritual and moral education / Clive Erricker
   and Jane Erricker.
      p. cm.
   Includes bibliographical references and index.
      1. Religious education. 2. Moral education. I. Erricker, Jane, 1948– II.
      Title.

BL42.E75 2000   00-022587
291.7'5—dc21

ISBN 0-415-18946-2—ISBN 0-415-18947-0 (pbk.)

Contents

List of figures   vii
Foreword   viii
Acknowledgements   xii
Introduction   xiii

1 True stories and other dreams   1
   CLIVE ERRICKER

SECTION I
Reconstructing the character and purposes of religious and spiritual education

2 A critical review of religious education   15
   CLIVE ERRICKER

3 A critical review of spiritual education   36
   CLIVE ERRICKER

4 Relativism, postmodernism and the spirit of educational enquiry   59
   CLIVE ERRICKER

SECTION II
Narrative, morality and community

5 Moral education as relationship in community   81
   JANE ERRICKER

6 Narrative constructions towards community   107
   JANE AND CLIVE ERRICKER

SECTION III
Pedagogy: putting theory into practice

 7 Principles of pedagogical practice   135
    CLIVE AND JANE ERRICKER

 8 Concept mapping: a starting point for narration   141
    JANE ERRICKER

 9 Developing emotional literacy   150
    JANE ERRICKER

10 Children's stories and responses   163
    JANE AND CLIVE ERRICKER

11 Reading pictures and telling stories   173
    CLIVE ERRICKER

12 Enactive storytelling   181
    CLIVE ERRICKER

    Postscript   189

    References   190
    Bibliography   199
    Index   206

Figures

1 Photosynthesis concept map   143

2 Earth and space concept map 1   144

3 Earth and space concept map 2   145

4 Concept map: myself and God   146

5 Adult concept map on loss 1   147

6 Adult concept map on loss 2   148

7 Italian soldier, Nicosia, 1943   174

8 The face of Christ (*detail*)   177

9 The raising of Lazarus   178

Foreword

It is a great privilege to be invited to write a Foreword to this book. In the first place it is an important book and I am pleased to be associated with it. Secondly it is also an erudite and well written book. Thirdly, its pedagogy is one that I have shared over many years.

As a publication it is what it proclaims. As I read it, I was reminded of Seamus Heaney's wonderful statement concerning the former Poet Laureate Ted Hughes's sense of the world, namely that he 'constantly beheld, behind the business of the usual, a sacred drama being enacted'. It links profound theory with basic classroom practice and the mystical with the ordinary but it is never patronising. There is never anything less than full respect for the reader as a person. Unlike all too many educational textbooks there is a genuine exploration of great ideas but these are never allowed to become mere abstractions. Again and again they are earthed in the lives of ordinary people, especially children. It is a very human book, not another list of bullet points churned out by curriculum manufacturers sitting in government offices remote from the classroom.

But the task of the writer of any *Foreword* is not to compose a eulogy so much as to attempt to set the work in the context to which it belongs.

It is exactly one hundred years since William James delivered his Gifford Lectures which were to be published in 1902 as *The Varieties of Religious Experience*. The book has remained in print right through the twentieth century. In his Introduction to the 1960 edition Arthur Nock wrote,

> His interest was in personal religion, acts and experiences of individual men (*sic*) in their solitude, so far as they apprehended themselves to stand in relation to whatever they may consider divine.
>
> (James 1982: 15)

If we add 'women, boys and girls' this is exactly what Clive and Jane Erricker are about.

But this does not mean a soft or soggy approach to children or to knowledge with the Errickers, any more than it did with James. He was one of the most mild mannered of scholars but one thing above all could be guaranteed to raise his blood pressure and his venom. That was the application of detached systematic analysis to this basic human sensitivity. Towards the end of that same book he commented, 'We must, I think, bid a definite goodbye to systematic theology' (James 1982:430). The parting is taking somewhat longer than he may have anticipated. These authors, however, are attempting to push the process along, certainly as far as schools and schooling are concerned; although perhaps more mildly than James himself, who regarded systematic theologians as the soulmates of taxidermists, killing off the natural in order to stuff its inanimate form to preserve as museum pieces.

> When I was a boy I used to think that closet naturalists must be the vilest type of wretch under the sun. But surely the systematic theologians are the closet naturalists of the deity. . . . What is their deduction of metaphysical attributes but a shuffling and matching of pedantic dictionary adjectives aloof from morals, aloof from human needs, something that might be worked out from the word, 'God' by one of those logical machines of wood and brass which recent ingenuity has contrived. . . . Verbality has stepped into the place of vision, professionalism into that of life.
>
> (James 1982:428)

If the Errickers question the continued existence of RE as a discrete subject in the curriculum, this is not because it is deemed to be worthless as some secularists would have it, but rather because its potential is too precious in the lives and inner experiences of the children with whom they work for it to be seen as detached from their human needs and turned into a cheap and meaningless abstraction. As it stands it has all the appearance of being zoned off from real life like the spiritual in the Millennium Dome. Theologians are as much responsible for that state of affairs as any number of secularists.

The answer lies in narrative and biography through the relating of human experience. That sounds trite. But it was William James' British successor at Harvard, Alfred Whitehead who graphically pointed out that, durable as some of them have proved over thousands of years, all religions have their origins in the narrating of an inner experience of a lone individual in such a way that it resonated with the lives of others. That was as true of Gautama Buddha sitting under his tree, as it was of the Prophet in the cave or of the lonely Man on the cross or in the wilderness. It has also been true of lesser movements within the great religions as, for example, when John Wesley founded Methodism on the basis of having 'his heart strangely warmed in Aldersgate Street'.

Religion IS narrative; it is theology that has become systematic in keeping with the culture of our age, which holds propositional language to be superior to narrative at all times. To look for the roots of the Errickers' concerns we go back then, not one century but at least two, to the Enlightenment with the onset of modernity. This book can surely be placed in the growing post-modern reaction to systems that demand first definition, then analysis and finally control.

In education it is the word 'spiritual'-which has come to the fore in that reaction. There is a clamouring for definition all around us but the traditional symbols demonstrate clearly why, as a matter of principle, definition is a nonsense. It would be to bottle the wind, to extinguish the fire and to damn the flowing stream. To define the spiritual is to define John Cleese's parrot, to make it an ex-parrot in the process, to play the taxidermist all over again.

A hundred years before William James, the Danish writer Soren Kierkegaard saw the dangers all too clearly during the birth pangs of the Enlightenment. His thoughts on curriculum are hardly known but he had some very pertinent thoughts on the appropriateness of method to subject. He was not anti-science but against human beings being treated as if their personal, social, moral, spiritual and religious experiences were somehow detached, external, objective, abstract, scientific phenomena, which had to be taught. He prophesied what would happen if this occurred. We would, he argued, turn our very selves into monstrous abstractions. We should cease to speak of people and talk of 'humanity' or 'the public' and its 'wretched opinion'. Mercifully, considering his temperament, he never contemplated 'human resources'.

This, for me, is the pedigree of Clive and Jane Erricker's book. It belongs to the long thin line of a minority protest, which has gone on down at least two centuries. The theoretical half of the book documents much of that story. The second half of the book shows, through their own practical research, just how much of the inner life of our own generation of children remains untouched by the monstrous abstractions of a scientific culture. But it also shows how education gives no help to them in living out their personal lives because it simply does not resonate with experience when it is 'delivered' as abstract knowledge. The impoverishment of English education in modern times is to be seen not so much in its content as in its verbs. There seems to be only teaching and learning. Imagining, creating, appreciating, enjoying are hard or impossible to find in the barren material of the Teacher Training Agency. But the real contribution of the Errickers is the emphasis they place on listening.

By that I mean listening to children before we can expect them to listen to us. God is not dead; he is alive in many of their stories. Morality is not an unknown concept: it is at the heart of their personal stories before any crude politicians come wading in with pronouncements about telling them the difference between right and wrong. Children, including young children, are perfectly capable of being active participants in their own social and spiritual education. It would be nice to think that all these concerns were about to be brought together under the umbrella concept of citizenship but the omens are not good.

Clive and Jane Erricker will no doubt be dismissed in some quarters for being too child centred, a phrase that has been turned into a negative by the Chief Inspector and others who have given no thought to its context. It was, in fact, George Archibald, the American founder of Westhill College, Birmingham, who introduced the term into British educational practice in the first decade of the last century but the context was all important. It had nothing to do with attitudes to learning multiplication tables or spelling. The context was religious and values education. It was an anti-indoctrinatory measure, a willingness to sit alongside children, to listen to them and to share stories with them. It worked wonderfully well. Westhill College is no more. But as one of its nine past Principals I am delighted that its vision is reborn in the pages of this book.

Jack Priestley

Acknowledgements

Thanks are due to various mentors, colleagues and partners in research. To Cathy Ota, our project colleague without whose constant supporting work this book could not have been written. To the children, teachers and schools we have worked with. To those from whom we have benefited in the academic world, especially Ninian Smart, John Rankin, W. Owen Cole, Bob Jackson, Jack Priestley, Ruth Mantin, Joyce Goodman and Joyce Bellous. To our own children Katy, Sam and Polly (in chronological order). To the Calouste Gulbenkian Foundation, University College Chichester and King Alfred's College Winchester, who have funded our work; and especially to Simon Richey who has given warm support at Calouste Gulbenkian.

Incorporated in this book are ideas and revised extracts from our own conference papers, journal articles and contributions to collected works, in particular the commentary on Nicholas Tate's speech in Erricker, 'Spiritual Confusion: a critique of current educational provision in England and Wales', *International Journal of Children's Spirituality*, 3(1), in Chapter 3; 'Spirituality and The Market Place of Education', *Panorama: International Journal of Comparative Education and Values*, 10(2), in Chapter 4 (the authors wish to thank the publishers of these two journals for permission to reprint extracts from their articles); 'Shall We Dance? Authority, Representation and Voice: the place of spirituality in religious education', *Religious Education* (forthcoming); Michael Grimmitt (ed.), *Pedagogies of Religious Education*, McCrimmon (forthcoming) and Andrew Wright (ed.), *Learning to Teach Religious Education in the Secondary School*, Routledge (2000), in Chapter 12; Ron Best (ed.), *Perspectives on SMSC*, Cassell (forthcoming); and 'Teachers Developing Spiritual and Moral Education', *Teacher Development* (forthcoming), in Chapter 12.

Introduction

Ways of reading this book

The most complete and systematic way of assimilating the argument presented is by reading cover to cover. However we are aware that practising teachers have little time to accommodate new theory and often feel that it requires conversance with an academic world that their professional duties, and other duties and responsibilities in their lives, have relegated to a past life. Even students immersed in their professional training often feel this way, given the current emphasis placed on training rather than education. The alternative way of reading this work is to acquaint yourself with this introductory chapter, which sets out the context and purpose, then move on to section three, which engages with principles and practices involved in teaching and learning. If this whets your appetite for the theory and politics that underpin the approach read it right through.

Reasons for writing this book

This book follows an earlier study, *The Education of the Whole Child* (Erricker *et al.* 1997), which was a report on the Children and Worldviews Project's research between 1993 and 1996. This research convinced us of the need to challenge current educational policy on the basis of numerous interviews with children in schools in southern England. During that research children often presented us with issues of deep emotional, existential and social complexity related to the circumstances of their own lives. Such issues were rarely addressed within their schooling and certainly not within curriculum study. Not only did this mean that the issues that mattered to them received no educational attention, but it became clear that their capacity to deal with these matters never came to light. In other words there was often a lack of awareness of the real achievements of the child because assessment occurred only in relation to curriculum attainment. Furthermore it became apparent that teachers, more often than not, lacked the time or the training to engage with children on this emotional level. However if this was not the raw material of spiritual and moral education it was hard to see what was. It convinced us of the need to challenge the philosophical, by which we mean rationalist, assumptions upon which our educational system is based, as well as the policy making that ensues from that base and two other shaping influences:

the economic purposes that underpin our education system; and, in terms of the scope of this study, the current approaches to religious and moral education. This work is the product of that aim.

Our aim is not to undermine the potential of religious and moral education but to put that potential to better use. Neither subject, at present, is seen as having significant importance within the curriculum. The latter is not even given curriculum time in England and Wales. Yet along with what is presently known as personal and social education or PSHE, they represent the obvious ways of attending to the development of young people beyond the cognitive domain. In other words they have the potential to help persons develop and grow, rather than just address knowledge and skills related to a body of knowledge. The introduction of spiritual, moral, social and cultural development (SMSC) into the aims of the 1988 Education Reform Act would seem to elevate the importance of these aspects of educational provision. However this has not proved to be the case. Much rhetoric has ensued since the introduction of that Act, but little purposeful change. Why is this the case? The introduction of the word 'spiritual' as an area of prime educational concern would seem to presage a reconsideration of educational goals; but this has not been the case any more than the inclusion of moral, cultural and social education. If we ask why, we have to return to our educational history to understand. Such terms are always enclosed within a political, economic and religious history. Our educational history always serves the ends of these other histories.

Sadly, despite being stated as one of the main aims of education that underpins the curriculum, the outcome has been to ensure only that there is evidence of addressing SMSC within curriculum subjects. This has led to a superficial observance of the educational necessity to attend to these terms without any rigorous consideration of what they entail. At the same time educational policy making has pursued an interpretation of these terms within a monocultural and nationalistic framework, as will be argued in subsequent chapters of this study. Spiritual development has not been a priority in this design and there is some danger that the radical potential of this term, and the embarrassment it affords in relation to the construction of educational policy, will result in its consignment to the margins of what schools attend to. This study argues that spiritual education needs to be taken seriously, that it can radically reshape our educational vision and practice, and that it can have a significant effect on religious and moral education. Importantly, the notion of spiritual should not be consigned to the margins of educational concern because it has significant implications for political, emotional and values education. It can reshape our educational map and our understanding of how to address the development and growth of young people.

There is an ongoing debate on the definition and circumscription of the spiritual in education and, more specifically, in religious education. In this study we have grounded the term within a particular approach to education, which we call narrative. This draws on a philosophical basis derived from relativist and postmodern thinking.

1 True stories and other dreams

Clive Erricker

Knowledge and education

The academic world and the professional world of education have long been held under a particular spell. This spell has an ancient Greek ancestry reinforced by the truth claims of religion, and Christianity in particular; the Enlightenment and its progeny, the project of modernism. Despite the tensions inherent in this uneasy alliance of historical traditions the glue that binds them is the belief in rationalism: a belief that epistemological constructions are the means to human progress. A belief that such knowledge is not only possible but also necessary to our survival as individuals and civilisations in all respects, whether it be metaphysical or empirical. This spell has had tragic effects as unnoticed as the fall of Icarus in Bruegel's depiction. In education, the handmaiden of academic, economic and political life, it has resulted in a lack of concern for the nurture of both the imagination and the individual. It is as if we have decided to construct a giant jigsaw puzzle in which the pieces are already made, but we have to determine the place of the pieces.

As a result we have constructed an equivalent of Escher's drawings, working in two dimensions. Our house of cards cannot take account of our temporal constriction or mortality; thus it poses answers to questions beyond our horizon, as if there were a certainty concerning the existence and specifics of such a further existence. Alternatively, such an existence is denied. These opposing religious and secular visions have one thing in common, they both claim to be knowledge to be passed on to the next generation. The consequences of such a venture, in educational terms, are to ensure that young learners inherit the puzzle we have constructed as though it is a reality to be cognised. Their task is to re-piece it together, as we have, and recognise their learning and progress thereby. This is a mundane and inadequate task, but it ensures social cohesion, the normalisation of morality and the possibility of economic gain. In other words it suffices for rational behaviour. Another way of stating this situation is that it creates a notion of reality that, spurning the waywardness of imaginative possibilities by consigning them to the fictional, allows for a consensus on the factual or objective world, despite the 'fact' that, ironically, it is built on the products of human imagination. This irony is the tragedy that underpins, as its substantial foundation, the venture of education as an historical institution. Religious and moral education are regulated according to this premise, despite their capacity to undermine it. It is this capacity we wish to explore in this study.

Despite the history recounted above there has always been an undercurrent of alternative opinion and commitment. At times this has received greater attention and assumed more respectability than at present. But it is still there, despite the label of 'progressive education' often attributed to it. Mary Hilton (1997:5) optimistically, affirms its recognition. 'Learning . . . in human beings has become recognised as an active process closely organised around affect. We learn because we are emotional beings, and what we learn and how we learn is closely related to how and what we desire, fear, sense and feel.'

This affirmation of the affective aspect of being human, learning and making sense of living has received rough treatment at the hands of rationalism. Education, despite the rhetoric that stresses the importance of citizenship and values, is constructed on the basis of curriculum. Curriculum is constructed on the basis of bodies of knowledge. Knowledge is constructed on the basis of knowing. Knowing, as the creed of rationalism intones, is value free. In other words it is objective, not subjective. This rules out the affective, emotions and feelings, and has always posed a threat to the educational importance of religious and moral education. To legitimate themselves as subjects with some right to educational provision religious and moral education have had to assert their curriculum credentials. Thus they have had to affirm their rational nature. In doing so we might say they have undermined their potential to change the course of education, to undermine the rationalist project; but it is hard to swim against the tide. If it is not too much to claim, this book attempts to do just that, at the risk of being charged with betrayal by those who have done so much to defend the subjects and their importance.

Whilst the aims of the 1988 Education Reform Act declared the importance of addressing spiritual, moral, social and cultural education within the curriculum it has proved to be a lip service that has impacted little on curriculum design, and if anything has worked in favour of a monocultural nationalism. As such it has reiterated the myths of our perceived heritage and traditional values. In effect, rather than being an exploration of difference and debate, these terms are meant to confirm consensus and prevent a perceived tendency for moral fragmentation.

Rethinking the purposes of education

Culture, used in the sense in which it applies to the arts, can, in different ways, attempt to reshape changing lifestyles and economic and social conditions such that values serve the aspirations of community life, without recourse to monocultural myths. Ken Loach, the film director, identifies the purpose of his industry as follows:

> So what is the function of Cinema? 'Well, what is anything for? What is writing for, what is theatre for, what is music for? It's to enable you to have

a deeper sense of who you are and the place you live in and the people around you, and have a sense of them and solidarity with them, and understanding and warmth. Because those are the only things weve got'.

(Loach quoted in Hattenstone 1997:40)

What if we understood the purposes of education, and specifically religious and moral education, in the same way? Implicit in Loach's view is the idea of valuing each other and what we can bring to a sense of community. This is a way of working from the inside out, from bottom to top, from the individual out, a form of democracy. If we conceive of the needs of learners in the classroom in this way we might do things differently. We might start with what is relevant rather than what is required.

Despite the constrictions in place, this can happen to some degree. The following is an example from the classroom, in relation to religious education and my experience in teacher education.

As this book was being written I was telephoned by a student whom I had taught the previous year, and who has just got a job in a primary school in Essex. She explained what she did with her pupils in her first teaching session. She asked her pupils 'Who likes RE?' Five hands went up (out of over thirty). She asked, of the others, 'Why don't you like RE?' The replies revealed it was 'boring', 'nothing to do with me' and 'I am not a Christian'. She went to the head of the school and explained how she wanted to change the way the subject was taught. She was asked to explain her ideas and it was agreed. The pupils in that school will benefit from a new teacher with child-centred, or rather person-centred convictions, a confidence in her capability to address their needs and adapt her teaching to them, a belief in what the subject can offer them if this is done, a head who will listen to a new, young and inexperienced member of staff, and a refusal to follow inspection requirements as a literal code of prescription.

This is not an anecdotal tale that can be readily applied to the experiences of all newly qualified teachers or all practising teachers. That is one reason for writing this book. We are fully aware that not all students, teachers and Ofsted inspectors are likely to read it, or having read it wish to agree with it, or even find the effort involved in reading it productive and relevant to what they understand as their immediate, practical and day to day concerns. The latter will tend to mitigate against the proposals we are offering insofar as centralised prescription and inspection take precedence for practitioners. But it is precisely this short-termism that is an indication of why religious and moral education and the issue of children's spirituality need to be targeted as a way of indicating the poverty of thinking and underachievement, in relation to the capabilities of children and young people, afflicting our educational system.

But why should children and young people think that religious education is about making you religious or, more specifically, only of relevance if you are Christian? Surely this is a misperception and we only have to inform them of that. Well, yes and no. My own degree students share the misperception of other students that to study religion they must be religious, which is one reason why the name of the degree was changed from religious studies to the study of religions. One interesting consequence of this change of name is that the subject attracts more students who want less Christianity. It is also the case that when asked 'What do you do for a living?', replying that I teach religious studies or religious education does not invite an enthusiastic response, but rather an uncomfortable pause. Ninian Smart's (1982) way of dealing with this is to say that he does 'worldview analysis'. Of course we can also explain to our pupils that the law prevents indoctrinatory RE and that its purposes are quite different. But this does not actually cut much ice. It is, after all, *religious* education. The point is that having spent many professional years employing the above strategies and attempting to teach in a way that engages learners, it needs to be acknowledged that they have a point. Their gut reaction reveals something more significant than RE teachers are often willing to acknowledge. It reveals something of the affective response to religion, and Christianity in particular, that we find in contemporary society. Despite changes in the law, beginning with the 1902 Education Act, and in approaches to the delivery of religious education, especially those advanced from the 1970s, the 'religious difficulty', as Barnard (1961:168, 214–15) describes it, persists. It can be most obviously identified in the 1988 Education Reform Act in the confusion of aims between religious education and collective worship and the continued inclusion of the withdrawal clause. Pupils are not insensitive to the messages this sends out, especially given that the subject is called *religious* education and that it is often the obvious provider of an unsophisticated *moral* education.

The purpose of this book is to interrogate a particular question. How can religious and moral education be of greater educational benefit to young people? The outcome, as will be argued to the conclusion of the text, is that we need to revise, retitle and reconceive what we do, in a practical as well as a theoretical sense. The idea of spiritual education can be of service in this respect.

Curriculum constructions tend to be conservative in design because they are structured on the basis of bodies of knowledge. Religious education, being heavily content laden, partly because of the diversity of subject matter at its disposal, is more so than many other subjects. Moral education, not being a curriculum subject, is inserted in various ways, often not particularly imaginative and reflective ways, into religious education and other spaces, notably PSE in secondary schools. With spiritual education, a revised initiative with little if any theoretical framework, the situation is even less satisfactory. The outcome of this is that, in practice, spiritual and moral education are seen as derivative outcomes of a content-led religious education; a result of 'learning from' in the parlance of the School Curriculum Assessment Authority's model syllabus attainment targets (SCAA 1994a:5, 1994b:5). This particular attainment, as Ofsted has reported, is insufficiently addressed.

Perhaps the major difficulty that brings about this state of affairs is that religion does not consist of a body of knowledge in the scientific or social scientific sense unless it can be justified on the basis of either theological truth claims or empirical investigation, as with other social sciences and humanities subjects.

Either way the existential significance of what religion deals with—faith in that which is beyond such forms of assertion and enquiry—is ignored or at least played down. Spirituality and morality are equally beyond purely rational and empirical investigation unless we restrict ourselves to normative ethics, the construction of rules. These areas of fertile existential reflection, depending on recourse to individual experience, are thus rendered of insufficient importance in an education system that overvalues constructed curriculum knowledge, as explained above. This impasse leaves us with the difficulty of effectively addressing the stated educational aims. In short, what we seek to teach often has little to do with the experiences of those who are required to learn.

Religious education and the role of the learner

As an illustration of the problem stated above we can reflect on the teaching of 'sacred books' or scriptures. In certain respects, given that scriptural teachings are most often regarded as timeless truths, the attempt to teach them as being regarded as such by those who belong to the traditions, can mitigate against the way in which learners try to reflect on their own experiences if they do not belong to a religion. Our point here is that we have a more complex problem than might be presumed. Adopting a phenomenological approach we might wish to enable the learner to understand how the believer regards and uses the scripture and to exercise his or her capacity for empathy in doing so. As a result the learner might attain a simple or more complex understanding of the concept of scripture, the sacred and so on, and how such concepts affect the worldviews and behaviour of those who belong to a certain religion and its membership groups. The learner is now more knowledgeable and has developed certain skills and capacities. RE thus reflects the style and aims of learning of religious studies in higher education.

However, for this learning to develop there has to be a desire to learn about such things. This is rare. We seek to develop such a desire as a result of our virtuosity as teachers. Why should education be such that our virtuosity is the basis of the desire to learn? A good teacher seeks to relate the content and method, their pedagogy, to the needs and experiences of the learner. At the centre of the learning process is the learner. Pedagogically this demands close attention to the action that ensues rather than a written script to be learned. A good drama teacher knows that memorising a script and repeating it is not good drama or drama education. For the teacher of religious education the issue is similar. The content must be a vehicle for the development of the learner in a much more significant way than that outlined above. It must impinge directly on the learner's experience and the events and relationships in his or her life, rather than obliquely or tenuously. The good RE teacher knows this and that is why the subject becomes so frustrating. Within the teachings of religious traditions there is much that is useful to this purpose and much that is not.

We arrive at two considerable problems. The curriculum is not so much a vehicle for learning; it is a script for knowing. Concomitantly, the aim of the pedagogy employed is topsy turvy—you might, at points, be able to address the learner's experience and development in a greater sense than those aims that exist academically, but most often you probably will not. The reason for this is principally that we are engaged in religious education and most learners are not religious. If we changed the aims of RE to resolve this issue things would actually get worse, not better. For example, the most obvious alternative approach would be a form of theological education. This would compound the problem. The point at issue is not what approach we should take to religious education but the frame of reference that religious education imposes as a curriculum subject. The problem is hermeneutical. Put simply you cannot, in the fullest sense, 'learn from' a subject whose conceptual frames of reference exclude your own. To illustrate using the scriptural example above, if the concept of 'scripture' or the 'sacred' is not one you employ to interpret experience and construct your own worldview, then the subject excludes you. If we were to change the frame of reference to make it hermeneutically inclusive the subject would no longer be RE. We would have to change the script or, more radically, recognise that the script is constructed in the classroom rather than by predesign. The conceptual issue at stake is not one of scripture but of authority and guidance. Enlarging the frame of reference in this way offsets the centrality of religion. This does not mean marginalising the concept of scriptural authority, for it will be important, in differing ways, for those who belong to religious groups. However this will place the experiences and sources of authority and guidance of the learners centre stage.

Robert Coles was confronted with this issue when talking to a ten-year-old girl from the North American Hopi tribe who, after some time, revealed to him her Hopi understanding of God and consecrated land. Coles then asked if she had explained this to her teacher. She said 'No', and then explained why:

Girl: Because she thinks that God is a person. If I'd told her, she'd give us that smile.

Coles: What smile?

Girl: The smile that says to us, 'You kids are cute, but you're dumb; you're different—and you're all wrong!'

Coles goes on to explain: 'My job . . . is to put in enough time to enable a child like the Hopi girl to have her say—to reveal a side of herself not easily tapped even by good schoolteachers' (Coles 1992:25, 27).

If we were to understand the issue Coles raises as one resolved by introducing diversity into the curriculum and impartiality as the teachers stance we would misunderstand the nature of the problem. The issue is one of children expressing themselves on their own terms and being heard. This is not the same as relating what they say to the curriculum. Indeed the point is that attempting the latter is unlikely to give the impression to young people that we really want to hear what they have to say. This examination of the problematics of religious education can, of course, be widened to a scrutiny of educational design and policy generally, but that is beyond the scope of this study.

Representational complexity

A further issue relates to the problem of representation in RE. To illustrate, when Anees Jung relates her own life and her experience of researching in India, she exemplifies two contrasting Muslim approaches, amongst others, to the purpose of their religion. One comes from her own father, the other from a mullah in Bihar. She relates her father's Shia views as follows:

> My father . . . talked of humanism as the focus of religion. *Purdah*, my father would say, is a state of mind. He would tell us the story of Zainab, granddaughter of the Prophet, who had the courage to set aside her veil to tell the world of the injustice of the tragedy of Karbela. . . . To seek knowledge men and women should travel and explore, said the Prophet. My father in his own way pushed the ideal. Stand on your own feet. . . . He trained me in a world of men to live like a woman.

Included in her account of her encounter with Jalaluddin Changezi in Bihar is the following:

> 'Times have changed but the written word has not', he intones, in the manner of an oration . . . . 'Today you see women walking down the streets with their heads bare, their faces revealed. A woman's place is in the home. . . . In the Koran she is described as *fitna*, one who tempts man and brings trouble. She should stay where she belongs, within the walls of her own home'.
>
> (Jung 1987:29–30)

When we compare these two commentaries it is difficult to believe we are listening to the same faith. This could be advertised as a reason for examining religious worldviews in their diversity and complexity, but why just religious worldviews? Her father's views, the mullah's and her own search are not just about religion *per se*. 'You don't look like a Muslim woman, people say. My religion has no face I tell them, and move on. Faith is an energy, which along with other forces, lends a dimension to my life. It is not as integral to my life, though, as it is to most women around me' (ibid.:29). She also relates how Hindu and Muslim come together in rituals 'around a shrine, a temple, a saint's grave' which do not reflect the distinctions in their faiths. 'They reflect a people's emotional fusion . . . a faith that grows out of meeting and confluence' (ibid.:29–30).

When we begin to analyse such snapshots of experience we find our religious classifications, with their rigidity and exclusivity, referenced to orthodox and ideological pronouncements, insufficient to convey the reality of cultural and social plurality, even in a particular Indian setting.

The following is a criticism of present provision in religious education that has been advanced previously: 'The fear is that religion may be presented as a series of ideal types that do not represent the complexity of living religious experience'

(Geaves 1998:20). However, here we are seeking to illustrate that the complexity of the lived reality renders religion one of a number of interwoven strands, creating patterns of fusion but also points of rupture. Religion, faith and belief are not divorced from this reality but are seamlessly woven into its tapestry. This occurs not by some rational design within which we can separate the parts, but on many levels and in accordance with and compliance to innumerable factors: personal, social, historical, cultural, political and ideological. To separate them out is to create a rational representational fiction. When such fictions are created we must ask whose purposes and desires they serve.

Jung's journey has a predisposed purpose: to understand Indian women and their situations, to register situations of gender disempowerment and their causes. It is not value free. Equally, in our attempts to educate young people we cannot pretend to be value free, nor to be neutral or impartial in our disposition toward the various roles within which religion guises itself and plays its part in the development or retardation of those influenced by its presence and power. To put it bluntly, religious education is neither a simple nor a purely descriptive enterprise. To put it more forcibly, religious education has the potential to be a highly political and socially coercive tool. The question to be asked and answered is, what is its purpose and what is its educational usefulness, in the light of the misgivings expressed above? We might ask the same question with regard to moral education.

Fact and fiction

By now it will be clear that this study seeks to relate our educational aims to larger social and political purposes. It is usual for books on education to deal with the discourse of educational theory and/or practice, and leave it at that. However this is of no consequence unless we place the debate in a larger setting. It is also true that to do so requires us to pay attention not only to 'factual' writing but also to 'fiction'. This is the case because the latter is often the only way of addressing the affective, the subjective experience of individuals and their imaginative capacities within our rationalist framework of 'knowledge'. As we shall see, this also requires us to deliberate on how such a distinction came into being. Alasdair MacIntyre (1988:357) argues that 'facts, like telescopes, and wigs for gentlemen, were a seventeenth century invention'. Adrian Thatcher (1996:125) responds that 'facts without values are already fictions'. The distinction between fact and fiction, we argue, owes more to political design than to the mimetic reflection of a reality. Biography and autobiography, presented in novel or poetic form, can disclose more than our rational persona and rational rules allow. In Dorothy Allison's *Two or Three Things I Know for Sure* (1995:3) we find a fine example:

> I'm a storyteller. I'll work to make you believe me. Throw in some real stuff, change a few details, add the certainty of outrage. I know the use of fiction in a hard world of truth, the way fiction can be a harder piece of truth. The story of what happened, or what did not happen but should have—that story

can become a curtain drawn shut, a piece of insulation, a disguise, a razor, a tool that changes every time it is used and sometimes becomes something other than we intended. The story becomes the thing needed.

Two or three things I know for sure, and one of them is what it means to have no loved version of your life but the one you make.

Such writing throws into conflict how we judge what is real and what really matters in spiritual terms. Allison learnt the italicised mantra from her Aunt Dot, who added an important caveat: 'Lord, girl, there's only two or three things I know for sure. . . . Of course it's never the same things, and I'm never as sure as I'd like to be' (ibid.:5).

Allison's writing has relevance to Randel Helms' (1988:16) definition of 'fiction', when he speaks of the Gospel narratives:

> but for now, suffice it that the [Gospel] scenes have a religious and moral purpose disguised as a historical one; we are, with these scenes, in the literary realm known as fiction, in which narratives exist less to describe the past than to affect the present. In De Quincey's phrase, the Gospels are not so much literature of knowledge as literature of power.

The concept of truth is, of course, applied in both realms, but meaning something different in each case. Spiritual truth is fictional in the sense applied by Allison and Helms, but it is also powerful. However, to be convincing as knowledge and taken seriously as such, it must disguise itself as 'fact'. Then it also becomes politically convincing—things I know for sure.

In schools we teach facts and fictions. Often we do so in an attempt to divide them up neatly. If I know the facts the fictions will look after themselves. Not so. Teaching 'facts' is a miserably impoverished form of pedagogy; investigating how 'facts' become wrapped in fictions is illuminating, but still insufficient; constructing and voicing our own fictions, within a listening community that reflects, supports and challenges, is spiritually and politically empowering—a different form of education. These three models should not be understood in a linear way—that is, age related. What we do with 15 year olds we can do with five year olds, we just do it differently. Whatever else we do in education this should be at the heart of it. This idea was expressed by a chief inspector for schools in England and Wales:

> The function of education is to foster growth. By some of my readers this statement will be regarded as a truism; by others as a challenge; by others, again, when they have realised its inner meaning, as a 'wicked heresy'. I will begin by assuming it is a truism and will then try to prove that it is true.
>
> (quoted in Shute 1998:1)

This was not the present chief inspector voicing his philosophy of education, but the first chief inspector, Edmond Holmes, in 1911. He was not representing a consensus view of the time, but acting more as a prophet in the wilderness. It brought him enforced early retirement. We still have that wilderness. *Plus ça change*. But the reason why this educational wilderness persists has a long history. Our judgement of what is knowledge, which structures the system of schooling, cannot escape the political history of the concept revealed in A *History of Reading in the West* (Gugliemo and Chartier 1999), and commented on in the review of it by Jay Griffiths (1999:9):

> It [A *History of Reading in the West*] details, for instance, literalist Christianity's special relationship with The Word, its sacrilising attitude to the Good Book, and its special hatred of the Tree of Knowledge from which Eve—curious, courageous Eve—snatched the fruit. You could read the whole history of reading as a grand replay of Eve's act, and as late as the end of the eighteenth century it was argued, reading was synonymous with original sin.

What applies to reading applies equally to knowledge. Once a text is pronounced canonical, in whatever context, it is the repository of knowledge. Deviating from its claims is an error because such deviation is deviation from what is true. Whether the text's claims are protected by the notion of absoluteness or objectivity, or both, these are then the criteria for knowledge. We are caught in a catch 22 situation. Other narratives are judged accordingly. But significantly, no other narrative can attain the same status as these texts. Their status is blighted by the authority already conferred on the canonical texts. Thus, although these authoritative texts are no different in structure, they too are narrative, whether religious or scientific in genre (we shall return to and elaborate on this point later when considering Lyotard's observations on this issue), tradition determines that knowledge is their preserve. This has devastating consequences. The theological judgement made on Eve, and the social judgement made on women as the progeny and type of Eve, is one. Another is the wedding of 'fact', 'truth' and 'knowledge', as three concepts utilised to preserve this hegemony. A third is the dispute over whether religious or secular authorities have the legitimate right to these terms. A fourth is the idea that education consists of framing learning such that learners imbibe both this knowledge and the rules on what constitutes knowing. The concept of fiction is constructed according to these rules, as is the whole pedagogical procedure in education. No matter that all we have are 'fictions', which differ only in relation to the status conferred upon them by this system. No wonder that the 'knowledge' of children is of no consequence in such a system. No wonder that Holmes' comment on growth can either be happily misconstrued, to be interpreted within this system, or regarded as a wicked heresy.

The interpretation of spiritual, religious and moral concepts in education will be quite different and used for different purposes, depending on whether they are understood according to the designs of this system or within a 'heretical' reading. Was Eve wilful and disobedient, or curious and courageous? The moral judgement is based on how you read the story. The question is placed within whatever educational parameters we are allowed to read it and to achieve those educational ends.

The liberal phenomenological approach to religious education was in part designed to overcome the ideological issues analysed above. By resorting to the idea of a broad descriptive study it was hoped that a different model of understanding could be developed, conforming to the aims and values of liberal education generally. As will be argued later, despite its interim value it is deficient precisely because it has ignored these issues. In seeking to circumvent them, by changing the content of RE and the approach to the subject, it has left the most significant educational issues untouched. The study of religious traditions, whether historical or contemporary, from an empathetic point of view, is still the study of traditions whose central principle, at least as far as orthodoxies are concerned, is that knowledge conforms to the principles of ideological design discussed above. This book argues for a more radical alternative, putting the spiritual education of the learner, from a 'heretical' point of view, at the centre of what we seek to achieve.

Section I

Reconstructing the character and purposes of religious and spiritual education

2 A critical review of the character of religious education

Clive Erricker

Introduction

This chapter investigates dominant issues in the development of religious education in England and Wales in the latter half of the twentieth century. It identifies the changes, tensions and debates that have given shape to the subject and determined its limitations. The chapter is divided into five sections, thematically arranged, that reflect this treatment. The central question addressed is, what is religious education and what does it exist for?

We can only answer this question by examining the history of religious education and asking what the conscious purposes of the subject have been. Thus we are presented with issues that arise in the struggle between various parties to influence the development of the subject within the social, political and educational frame of an historical period in a particular national setting. We can best answer our question not by providing an historical survey but by identifying the purposes and attitudes that lie behind and within significant and influential statements and writings during this period. When individuals and groups pronounce on the value of religious education they necessarily reveal certain personal and often ideological positions. In other words there is no neutrality in the positioning of the subject in the curriculum. It does not exist purely for its own sake but also for other specific and extrinsic purposes. The aim of this chapter is to identify those purposes by analysing the issues at the centre of the debate.

Religion and secularity

We shall start with a recent reflection on why religious education is perceived to be a necessary part of the curriculum in England and Wales:

> However 'bad', judged as education or theology, RE may sometimes have been, its removal from the curriculum altogether, a vague spectre that hovered around it from the early fifties until the early eighties, would have been far worse. For then implicit secular indoctrination in the curriculum might have reigned unchecked, pupil choice would have been further reduced and perceptions of religion among children would have been left to

scandals misreported in the tabloid press and the more or less beguiling
doorstep purveyors of religion.

(Copley 1997:x)

Terence Copley's observations in the above quotation are pregnant with meaning
and significance. They are pregnant in more than one sense. By using this term
we usually refer to the fullness and importance of what is actually stated. I think
this is true of the above, but there is also a pregnancy in the hidden sense of what
is not overtly stated by Copley yet is clearly there, underlying both his concerns
and his judgement. My concern is with this hidden pregnancy. We may approach
this by deconstructing the statement and placing it within the social and
educational context from which it emerges. This will allow us to investigate
further the particular character of religious education in England and Wales and
its purposes. At the outset it is also important for the reader to know my position
in reviewing the subject. The purpose of my analysis is to construct and defend
an understanding of the subject as insufficient due to the way in which it has been
influenced, largely by ideological and political rather than educational policies.

Why should Copley begin by considering a negative judgement of the subject?
Why should he consider the negative judgement to be accorded from the two
different disciplines of education and theology? At this point we can observe the
difficulty that derives from the disparity between the two disciplines. Education
is secular in character and has been since the period following the Second World
War, precisely the period with which Copley is concerned. This we can identify
as the point when the church, and more specifically the Anglican Church,
increasingly lost its influence over state education and religious education. The
theological reference thus becomes important because theological criticism is
unlikely to concur with educational criticism of the subject but will be in
opposition to it. Thus religious education is pulled in two opposing directions.
These directions represent the struggle for secular or religious hegemony in our
society. Religious education is a particular battleground upon which the Christian Church(es) is able to marshal its forces, defend its place and position, and
either fashion an honourable retreat or still claim a place in the educational
purposes of society.

Copley's judgement that bad RE is better than no RE is therefore made on
the basis that secularity (which, ambiguously, must lead either to a lack of
Christian/religious nurture or to religious literacy, it is not clear what is being
implied here) is to be avoided at all costs. His use of the term 'secular
indoctrination' is particularly significant because it implies that there is no neutral
ground between that and religious/theological education/indoctrination, although
he does not state this. The point I am making here is that we are not given a clear
message about the purposes of religious education, beyond stemming the tide of
secularism, and these purposes can and do vary considerably among those who wish
to defend the subject. However what now emerges is the message that secularists,
whether explicitly or implicitly, have responded to during this historical period:
religious education is indoctrination into religion, or at least indoctrination against

secularism. This in turn is interpreted as religious education not being conducted according to educational principles, that is, it is not really education at all. As evidence of such an attitude already operating, due to suspicion about the purposes of RE, we can observe the general lack of cooperation and collaboration between religious education and its apparently closest curriculum companions—PSE, multicultural education and antiracist education. Four curriculum bed-fellows in a rather narrow and uncomfortable bed.

The last part of Copley's observations is especially interesting because it points to the ambiguity in religious education. Theology is not the same as religion. Thus when Copley defends the importance of religious education he points to the need for children to have an accurate understanding of religion. This is a reference to the changing aims in religious education that emerged in the late 1960s and gained favour in the 1970s and 1980s until (paradoxically and politically) both were held in check and officially sanctioned by the 1988 Education Reform Act (ERA).

Copley's report, both sad and amusing, of the passage of the bill through the House of Commons and the House of Lords (ibid.:128–46) is instructive for identifying misunderstandings about the role of RE in education, the lack of interest in it from those who had no strong religious commitments, and the influence of different Christian factions in determining the nature of the debate. He quotes the then Bishop of London (Graham Leonard, who was an important agent in defending the bill against right-wing Christians), who made the extraordinary assertion that 'the churches should supply good men and women as RE teachers and not expect the government to do their job for them' (ibid.:139).

The notion of a descriptive, objective and accurately informed approach to the teaching of world religions, which changed the overt character of RE in the 1970s and 1980s, is a significant deviation from a theologically informed education to promote religious nurture. Copley seems to endorse the former as a necessary development—with some misgivings, to which he later draws attention—but on what grounds? His argument is an antisecularist one and thus the message is confused. Do we wish children to know about religion so that they do not become antireligious? Do we wish them to acknowledge the importance (and higher value?) of religious ways of understanding human experience? Or do we simply want them to become knowledgeable about the worldviews of other people, and if so, to what end? The confusion in Copley's argument and the implicit message it sends to educationalists about the ambiguity of the aims of RE are an example of the difficulties that confronted the subject in the latter half of the twentieth century. Why does Copley defend bad RE against no RE? Not primarily, it would seem, on the ground that knowing about religion is in itself educationally important, although that is acknowledged, but on the ground that secularist indoctrination is worse than religious indoctrination.

His argument reflects the confusion, ambiguity and problematics inherent in the defence of the subject in the period he defines, in relation to how it was understood within different institutional contexts and by different groups: from schools to churches and from parents to parliament. His own statement is an example of why RE still exists and why it is educationally incoherent. Whatever aims it seeks to serve it is first and foremost, we are given to understand, antisecularist. But the reasons why it is so are different and conflicting, according to the different factions within and beyond those speaking in its defence.

In support of his own view, Copley (1997:181–2) cites Brenda Watson's view that the most fundamental problem facing religion and religious education is secularism, despite, in her judgement, the philosophically formidable case against secularism (Watson 1993:41). What is interesting about Watson's defence of RE is that it is bound up with a defence of religion, the automatic assumption being that those who seek to defend an educational subject are doing so from a religious position, as insiders we might say. However Watson is particularly concerned with the development of the imagination and with linking the religious and wider values that pertain in society. This alerts us to a fundamental characteristic of the debate on the purposes of RE over the last twenty or more years: that there is disagreement about both the scope of its enquiry and what its function is in relation to the development of the learner. Jackson (1997:10–11) draws attention to the views of Cox (1983:132), who in some respects adopts a similar position to Watson in arguing for the need to address the 'motives that prompt [religious] behaviour', rather than being concerned with its external expressions, for example in religious ceremonies. He goes further, however, by asking whether religion can be deemed of sufficient interest to young people to substantiate its claim as a curriculum subject. Cox suggests that RE needs to situate itself within a larger frame of reference as a form of values education that includes the secular as well as the religious, and whose main purpose should be to enable pupils 'to move towards coming to terms with their own life problems by means of a coherent and conscious set of beliefs' (Jackson 1997:11; Cox 1983:135–6).

At this point we can identify the following questions as requiring attention:

- Is RE about investigating the concepts and concerns intrinsic to religious belief, such as God and the transcendent?
- Is RE about understanding the diverse forms that religion takes, primarily constituted by a study of 'world religions'?
- Is RE about understanding different value systems and, primarily, about enabling pupils to develop their own?

These questions have emerged within the debate on what religious education's primary educational responsibilities are. They operate as a guide for the enquiry that follows in this chapter and, in part, for the rest of this study. We begin with a consideration of the shaping role that phenomenology has played in the construction of present RE provision.

Phenomenology and the representation of religion

This section and those that follow are concerned with the major issues that have arisen as a result of RE being largely influenced by phenomenology since the late 1960s. Robert Jackson has offered a detailed study of this in presenting his case for an interpretive approach to RE. Here I wish to consider Jackson's understanding of the main concerns that he seeks to address as a way of both constructing an agenda for this part of our own study, and in order to move on to consider the question of spiritual education in more detail in Chapter 2.

In developing an approach to RE that builds on Ninian Smart's (1971, 1973, 1983, 1989) phenomenological stance but critically refines it through ethnographic study, Jackson (1997:6) uses the term 'interpretive'. Here Jackson recognises the difficulty of understanding the phenomenon of religion and, crucially, cites the problems inherent in representation, in relation both to faith groups, as represented in classroom materials, and to pedagogic practice, in relation to the method of enquiry. Jackson points to the difficulty of outsiders seeking to understand insider's worldviews, and the procedures through which his and his coworkers' ethnographic fieldwork in England revealed ways in which previous representations needed to be challenged as a result. He is concerned with this at a number of levels. First, there is the question of approach, within which he draws on phenomenological and social-anthropological methods and considers the contribution of Wilfred Cantwell Smith's use of 'faith' and 'cumulative tradition' as alternatives to the term 'religion'. Second, there is the difficulty of extrapolating religion from culture. Third, there is the difficulty of conveying a sophisticated understanding in the classroom—the teacher's role. Fourth, there is the associated issue of the relationship between religious education and religious nurture (ibid.:4). In the context of debates on Christian RE in Britain, these last two terms have taken on distinct and opposed meanings that invite reconsideration, in Jackson's view. The first issue we wish to consider is that of approach.

Phenomenology has been the approach underpinning the idea that RE is primarily about the study of world religions. This approach to the subject has drawn on the way in which phenomenology has influenced the study of religion and attempts accurately to represent religions. Accordingly, representation within the subject of religious studies has become an issue of importance within RE. Within phenomenological approaches it has always been at the centre of debate. To examine this is an instructive first step towards the construction of a new theoretical framework. Broadly speaking the phenomenological methods of enquiry fall into two camps: descriptivist and interpretative. Descriptive approaches, sometimes referred to as empirical or morphological because of their aim systematically to classify or typologise religious phenomena, tend to take for granted that the phenomenon as it is perceived is the phenomenon as it is. The major aim is then to classify the subject studied (ibid.:15–19). This approach emphasises the study of religion as a social science. In its early days this was a way in which scholars of religion could justify the importance of the discipline in its own right, as distinct from theology, and within a frame of academic research that was otherwise secular in its concerns (Erricker 1998:74ff).

The interpretative or hermeneutical approaches were concerned with the philosophical implications involved in knowing or understanding the phenomenon (Jackson 1997:19–21; Erricker 1998:76ff). Here the idea of objectivity was called into question. The study of religion was more closely aligned with the arts as a discovery of something that was also transformative for the student or enquirer. Within the former camp we can place Chantepie de la Saussaye, William Brede Kristensen and Eric Sharpe. Within the latter we can place Gerardus van der Leeuw, Jacques Waardenberg and Rudolf Otto. This classification is nevertheless crude. We may think of the relations between these two positions as lying on a continuum with the figures occupying different spaces, but in some cases their work actually shifts and overlaps to some degree as it develops. Smart's work is a case in point, to which we shall return later. However this classification does help to identify some important issues.

One issue is whether the Husserlian understanding of phenomenology is achievable. This is based on the need to arrive at an understanding of the phenomenon by utilising two different methods: eidetic vision and empathetic awareness. Essentially this means being aware of and 'bracketing out' one's own understandings and preconceptions in order to identify with the understandings, or worldviews, of others. The critical appreciation of this by Jackson (1997:21–4) is an example of exposing the naiveté of this endeavour. What is exposed is the hermeneutical inadequacy of the model in attempting to arrive at an accurate representation of the phenomenon that is consistent with insiders' understandings, and can be posited as objective in the sense that accurate representation demands.

A second issue is that of essence. The idea behind representation is that what is represented is the essential nature of the object of investigation, what characterises it as distinct from anything else and on what basis this can be said to be the case. Rudolph Otto's *The Idea of the Holy* (1959) is the most obvious example of this. In Otto's eyes, his identification of the numinous as the prime characteristic of religion not only served to justify it as a phenomenon in its own right, but also served to justify the existence of the numen itself. In other words he was calling into question the assumption of secularity as a basis upon which the study of humanity could be appropriately carried out.

The idea that there is an essence to be discovered has been under attack for some time. Critically speaking, we can say that the 'essence' acts as a metaconception introduced by the researcher into the subject of enquiry as a classificatory means of determining what is and what is not the nature of the subject. As such it is an outsider seeking to construct the subject from his or her point of view. This does not accord with the notion of self-definition as a hermeneutical principle and the researcher's need to understand that self-definition as a methodological criterion.

Summing up the critical position so far, we may say that the search for essences is flawed and incommensurable with the idea of empirical enquiry, and that empirical enquiry can never result in a normative accuracy in the representation of a religion. The issues are simply too complex for this sort of study, and this has been reflected in the tensions between different phenomenological approaches.

Attempts to overcome this representational problem by what Jackson refers to as 'new style' phenomenology, citing Waardenberg's (1978) approach as the chief example, move towards interpretive anthropology. Jackson's explanation of interpretive anthropology principally follows the method of Clifford Geertz (1973, 1983, 1988). Here there is a recognition of the role of the researcher as an actor in the whole process, in other words we cannot regard the one who seeks to represent as being outside the process of representation itself. This removes the distinction between the subject studied and the student of the subject as discrete entities, so that the latter can in some sense both 'discover' and 'represent' the former. What we shall go on to discover, as well, is that the concept 'religion' is in itself problematic. As Bauman (1998:55) observes:

> 'Religion' belongs to the curious, and often embarrassing concepts, which one perfectly understands until one wants to define them. Postmodern mind . . . resigns itself to the tendency of definitions to conceal as much as they reveal and to maim and obfuscate while pretending to clarify and straighten up. It also accepts the fact that all too often experience spills out of the verbal cages in which one would wish to hold it, that there are things of which one should keep silent since one cannot speak of them, and that the ineffable is as much a part of the human mode of being-in-the-world as is the linguistic net in which one tries (in vain as it happens . . .) to catch it.

Bauman's observation will prove to be of crucial importance in determining how we should reconfigure our task as educators in relation to the content of RE and its relationship with spirituality. He also introduces us to the fact that so far we have only touched the surface of the complexities involved in the epistemological and hermeneutical issues that face us when we take account of the postmodern and relativist contributions to them. These and what Bauman refers to as 'the linguistic net' will be considered later, mainly in Chapter 4, but first we shall consider the issue that Bauman refers to as the 'ineffable', or the question of faith and its relationship with religion.

Faith and religion

Here we return to two writers who have been influential in the study of religion due to the distinctive approaches they have offered, Wilfred Cantwell Smith and Ninian Smart, and to consider the contribution of John Bowker. We shall also consider Jackson's comments on the former in constructing his interpretive approach to RE.

Smart proposed, and was an instigator of, the study of world faiths within higher education, and later within the school curriculum (Smart 1968), by directing the Schools Council Project, *Religious Education in Secondary Schools* (Schools Council 1971), in the late 1960s and early 1970s. Significantly, however, Smart's later work in religious studies, in which he broadened his understanding of the subject to include worldviews that extended beyond the traditional classification of 'religions', never made an impact at the curriculum level. More recently Smart has favoured the inclusion of 'so-called secular worldviews like Marxism' (Smart 1998:ix–x). But it is important to note the underlying values position that Smart holds. He states:

> A multicultural or pluralistic philosophy of religion is a desideratum, and it has been amazing how culture-bound so many Western philosophers have been: an unconscious (to be kind) imperialism. . . . We have surely passed beyond a stage in human life when national values stand supreme, after all the horrors national wars have caused during this passing century. Nationalism sometimes makes good politics: but its dangers are well advertised. We need to see religions in the same sort of context: just as democracy is a way to eliminate violence in the choice of policies: so a kind of spiritual democracy should eliminate inter-religious and inter-ideological violence . . . we need an overarching worldview for all human beings.
>
> (ibid.:xii–xiii)

Smart's admirable utopian vision is built not upon the credibility of religious truth claims and ideologies, but upon religion's contribution to an overarching, democratic human unity. In fact Smart is primarily concerned with specific values and a certain political order.

It is interesting to contrast Smart's benign approach to the possibilities that religion has to offer with Bowker's apocalyptic vision of religion's contribution to the future: 'For years I have been pointing out that religions are likely to destroy human life as we know it now on this planet. Religions contribute to virtually all the intransigent and seemingly insoluble conflicts in the world' (Bowker 1996:3). Whilst Smart stresses the importance of religious education in moving us towards a liberal and plural democratic culture, with RE operating as a vehicle for a particular form of values education, for Bowker the importance of including the subject in the curriculum is as follows: 'One reason undoubtedly stands out. On pragmatic grounds alone, the study of religions is necessary, since without it, it is impossible to understand the nature of so many bitter conflicts in the world today' (ibid.:3).

The contrast between these two views alerts us to the fact that there are very different reasons why religious education can be thought of as important, and the differences in the conception of the value of the subject are underpinned by different attitudes towards religion. In other words there is not just one subject—distinctions lie across ideological fault lines, constructed by religions themselves. For Smart, we should play down the importance of these fault lines and study the enriching possibilities offered by religious teachings and traditions. For Bowker, there is no doubt that the earthquakes will happen, so it is important to acquaint ourselves with some ideological geology.

Cantwell Smith, in contrast to Smart and in even greater contrast to Bowker, emphasised that the descriptive study of religious practices and the phenomenological understanding of religious beliefs fell short of the task that the student of religion, and by implication the religious educator, needed to undertake. His concern was with the understanding of faith. His ideas are worth revisiting in the light of the shift in the educational debate that the term 'spiritual education' has engendered. Smith uses the term 'faith' to refer to 'personal faith'—'For the moment let it stand for an inner religious experience ... the impingement on him [the individual] of the transcendent, putative or real'— and he coins the term 'cumulative tradition' to refer to the entire mass of overt objective data ... of the past religious life of the community in question ... anything that can be and is transmitted from one person to another' (Smith 1978:156–7). Smith's contention is that the term 'religion' can be replaced by the above two terms and the focus of study will then become 'The expressions of the faith of individuals [which] then become part of the organically changing cumulative traditions' (ibid.:187).

Smith's approach had no obvious impact on the development of RE in the UK during the 1960s and 1970s as the curriculum moved in the direction of a 'world faiths' approach, championed by Smart. Nevertheless critics of this approach often pointed to its tendency to emphasise the outward practices and observable structures and phenomena, rather than the inner motivations of believers. Those who defend the teaching of world faiths have not been insensitive to this criticism. They have often been divided in a similar fashion to the different phenomenological approaches taken in the study of religion academically. This has been documented by Jackson (1997). Therefore we need to recognise the existence of different 'world faiths' or 'multifaith' approaches in RE, which have been the subject of ongoing debate.

Within this debate there has always been a concern with the relationship between curriculum content and the aims of pedagogy, in the context of which the question of faith, in relation to believers in the traditions studied and the learners themselves, has featured prominently. Nevertheless it has been the case that this debate, which is sophisticated in character, often did not influence the way in which the subject was taught in many schools. Also, there was a desire to avoid any sense of nurture, as it was understood within earlier RE teaching, related to Christianity, and a need to defend RE as a 'proper' curriculum subject with its own body of knowledge: religion. For these reasons, amongst others, Cantwell Smith's approach did not have the influence it might have had, since it did not suit the climate of debate. However a reconsideration of Smith's approach makes clear, when translated into the situation in England and Wales, that we have made no accommodation for the development in children of any sense of 'faith' to replace the understanding of it as Christian nurture, once the latter became educationally unacceptable during the above period, and legally so after the 1988 Education Reform Act. Jackson (ibid.:4) indicates that the relationship between the terms 'education' and 'nurture' needs to be recon-sidered. I shall argue that a reconsideration of this issue, and of the term 'faith', has radical implications for our reassessment of RE.

Jackson presents and uses Smith's ideas well. By sympathetically critiquing him, Jackson shows the virtue of Smith's emphasis on organic change and hermeneutical method. His most significant criticisms amount to recognising the problem with thinking that, as an historian of religion, you are dealing with 'objective data' and the political naiveté of Smith on the issues of power and representation. Here Jackson (ibid.:63) points to the observations of Said. Most significantly, Said pointed out in *Orientalism* (1978) that 'all academic knowledge is tinged and impressed with, violated by, the gross political fact'. In this and later works, for example *Culture and Imperialism* (1993), Said develops the argument of the disempowerment and misrepresentation of the 'Other' by the construction of imperialistic discourse. His point is that 'knowledge' in one cultural context— and he is particularly concerned with Western constructions of knowledge— creates its own images of that in other cultures in order to gain power over them. Said's observations will prove of value later in this work in relation to constructions of childhood.

There are two ways in which Smith's understandings and Jackson's use of them seem to fall short of what is still required for the transformation of religious education. First, in Smith's model the outside observer takes account of what is occurring within traditions in relation to the developing faith of individuals. In doing this, whilst not wishing to use the term 'religion' and yet continually finding it necessary to do so, it becomes clear that he, as an insider in his own tradition, presumes the boundary of investigation to be that of religions, with the presumption that the student has his or her own 'religious' faith. This is not to say that agnostics cannot be involved in this enterprise, but rather that the agnostic cannot by definition of the area of study have a faith. The difficulties with this approach, whilst not necessarily problematic within the academic study of religion from Smith's or Jackson's stance of liberal enquiry, become more so when we follow this approach in religious education.

In religious education we need to take account of the faith of the learner—who is, by definition, able to undertake the academic task but is excluded from the developmental process involved in the spiritual if he or she lacks a 'faith' in Smith's sense, which is intrinsically religious. In other words, by putting faith and cumulative tradition at the centre of enquiry the subject frees itself from being a study of the generalised construct 'religion' and yet excludes those without religious faith from the reflexive processes involved in such enquiry. It is not enough to say that the spiritual development of any learner will occur by virtue of gaining understanding of the spiritual dimensions of religious traditions and the faith experiences of individuals within them, when the subject of enquiry has an epistemological and hermeneutical bias towards religious constructs.

The above understanding is implied in the phrasing of the two attainment targets of the SCAA model syllabuses (SCAA:1994a and b), 'learning about' and 'learning from'. However the learner who has no religious faith is outside the frame in the same sense as Anees Jung explains in connection with women in *Unveiling India* (1987:14). (This point will be elaborated on in Chapter 6.) It is also not sufficient to suggest that the learner's spiritual education will be addressed elsewhere in the curriculum and their schooling.

This situation creates a sense of exclusion and disempowerment—the creation of otherness, as identified by both Said and Jackson, in relation to those represented as the subjects of study, which pertains equally to the learner when considering pedagogic practice. This demands radical change to ensure the effectiveness of the subject. Thus we arrive at one of the reasons for the need for transformation. Of course this does not mean excluding the study of religion, but it does mean that the barrier that is still in place between the religious and the secular must be dismantled. This in turn involves revisiting our understanding of the terms 'faith' and 'spiritual', which will be addressed in Chapters 3 and 4.

The second shortcoming of Jackson's approach is revealed when he proceeds to incorporate Smith into his own empirical research and subsequent school resources. His aim is to record young people with traditions speaking of their faith and how this is put into practice in the context of tradition and membership group (Jackson 1997:95ff). The question is whether the children represent themselves or whether they are representatives of the tradition/membership group? This might seem to be a false dichotomy until we take account of the political processes involved in such research and the ethical questions posed. Here the question of representation is highly ambiguous. Who decides which children and from which families representing a particular membership group (say Orthodox Jews or Roman Catholics) will be researched and presented in materials representing that group? Who decides which membership groups will be represented in a faith tradition? Who decides what questions may be asked in interviews and what responses published? In a sense, of course, these questions are rhetorical. In an area of such political sensitivity, and with the researcher's wish to promote positive images of these groups and the need for these groups to agree to the publication of the findings, the process of representation that needs to be followed becomes clear. Jackson (ibid.:107–11) makes reference to some of the issues involved as matters of negotiation. My point is that the spiritual life of children, which I am equating with 'faith' at this juncture, as they seek to comprehend and grapple with the existential issues involved, and the complexity entailed in their experiences and relationships are not going to be fully revealed or centrally addressed in this context. We may be given an understanding of what children do and why they do what they do in the affairs and practices of the family and group and the surrounding culture, but that is not the same as coming to understand their spiritual lives. Thus we can say that, valuable as such research and representation is in understanding the membership groups and the variety of expressions of a tradition, and as a way of representing the complexity of religion as lived practices and teachings, it does not deal with the depth and complexity of what Smith refers to as 'faith', nor does it, given Smith's religious exclusivity in his use of the term, help us to cross that barrier of the religious and secular in addressing the spiritual with learners in a fully inclusive way.

Taking these two points together we may start to investigate the underlying issues that emerge from them, which can be contextualised within the concept of representation. These will be elaborated on later, primarily in Chapter 6, but the thrust of our argument is that children's spirituality cannot be effectively represented in RE in relation to the content and materials produced when what is being studied and represented is religious traditions or membership groups; and that children's spirituality cannot be expressed and reflected on by the children themselves in RE as long as the subject enquired into is defined by the concept 'religion'.

Religion and culture

In this section we shall focus on Jackson's examination of the relationship between religion and culture, and on Bauman's notion of cultural variety. Distinctive among Jackson's concerns is the difference between more closed and more open or flexible understandings of 'culture'. An example of the former is that of John McIntyre, where a culture is 'the expression of the fundamental concepts and values of a community' (McIntyre 1978:1.1; Jackson 1997:16). Jackson goes on to identify McIntyre's understanding that 'in western society, it is religion, and in particular, the Christian religion, which has been the source of the values and concepts from which culture has sprung' (McIntyre 1978:1.6; Jackson 1997:16). Jackson observes that for McIntyre the nucleus of Western culture is Christian. Thus McIntyre's view is that the values of the dominant culture must be maintained if the culture itself is to be sustained. This in turn means rejecting any 'outside' or critical influence on the values of that culture, even from within the society in which it has dominance (this view was reflected in much of the debate on the 1988 Education Reform Act, and it continues to be held by such figures as Nicholas Tate, former chief executive of the Qualifications and Curriculum Authority and now Headmaster of Winchester College). At the other end of the scale is Carrithers' more open and fluid idea of culture, where the emphasis 'shifts . . . from a generic idea of the "culture" of a people to "sociality", the study of individuals in relationships and the interactive nature of social life' (Carrithers 1992; Jackson 1997:19).

In relation to this study the issues raised above are of great importance, not least because of the question of authority involved. Jackson wishes to ensure that religion is understood in terms of cultural settings that are dynamic and changing, which will affect the representation of religion, the way in which religion is understood in relation to culture, and the debate on education and nurture in the context of the situation in England and Wales. Jackson's discussion of culture and nurture in relation to religious education (1997:4, 75, 136) allows us to reflect further on Copley's position.

As Copley's (1997) description of the changing character and aims of RE unfolds, it is precisely the question of what values and purposes RE exists for that continually recurs. The values question is intimately related to the perception of culture employed. Although he does not use the term, Copley's cultural categories are primarily fixed and wedded to his distinction between religious and secular and his recognition of their opposition. McIntyre supports such a classification with an overt emphasis on the importance of Christianity providing the dominant cultural values to be conveyed to children (though Copley is not supporting this view). In contrast Jackson supports the understanding that the dynamics of cultural and religious change have to be understood and represented, so that the distinction between 'our culture [the dominant group] and the cultures of others' [the minority groups] does not prevail.

Jackson, following Geertz (1973), wishes cultures to be understood as, first, containing within them 'a considerable amount of diversity'; second, following Clifford (1986), 'internally diverse and actively contested, thus inevitably represented and influenced by those attempting to interpret it (both insiders and outsiders)'; third, following Said (1978), 'negotiated, present processes'; and lastly, following Barth (1994), 'people *engaging with* culture, drawing on different "cultural funds"' in constructing their 'social identity, which might be shaped by a variety of cultural influences' (Jackson 1997:80–2). Jackson illustrates something of the intricate character of this debate when he goes on to discuss the complicated relations between culture, ethnicity and nationality. He speaks of the difficulty that arises in the employment of these terms, and that if they are used in a closed sense they can result in disempowerment and the conferral of 'otherness' within the representational construction of society (ibid.:83-8).

Bauman (1999) offers his own critique on this issue using the terms 'multi-culturalism' and 'multicommunitarianism', both of which 'deal with a similarly diagnosed situation: the co-presence of many cultures within the same society' (ibid.:xliii). His point is that the diagnosis is false to start with; rather than dealing with a variety of cultures in society we are living in societies with cultural variety. The difficulty arises from conceiving culture as a complete system, when in fact 'fragmentation has affected all fields of life, and culture is not an exception' (ibid.:xliii).

Thus the communitarian concern to establish a culture as a self-enclosed totality is an extension of state promotion of national culture. Its tendency is assimilative and coercive. Multiculturalism, on the other hand, whilst opposing multicommunitarianism in seeking to celebrate the universally enriching effect of cultural diversity, still understands this sense of difference in a static sense of systems operating in close proximity to one another. Bauman's point is that

> Identities do not rest on the uniqueness of their traits, but consist increasingly in distinct ways of selecting/recycling/rearranging the cultural matter which is common to all, or at least potentially available to all. It is the movement and capacity for change, not the ability to cling to once-established form and contents, that secures their continuity.
>
> (ibid.:xlv)

Thus the issue is not one of protecting present cultural systems, understood according to either of the above positions, but to accept the dynamics of cultural transformation. Within this the notions of nationhood, religion and values are rendered equally fluid.

The importance of this discussion resides in how we determine the value and position of particular groups and individuals within a society, the classificatory terms used, and how those terms relate to one another. At issue is who decides upon this. Thus, for example, is it a question of whether I feel myself to be British, or whether I am considered British? Indeed we can ask: what does Britishness mean? What does it stand for? How does the term British relate to other religious and cultural categories?

This issue features in Eleanor Nesbitt's (1998) study 'British, Asian and Hindu: identity, self-narration and the ethnographic interview'. In her research on self-identity among young British-born or British-raised Hindus, ' "Hindu" emerges as a trans-generational, core identity, but with significant differences from ... young South Asian Muslims' preferred Islamic identity' (ibid.:189), which is the subject of Jacobson's (1997) research. However Nesbitt discerns that the term 'Hindu' is not understood by her respondents in an unequivocal way, such that we can classify it as either religious or cultural. Such a classificatory distinction cannot be placed upon its usage. Rather, what we find is that it operates as a 'narrative thread' (Nesbitt 1998:197), with the purpose of 'conveying the nature of identity as an ongoing, complex and affective process' (ibid.:196). Similarly Ota (1998), interviewing primary school children, finds that the terms 'Asian', 'Indian', 'Pakistani', 'Bengali', 'Punjabi', 'Hindu', 'Sikh' and 'Muslim' are used by the children in a variety of ways and for different purposes to situate themselves in relation both to each other and to 'Britishness'.

Nesbitt notes that the use of the term 'Hindu' does not operate in a similar way to the term 'Muslim' in Jacobson's study, in which 'Islam inspired Jacobson's young Muslims with its universal relevance and clear-cut boundaries' (ibid.:197). This should alert us to the inappropriateness of seeking to use such terms as though they were similar religious concepts operating for similar narrative purposes. To do this would be to distort and to simplify self-representation. We might argue that creating a discrete subject of study called religious education is a first step towards imposing this distortion, and we would expect children, in attempting to give voice to their own self-narration, to be the first to recognise this, whatever position they occupy. Similarly we must be careful with the use of the term 'faith'. Whereas for Jacobson's Muslims this might operate as a synonym for religion, for Nesbitt's young Hindus the two terms are much more confused. As one interviewee, a devotee of Sathya Sai Baba, explains 'I would say I'm born a Hindu, I'll die a Hindu. But then, maybe, I shouldn't call myself a Hindu in the first place because I don't actually practise Hinduism' (ibid.:196). One might suppose that this interviewee would, however, wish to articulate an idea of her religious faith even if it is not appropriately circumscribed by Hinduism.

It is interesting to reflect on how a young person whose self-narration had no reference to religious identity would be able to articulate his or her 'identity', 'spirituality' or 'faith' if these terms have authenticity only within the parameters of religion. Reflection on this issue of narrative construction leads us to consider a fundamental question that underpins all this discussion. It is not a question of what classifications are in place, the conceptual constructions within which we live, that constitute the site of enquiry, but how these constructions become articulated, by whom, on what basis and why. Self-narration as a classroom activity releases these sorts of questions.

Thus we come to realise that the activity we are engaged in is one of construction in all respects; in relation to the concepts of nationality, religion, culture and values. We are political players in a particular game in which classification, representation and power are the key interrelated currencies out of which the constructs that we call religion, education and religious education are created. What we have to ask is where power is situated, what representations arise as a result, and what effect that will have on the enculturation of pupils and the values underpinning that enculturation. This leads us to an investigation of the role of tradition and religion as ideology.

The role of tradition in religion and religious education

The primary concerns of this section are the problematics inherent in seeking empathetically or sympathetically to represent faith traditions without taking account of religion as an ideology. We started this chapter by looking at the antagonism between the religious and the secular that has been a prevailing feature in the construction and maintenance of RE in England and Wales in the twentieth century. Such antagonism is a result of ideological difference. Here I want to investigate the limitations and fractures arising from failing to acknowledge traditional religion as ideological, politically conservative and often morally ambivalent.

In *Licensed Insanities*, Bowker (1987) speaks of the unacceptable face of religion. In citing the strong religious components involved in bitter conflicts (ibid.:1–3) he suggests, as noted previously and below, that this destructive characteristic of religious ideologies constitutes an important reason why religions need to be studied: 'it would be the strongest possible argument for devoting far more time . . . to the attempt to understand such insanity a great deal more clearly than we do. Insanity . . . can be a lethally dangerous phenomenon' (ibid.:4–5).

His understanding of religions as systems is that they are organised for 'the process, protection and transmission of information' (ibid.: 9). It is for this reason that the operators of religious systems are boundary minded and why, as a result, we can continually expect 'border incidents' (ibid.:14).

However Bowker's thesis is that despite their tendency to repress individual creativity and freedom of thought, and to promote conservatism, stasis and imperialism, together with the ever present possibility that they will succumb to self-interest, religions are necessary formulations for humans to improve and reach beyond themselves. For Bowker they have an intrinsically noble aim or first purpose: 'the first purpose of the Christian system is to draw us into the worship and adoration of God' (ibid.:135).

New questions now arise about our purpose in teaching RE and representing faith and religion. How do we separate faith narratives from religious ideology? What exactly is it that we should be teaching? Following Bowker we could start with the idea that the conceptual framing of the world is at the heart of religion and religious traditions. The continuance of a tradition is based on allegiance to this conceptualisation. This is called belief. Belief is institutionalised, thus it is expressed in creedal rituals that are constructed by tradition. Disruption of tradition resulting in new branches of a tradition is based on the premise that the institutionalised form of the religion in place does not reflect the original vision and its teachings. Thus we have renewal, which involves a renewed concep-tualisation. 'New' religions operate *vice versa*, by claiming that a new revelation of truth makes inferior the previous truth claims. By virtue of charting this process we arrive at the history of religions. This is one thing we could teach, but we then have to ask to what purpose we would teach it and why?

We can, alternatively, regard the history of religions as something worthwhile to academics but not central to pedagogical practice in schools. Rather we might deal with the contemporary manifestation of religions. This is the present situation, underpinned by phenomenological methods. What the phenomenologist studies is what has arisen and is a result of what tradition has done and is doing. Herein lies a problem. Phenomenological approaches translated into representation and pedagogy in the classroom or in teacher education necessarily operate with a particular model of conceptualisation and representation. This model presumes that what is to be studied is what tradition presents, or at least what we interpret tradition as presenting, even when conveyed through the plurality of its membership groups. What has been edited out is what tradition has discarded as heresy rather than orthodoxy, or has reinterpreted to conform to its orthodoxy.

We can refine the phenomenological enquiry to ensure greater discrimination and accuracy by studying groups within traditions. Thus we have more complex and diverse forms of representation but still within the compass of tradition. We can refine the method of enquiry with ethnographic fieldwork to ensure that there is greater precision in relation to the representation of the empirical reality, and to signal the difficulties and inadequacies involved in the interpretation of the same. We are still working within a conceptual model that is determined by tradition. What we study is what has survived and been legitimated. This is the case even if we regard tradition as dynamic and cumulative. What we study is what the gatekeepers or authority figures in traditions, communities and groups wish to be acknowledged as the representation of themselves. This operates not only within the smaller group but also within the metanarrative that tradition has constructed, which frames the whole enterprise. What is never contested is the metanarrative itself, even though it may be understood differently by different groups. In moving away from constructions that have been presented by academics, the approach is now confined to a different interpretive context defined by representatives of 'tradition', even if presented by their interpreters.

In effect we are still examining the world from the standpoint of ideological perspectives, if we wish to study religion *per se*, and these perspectives have political implications. They communicate within political contexts, locally, nationally and globally. This makes them inherently conservative in their values and stances in relation to cultural change and wishing to call upon authority that transcends the historical to legitimate their voice. These are the predominant characteristics of religions, even though we can point to movements, groups and individuals within them who are dissenters—perhaps the Quakers would be a good example—or who are committed to a different sense of mission derived from teachings within their faith—liberation theology could be seen in this way. Similarly, in the realms of religious education John Hull is one individual who stresses the need for a religious or theological education that is anti-ideological and based on an understanding of Christianness rather than Christianity (Hull 1998:passim). However, by playing down ideology, emphasising the importance of values derived from different faith teachings and striving for inclusivity we find ourselves moving towards the justification of a subject that cannot be suitably described as *religious* education. We also find ourselves unwilling to acknowledge that ideology is a central feature of religion. Claims to truth are proclaimed with a capital T.

The problem with working within this frame of reference is that we cannot easily engage with issues and questions that lie beyond it, that is, those that tradition will not allow to be voiced. There are no representatives for these sanctioned by tradition, insofar as tradition weds itself to ideology. They have either been lost with what tradition has exorcised or they exist in the minds of communities but cannot be voiced in the context of this model of representation, except insofar as they represent an alternative voice that orthodoxies do not willingly accommodate. Although scholars of religions and religious education can take sides in these disputes, they do so—especially in the case of RE—in the knowledge that representation of a tradition starts with attempting accurately to map the 'orthodox' positions and their truth claims. By orthodoxy we do not mean just those branches of religion that are accepted to be of an orthodox form, but also those branches that oppose such orthodoxies with a new 'orthodoxy', an institutionalised representation. This inevitably applies a bias to representation in favour of the idea that the truth claims of 'orthodoxies' occupy the central position in any attempt to understand religion—a sort of fixed (ahistorical) point from which there is only (temporal) deviation. This model is underpinned by a judgement that, despite their shortcomings, as Bowker observes, religious systems are intrinsically valuable.

It follows that, despite their tendency towards deviance and corruption, religious orthodoxies are to be trusted and supported as vehicles for human progress towards wisdom, even if we have some or, in Bowker's case, many misgivings. They are spiritually necessary, even if they are ultimately destructive. As a result, however much we may advocate internal criticism as part of the dynamic of their maintenance, we do not regard it as suitable, in relation to our educational purposes, to undermine their truth claims. We may do this by seeking to occupy an impartial position. In other words the assumption behind this sort of study is an implicitly religious one: defence of our subject as it represents itself to us, and defence of its claims to knowledge, or at least the right to those claims, however much we may observe conflicting expressions of such claims.

An alternative model is to understand that such a map is precisely the one that orthodoxies wish to impose as a representation of religion in order to gain hegemony over both deviance (heterodoxy) and secularity. The map acts in the self-interest of orthodoxies and their truth claims. Were we to chart things differently we would recognise that the term 'orthodoxy' has been utilised by various groups over the course of history and within different religions to sanctify their own claims. There is no special status to be accorded to 'orthodoxy' in mapping religious tradition. We can, alternatively, investigate what purposes 'tradition' and 'orthodoxy' serve.

Tradition can be understood as less engaged with ideology. Cantwell Smith (1978) moves in this direction when he makes a connection between individual faith and cumulative tradition. In this model orthodoxy figures much less prominently as greater autonomy is placed on the shaping of the faith of the individual by the individual. But his idea of 'drawing on' rather than inhabiting that tradition does not do justice to the intricacies of this situation, and it objectifies tradition rather than seeing it as a powerful shaping influence, a proactive and self-conscious force. Cantwell Smith is vulnerable to criticism once culture is perceived in a more complex and fluid way in relation to the models of Barth and Bauman, with the political motivations analysed by Said. If we turn to the interpretive ethnographic model offered by Geertz and Jackson, we still find difficulties, but of a different kind. Bauman comments on the difficulty of cross-cultural translation in *Culture as Praxis* (1999:xlv–lii). Under the heading 'Relativity of culture and universality of humanity', he points to what Castoriadis calls 'the lack of equivalent codes' (ibid.:xlvi) for the ethnographer to work with when translating from the culture studied back to his or her own culture, and of the process of translating identity, and the precariousness of the same, that the cultural anthropologist undergoes. Effectively, he states:

> We are often worried by what is 'lost in translation'. Perhaps we worry unduly, or we worry about the wrong thing: what is truly lost we will never *know*, anyway, and if we come to know, we won't be able to *share* our knowledge with those for whom we wished to translate. . . . There are things which can be gained only in translation.
>
> (ibid.:xlvii)

Previously, he states, we had thought that the interpreter 'was a mask of the legislator . . . expected to reveal the truth of what the experiencers of the interpreted experience' (ibid.).

We may observe that in religious education we still retain the notion of the interpreter being a mask of the legislator to a large degree. If we examine the implications of Bauman's assessment we arrive at certain more radical conclusions as to what is going on in relation to tradition within and across cultural difference. Tradition, insofar as it wishes to ensure the continuance of cultural separation and maintain a closed system with its own ideological truth, works against the idea that there can be a cultural plurality in which communication is exchanged and translation occurs. This affects what is communicated and the purposes of communication, and works against acceptance of the idea that what is lost in translation we do not have to worry about unduly. Insofar as this model of communication is concerned with the communication of specific truths to those outside their own closed culture, it operates within the earlier model of passing on the truth of the experiencer. This can involve acceptance of the pluralism of cultures, but also preservation of a fixed identity within each culture. Applied to religion as a specific category and subject of study, this leaves the interpreter in an invidious position. He or she is required either to accept the truth claims of the subject at face value, or to subject them to scrutiny in a different hermeneutical context that will distort them, at least insofar as the claimant understands them (they are no longer given the status of truth accorded by the tradition). This leads us to levy a charge against the style and limitations of 'new phenomenology' or 'interpretive RE'. Despite Jackson's tendency towards ambivalence on this issue (Jackson 1997:82, 122–6), and his guarded defence at another point, 'contrary to the accusations of some of its critics, the phenomenological method does not imply a relativistic stance on the part of those who use it' (ibid.:14). The interpreter must side with the relativists or accept the 'native' view, at least by virtue of not contesting any of its claims. In effect this places the interpreter in a position that is provisional upon whether he or she addresses questions on values in his or her role. As teachers it is incumbent upon us to do so, and thus the interpreter ultimately makes judgements and places him- or herself on one side of the fence or the other.

Thus we arrive at a crucial hiatus in our study that will be pursued more thoroughly later. The researcher and the teacher necessarily take a relativistic or foundationalist stance, at a hermeneutical level, in being the interpreter of his or her subject of study and the claims of tradition. Insofar as they are understood to be truth claims and value claims they are reflected upon differently in accordance with the interpreter's/teacher's stance. It is precisely this issue which divides those who press for the defence of RE; whether maintaining its necessity as a defence against secularity, or recognising it as a preserve of openness against a closed, monocultural education system. It is difficult to side with the relativists when seeking to represent those making truth claims, and if you also belong to one of the traditions represented, as another aspect of your identity, you will have no wish to do so. This distinction between advocates for the subject has deep repercussions. Those committed to a fixed position in relation to the veracity of the bond between tradition and truth will understand this to be for the social good. Those who recognise the exchange of understandings as being propitious will pursue this as advantageous to the social good, without determining particular outcomes in terms of truth claims. The teacher who claims professional sufficiency without taking account of his or her insider role in relation to shaping values and the obligation to promote pupils' capacity for making judgements, is suggesting that he or she is situated in some impartial space, in the same sense as the phenomenological interpreter, which is his or her sole preserve. This is an illegitimate claim, and as far as the teacher is concerned it is professionally indefensible.

Bauman suggests that we would do well to heed Michel Foucault's warning that 'What is good, is something that comes through innovation. . . . The good does not exist . . . in an atemporal sky . . . the good is defined by us, it is practised, it is invented. And this is a collective work' (Bauman 1999:li; Foucault in Bess 1988:13).

It is probably clear by now that we are suggesting that the centre cannot hold and that the epistemological ambivalence of RE as a discrete subject of study has to be reexamined, as does its overall remit. This discussion on tradition has brought us to the point of reflecting on our own epistemological position as teachers and researchers of the subject. Our contention is that this is not just a question of how we teach the subject appropriately; a more significant issue also has to be addressed: whether we think the subject has an *exclusive* worth. If we think it has we will advocate it as a discrete subject because we side with religion's claims. We are epistemologically and ideologically religious. We may contrast this with defending the subject because of its *inclusive* worth. In Jackson's case this amounts to thinking it important that we educate into an understanding of different faith positions as part of a worldview awareness resulting in edification (Jackson 1997:130–1). In Hull's case it becomes part of a critical enquiry into values that resist ideological enclosure, within which the voices of different faiths should be heard (Hull 1998:20, 27). Taking an inclusivist position means we are situated differently and more ambiguously in relation to the subject as a discrete area of enquiry. In fact the subject and the reasons for studying it are quite different. From this point of view religion is to be understood as part of the diversity of cultural formation, of intrinsic importance to adherents in relation to identity but in significantly varying ways. From this advocacy of the subject religion becomes one phenomenon among many, and not entirely discrete from the others in its manifestation. It also becomes an aspect of values education, conceived of in a radical and critical sense. Thus in our view any argument on these grounds for religion to be studied discretely is undermined, and the only reason for maintaining the status of the subject is a pragmatic one—that is, the incorporation of an understanding of religion into education is of value and politically this can only be achieved by ensuring that the subject remains in place. In terms of educational and pedagogical principles this is highly unsatisfactory, despite its expediency. It also affects the effectiveness of inclusivist approaches.

To summarise, for advocates of religious education it appears that religious tradition can be understood in two distinct ways, as illustrated by the following extract:

> In the earliest days, to be a Christian was to be a member of a community animated by a faith and sustained by a hope—faith in a person and hope for a coming event. The morality of these communities was a custom of behaviour appropriate to the character of the faith and to the nature of the expectation. . . . The nearest thing to a moral ideal known to these communities was the ideal of charity; the nearest thing to a moral rule was

the precept to love God and one's neighbour. . . .

[B]ut over these earliest Christian communities, in the course of two centuries, there came a great change. The habit of moral behaviour was converted into the self-conscious pursuit of formulated moral ideals—a conversion parallel to the change from faith in a person to belief in a collection of abstract propositions, a creed.

This change sprang from . . . the necessity of translating a Christian way of life into a form in which it could be appreciated by those who had never shared the original inspiration and who, having to learn their Christianity as a foreign language, needed a grammar.

From this time in the history of Christendom a Christian habit of moral behaviour (which had sprung from the circumstances of Christian life) was swamped by a Christian moral ideology, and the perception of the poetic character of human conduct was lost.

(Oakeshott 1962:77–8)

Oakeshott identifies the distinction historically, with particular attention being paid to the movement from habits of moral behaviour to moral ideology. However, explicit in this is the development of creedal formulas that provide the truth claims, in an ideological sense, upon which the systematic formulations of ethical injunctions are based. Faith communities, as Oakeshott identifies them, are constituted differently, with different ends and purposes from religious ideologies. Proponents of the study of religion in education treat their subjects of study differently according to the principles behind the approach. Phenomenological approaches treat them as faith communities, with empathetic consideration, or at least sympathetically in wishing to understand their grammar. Alternatively, like Bowker, they warn against their ideological tendencies and the likely political outcomes that will ensue. Alternatively again, they argue for the importance of teaching these truth claims to ensure theological literacy and the creation of a more moral and just society. Underlying these different approaches are convictions about the way in which religious education can best contribute to values in the shaping of the future world. Oakeshott's historical distinction is still being played out on the contemporary stage in the different ways in which religions are affirmed or criticised. As we shall see in Chapter 3, this has a distinct bearing on different conceptions of spiritual education.

3 A critical review of spiritual education

Clive Erricker

The spiritual has been identified as having a place in state education since the involvement of the churches in the national system of education in the first half of the nineteenth century. Nevertheless it has never taken a central position in the purposes of education. The initial responses to the idea of mass education hardly had spiritual wellbeing in mind, as Chadwick notes when quoting Henson: 'The ignorance of the masses was thought by the ruling class to be the best protection of society against the destructive idealism of minds which had been so far enfranchised by knowledge as to feel hardship and to resent oppression' (Henson 1939:189; Chadwick 1997:5).

The churches' role in such a venture was not deemed to be one of providing spiritual edification but to guarantee moral order and social stability through the delivery of a catechism that was not distinctive of any particular denomination (Chadwick 1997:11), and by 'inculcating' Christian values (ibid.:5). Such beginnings, not easily accomplished in themselves, alert us to the political and ideological character of the environment of educational policy making within which any notion of spiritual education would have to be shaped. This also alerts us to the pragmatic function for which any 'spiritual' education would be deployed. Indeed, arriving at the 1944 Education Act, according to Jack Priestley, we might well be suspicious of the purpose of including the term 'spiritual', and that its usefulness lay in its vagueness.

Priestley (1996) notes that the key moment in the use of 'spiritual' in modern educational usage was its appearance in the 1944 Education Act, preceding 'moral, mental and physical' in the first sentence of the Preamble. He also remarks that it owes its presence to 'a simple piece of archipiscopal jiggery-pokery' (ibid.:2). He explains this by relating that the author of that part of the Preamble was Canon J. Hall, chief officer of the National Society, who was chosen for the post by William Temple to gain 'the confidence of local authorities, directors of education and the teachers in their organisations' in order to bring about a coming together of church and state schools. When Hall was asked why he had used the word spiritual rather than religious he replied 'Because it was much broader', explaining that 'If we had used the word religious they would all have started arguing about it' (ibid.:8). Ironically, and by contrast, Priestley also relates how, in 1977, the word was almost lost when the Department for Education and

Science (DES) published its list of relevant areas of experience in Curriculum 11–16, when one view offered was that 'Spiritual is a meaningless adjective for the atheist and of dubious use to the agnostic' (ibid.:2). He also states that such views often flew in the face of, or were simply ignorant of, relevant educational research, such as that published by David Hay at Nottingham University during that period. This was and still is not an uncommon phenomenon. The most significant points to note about Priestley's observations are:

- how the notions of spiritual and religious are overlapping but distinct;
- how contentious the word spiritual is in modern society;
- how the notion of the spiritual has a particularly ambivalent place in the idea of a curriculum.

In recent years, largely as a response to the word spiritual being included in the 1988 Education Reform Act, but also as an ongoing concern in the British educational system, especially in relation to the purposes of religious education, the question of what it means to address the spirituality of children and young people has produced a body of literature and a flourishing debate. Within the divergent views expressed a number of ideological and epistemological positions have emerged in attempts to establish the principles according to which spiritual education can be appropriately taught, learned or developed. The value of this debate lies in much more than the question of how the spiritual can be inserted into education. It has reinvigorated the concern for the philosophical basis of education and reflection on the historical differences in educational philosophy that have been in tension in Western societies since the Enlightenment.

Before entering that debate, the following section will begin with a critical review of how spiritual development has been addressed by Ofsted (Office for Standards in Education) and the SCAA, now the Quality Curriculum Authority (QCA), in response to its inclusion in the main aims of the Education Reform Act. The purpose of this is twofold: to illustrate how the vagueness of the term 'spiritual' is maintained; and to show the political usefulness of this strategy.

Government directives and guidelines: (cl)aims without commitment?

In the 1988 Education Reform Act and Circular 1/94 (DFEE 1994) there is an expressed commitment to the spiritual in education. The first paragraph of the circular establishes the context for curriculum provision in relation to the overarching aim of education: 'The Education Reform Act 1988 sets out as the central aim for the school curriculum that it should promote the spiritual, moral, cultural, mental and physical development of pupils and society, and prepare pupils for the opportunities, responsibilities and experiences of adult life' (DFEE 1994:9). Given this starting point we can chart the pursuit of this aim, with particular reference to the spiritual development of children: 'The Government is concerned that insufficient attention has been paid explicitly to the spiritual, moral and cultural aspects of pupil's development and would encourage schools to address how the curriculum and other activities might best contribute to this crucial dimension of education' (ibid.:9).

Supportive as these comments were of addressing the spiritual in education, there was criticism of what might be realised in practice, for example by John Hull in his Hockerill Lecture (Hull 1993), which was a response to Circular 3/89 (DFEE 1989), and in his editorials in the *British Journal of Religious Education* during that year and subsequently (Hull 1998:122–6). Hull is directly concerned with the wording of the Act and its interpretation in relation to religious education, the cultural prominence given to Christianity, and the type of Christian theology lying behind this. As we shall see, this 'political theology' also affects the interpretation of 'spiritual, moral, cultural and social development' and the current moves towards the implementation of citizenship education in 2002.

Initial concern was also expressed about the circulars' reference to spiritual development being included in collective worship as there was ambiguity as to whether a suggestion of Christian nurture was implied. At the same time no specific examples of how spiritual development should be included in curriculum subjects other than RE was provided. In effect, in the Act itself and the circulars that followed it there was a directive to deliver across the curriculum and beyond with insufficient guidance. The result was confusion, a vacuum that Ofsted was subsequently required to resolve. The difficulty for Ofsted was that it was and is not a policy-making body. Thus the Ofsted definition below can be subjected to the same criticisms as those made previously. In its framework document, which moves between being a discussion paper and a directive, interesting statements are made that deserve to be viewed in relation to one another. It starts with a description of the scope of spiritual development, under the title 'definition':

> Spiritual development relates to that aspect of inner life through which pupils acquire insights into their personal existence which are of enduring worth. It is characterised by reflection, the attribution of meaning to experience, valuing a non-material dimension to life and intimations of enduring reality. 'Spiritual' is not synonymous with 'religious'; all areas of the curriculum may contribute to spiritual development.
>
> (Ofsted 1994:8)

One of the obvious difficulties that this move towards inspection created was identifying the criteria and context in which development could be assessed. Schools with a religious foundation could take recourse to theological principles and community practices relating to values, attitudes and ethos, but Ofsted was at pains to make clear that this was not expected in state schools generally. One of the reasons given for this was that it might result in the confessional teaching of RE, 'which legislation since 1944 has been at pains to avoid' (ibid.:15). Regrettably, in its attempt at even-handedness and broad definition, the Ofsted framework could be said to be the opposite of a framework because it supplies no generally acceptable criteria or context. The result is a stress throughout on the importance of the development of the individual and the uniqueness of each individual's conception of spirituality (ibid.:10). This has attracted criticism from different quarters. Adrian Thatcher comments that: 'The Ofsted approach to spiritual development is gripped by the notion of individuality and the problem of the individual's reflexive relationship to herself...there is a complete lack in Government literature of any mention of neighbour love, or (to use an equally biblical word) justice' (Thatcher 1996:119). This criticism exposes how in-dividualistically oriented notions of spirituality are perceived to fail to address values, common notions of human responsibility and the creation of a just society. A further criticism, by Andrew Wright (1997a), drew on Alasdair MacIntyre's statement:

> The story of my life is always embedded in the story of those communities from which I derive my identity. I am born with a past; and to try to cut myself off from that past, in the individualistic mode, is to deform my present relationships. The possession of an historical identity and the possession of a social identity coincide.
>
> (MacIntyre 1985:221; Wright 1997a:16)

Wright concludes that it is therefore necessary to understand spirituality in terms of national identity, which must begin with 'recognising and nurturing children into the specific spiritual tradition they bring with them to the classroom' (1997a:16). In contrast he suggests that a 'spiritual education that seeks to dislocate itself from any specific tradition' will end up 'indoctrinating children into the spiritual tradition of romanticism' (ibid.:17), which he identifies with the teachings of Rousseau and those of progressive, childcentred educators.

Both the above criticisms point to a nurturing by default into an inadequate form of spiritual development precisely because a lack of responsibility has been taken over the educational and social implications that attach to spiritual development in schools. Whilst Thatcher criticises the lack of attention to Christian theology, Wright identifies the lack of any hermeneutical underpinning in policy making.

Ofsted ends its framework document with four questions, or 'Points To Consider'. This is perhaps evidence that Ofsted itself was unsure of the workableness of its own approach.

A comparison of the guidance and inspection documents investigated so far reveals certain similarities in character. For example they identify religious education and collective worship as significant areas in which spiritual develop-ment can take place; and they suggest that spiritual development should be addressed across the curriculum and beyond, but do not illustrate how, which *is* done with religious education and collective worship. When illustration is given (DFEE 1994:13) it relates either to knowledge and understanding, for example of beliefs and worldviews (including scientific), or to values, moral development, behaviour and attitudes, with regard to personal reflection in the case of RE. It becomes particularly problematic with regard to collective worship, with the requirement to focus on Jesus Christ being included, particularly as the framework document emphasises the 'process of exploring' (ibid.:11).

It appears that these documents, whilst not necessarily making overtly contradictory statements, do not provide a coherent explanation of what is being addressed or how it can be addressed. The statements effectively compete with one another rather than offer progressive clarification, whether we scrutinise one text or the texts in relation to one another. This tension and ambiguity is due both to a lack of conceptual clarity and to the attempt to identify a process in the context of a knowledge-based curriculum and a wider educational context (that of collective worship, moral development, school ethos and policy making) that had been insufficiently addressed previously. The outcome is competing claims about the direction such provision should take and a suspicion as to what exactly the policy makers were seeking to achieve.

When we inspect the framework document's statements on inspecting 'spiritual development' (the quotation marks are included in the document) we become aware of the tentative nature of such an activity (ibid.:12), within the description of which the word spiritual does not appear but values, attitudes, ethos and climate do. Highlighted is the need to be distanced from a partisan view of spiritual development and any attempt to assess individuals. What is worrying at this point is the lack of criteria for inspection. This necessarily determines that it is the individual inspector assigned to the task who constructs, or not as the case may be, a coherent means of assessment. Such a situation is clearly flawed. The question that remains is what to do about it. The following possibilities might have been envisaged:

- Abandon all talk of spiritual development and concentrate on values and moral development.
- Work towards a more rigorous (exclusivist?) attempt at definition.
- Conduct/consult educational research in the area.
- Recognise the need to address how cross-curricular issues can be firmly identified in curriculum subjects.
- Take this as an opportunity to revise our understanding of the relationship between the curriculum, religious education and collective worship, and values education.

A number of the above options would have required a seriousness of intent in terms of educational purpose, and would have brought particular political issues to the surface in relation to approaches to education and religious influence on education that the government and administrators wished to avoid. It is interesting to identify how this was dealt with under the auspices of the School Curriculum and Assessment Authority (SCAA), which replaced the National Curriculum Council (NCC) and later became the Qualifications and Curriculum Authority (QCA).

It is worth noting that SCAA had already produced model syllabuses for RE (SCAA 1994a and b). These had attracted criticism as being too content led, but have become influential throughout the latter half of the 1990s. At the time of writing this influence has reached the point where they must be included in the material used for initial teacher training. Their promotion as the guide for delivery of RE in schools and subsequently initial teacher training by the Teacher Training Authority (TTA) and, probably more importantly, through the use of their two attainment targets as a basis for inspection of schools by Ofsted, and of LEA agreed syllabuses and teacher training courses, have been the significant factors. This exercise in centralising the monitoring of provision was an adept political strategy that circumvented the legal authority held by local education authorities (LEAs) and their agreed syllabuses.

During this same period the SCAA launched the 1995 'Education for Adult Life' initiative with the republication of an earlier NCC document on spiritual and moral development (SCAA 1995). At this point it is important to note how this initiative was managed. A forum was set up to ensure that the process by which policy and provision was constructed would be democratic. A succession of documents followed as this procedure ran its course: Discussion Paper 6 (SCAA 1996a); the findings of the forum (SCAA 1996b); and an illustrative matrix for schools to use as guidance, and still in operation at the time of writing. There were seven groups representing different areas of education: PSHE and Citizenship being two examples of groups reporting on findings in their own areas. The object of these groups' reports was to suggest the best way in which the Education for Adult Life initiative could be provided for. At this point it is not necessary to investigate these documents in detail, some of which are bland and vague to the point of distraction. A critique of their approach will be presented in Chapter 5.

Underlying this process has been a political will to ensure that a certain type of values education prevails in state schooling to serve national and economic interests. This was clearly revealed in the speech by the chief executive of the SCAA at the inaugural conference in 1996. What follows is a close examination of the text of that speech and a deconstruction of its message. This is undertaken not just because the speech was important for setting the educational agenda that followed, but also because it is a model of rhetoric for all political pronouncements on the relationship between education, values and the cohesion of modern society. It is the dominant script to be followed. The SCAA agenda was outlined by its chief executive, Dr Nicholas Tate, as follows:

> The issues we are here to discuss are not just ones for schools. Moral and spiritual education in schools is only possible if the society which maintains these schools is clear about its ends. . . . As the statutory custodian of the school curriculum, the School Curriculum Assessment Authority is perhaps uniquely placed to initiate a national debate on these issues. But we hope to do more than just that. Our objective today is to come up with an agenda for action.

> (Tate 1966:point 5)

He subsequently identified the reasons for the present moral and spiritual malaise:

> What has done most to undermine our surviving moral language has been the spread of an all pervasive relativism. . . . By relativism I mean the view that morality is largely a matter of taste and opinion, that there is no such thing as moral error, and that there is no point therefore in searching for the truth about moral matters or in arguing and reasoning about it.
>
> (ibid.: points 14–15)

He identified the decline of religious faith as one of the main reasons for the spread of moral relativism:

> As the Archbishop of Canterbury has recently said, people ever since the Enlightenment 'have been living off the legacy of a deep residual belief in God. But as people move further away from that, they find it more and more difficult to give a substantial basis for why they should be good'. This is one reason why religious education must continue to be a vital part of every child's curriculum. . . . It is also a reason why children's development is so important, as the origin of the will to do what is right.
>
> (ibid.:point 23)

He also suggested that in personal and social education:

> We need to review dispassionately the emphasis it often gives to the promotion of pupils' self-esteem . . . . Is it too heretical a thought that it is possible to place too much emphasis on self-esteem (a peculiarly late twentieth century occupation) and too little on some of the traditional moral qualities?
>
> (ibid.:point 36)

Nicholas Tate's speech was seminal insofar as it made very public and reoriented the debate on spiritual and moral development. The fundamental reason for this was the close association it made between children's education in these areas and the perceived state of moral decline in society. A closer analysis of the speech may reveal for some the following agenda:

- Shoring up the moral fabric of society (point 7).
- Helping to keep the beacon of civilisation alight (point 8).
- Promoting a virtuous society (point 10).
- Promoting the moral and spiritual well-being of society (point 11) by reaffirming the transmission of a set of rules, precepts and principles (point 12).

This could be achieved by challenging 'the spread of an all pervading relativism' (point 14), which has eroded our ability to 'assert that any value is objective and enduring' (point 14) and left us 'profoundly disabled' (point 21). Since we had lost the 'religious basis for morality' (point 23), people were finding it 'more and more difficult to give a substantial basis for why they should be good' (here he was quoting the Archbishop of Canterbury). Furthermore there was a need to counter the 'full flowering of postmodernism with its simultaneous and dispiriting rejection both of universal values and our traditional sense of the significance of the culturally specific' (point 24), and to recognise that 'If ever a dragon needed slaying, it is the dragon of relativism'.

The suggested ways forward included a 'commitment to a set of core values' (point 28), 'broader national agreement on those values that society is *authorising* schools to teach on its behalf' (point 29, emphasis added), and recognising that 'there are some moral matters which should not be called into question. This is how it is; this is how it has been; this is how it must be' (point 30). The values being taught should not 'separate the public from the private' (point 31).

This led to Tate identifying certain matters that needed to be addressed, taking account of the assertion that '70% of people believe in God' and that research had shown that 'young people are more likely to find life worth living, to think it has a purpose, and to show concern for others and for the environment if they are either practising or non-practising believers' (point 34). He also spoke of the need to review dispassionately the emphasis that personal and social education often gives to the promotion of pupil's self-esteem, 'and how it can contribute to society's efforts to maintain structures centred on the traditional two parent family' (point 36). To these ends he proposed the establishment of a national forum to 'look further into the issues and suggest courses of action' (point 37).

Taking the analysis one stage further, we note the following:

*   The use of terms. If we total the number of times significant terms are used in the speech we discover the following: Moral and spiritual education/development eight times, with moral invariably preceding spiritual: moral(ity) 21 times; value(s) 10 times; spiritual(ity) once; religion (religious/faith/community, excluding RE) six times.
*   The predominant emphasis on morality over and above spiritual development. One of the issues that arises from this is the relationship between the two. Is spiritual development the handmaiden of moral education? If so how, in practice, are the two to be related? Also, can we really arrive at an understanding of spiritual development without recourse to a specific doctrinal understanding embedded in a religious tradition? This is the same question that was raised in response to the earlier document (Discussion Paper 3) and we shall address this issue below.
*   The construction of a social and educational reality. The argument used and reality presented make interesting reading in the context of the professed purpose of the speech: to initiate a debate in order to arrive at consensus.

Clearly, those holding a relativist position cannot enter into this debate since the terms of the debate exclude them, having been identified as a 'dragon to be slain' on the basis of their significant contribution to moral decline. Also, in the list of those invited to contribute to the debate—'people from all sectors of the community' (point 5)—there are no children, presumably because they have been identified as being corrupted by the dragon and still under its spell, and thus their voices are of no account. Note also that the debate is not about the veracity of the picture painted by Nick Tate, but about 'an agenda for action' (point 5), which implies that we already know why action is required, against what state of affairs the action is to be directed, and towards what ends it is to be undertaken. The analogy that springs to mind might not be a forum, but a council of war. The enemy has been established (relativists and postmodernists), the victims have been identified, specifically in the martyrdom of headteacher Philip Lawrence, and the corruption of children and society. The weaponry has been chosen in the form of values that are 'objective and enduring' (point 14), and the troops are to be led by tried and trustworthy traditional figures, such as Shakespeare and Schubert (point 22), the Chief Rabbi (point 8), the Archbishop of Canterbury (point 23), historian Richard Hoggart (point 14), columnist Melanie Phillips (point 9) and, last but not least, Lord Rees-Mogg (point 18).

This nationalistic fervour against the enemy within is nothing to do with the development of children's spirituality, in the sense of addressing their stated needs. Rather it is a crusade to exterminate those who have afflicted 'the whole moral consciousness of present-day Britain' (Lord Rees-Mogg, point 18). No room for any conscientious objectors here.

Thus we have an interesting situation that could be analysed as follows. Perhaps Nick Tate is more of a Don Quixote than a St George. Rather than a dragon we have windmills at which he is tilting; or just an Aunt Sally that he has constructed for his own purposes. Relativism is, in fact, something different from the account Tate constructs. The relativist position could be said to be the only one to provide the possibility of arriving at consensus. The case for this will be argued in Chapter 4, at which point we shall have to determine exactly what we mean by relativist, whether those who adhere to absolute values can operate in a relativist framework, just whose voices should be consulted or excluded in attempting to arrive at a consensus, and whether consensus is possible or desirable.

The purpose of the above examination has been to map the political territory within which educational debate on and research into spiritual education can be situated. I shall now turn to those who have conducted research and written in this area in order to identify the positions held and the issues to be resolved.

Theological defences

Adrian Thatcher, a virulent critic of the SCAA documents, has been a significant advocate of a theological foundation for spiritual education. Theology also provides the identifiable ends to which spiritual development should lead. Indeed he states that the lack of theological direction has seriously undermined religious education, and that 'one of the most important tasks for the theologian is to draw attention to *the climate of unbelief* within which the religious educator operates' (Thatcher 1990:274). This he parallels with Alastair MacIntyre's charge of emotivism, the doctrine that 'all evaluative judgements and more specifically all moral judgements are *nothing but* expressions of preference, expressions of attitude or feeling, insofar as they are moral or evaluative in character' (MacIntyre 1985, quoted in ibid.:274). Thatcher arrives at the conclusion that what in the moral case can be identified as the need for contemporary society to recover a sense of virtue, in the theological case amounts to a need to recover religious truth (ibid.:275).

Thatcher's argument proceeds from a critique of the phenomenological approach to religious education, which, he claims, reveals the problems that arise from taking up a relativistic position that is supposedly value free. On the contrary, he observes, it operates on the assumption that 'in treating religions as equal or religion as a universal feature of existence, the stipulation that no religion is absolute is as absolute as the stipulation that any one religion is absolute' (ibid.:279). The consequence of this is that securing religious commitment ceases to be an aspect of religious education. This relativism becomes problematic when addressing spiritual development since no religious stance, and in particular one based on the distinctiveness of Christian commitment, can operate as the basis of spiritual development. Thatcher considers that the SCAA model of consensus suffers from the flawed premises that derive from the climate of unbelief within which it operates, despite an (ironic?) consonance of view with the remarks of Nicholas Tate. Thatcher is also concerned that, in the absence of a theological foundation, there is no obvious connection between spiritual and moral development.

Andrew Wright adopts a similar position to that of Thatcher. However, his position will be given more detailed attention since it can introduce us to the hermeneutical complexities involved in seeking to address spiritual education. In his articles on 'Hermeneutics and Religious Understanding' (Wright 1997b, 1998a), and in his *Spiritual Pedagogy* (Wright 1998b), he argues from the position of Trinitarian Christian Orthodoxy, relying on an interpretation of the critical realism of Gadamer and Habermas to construct a new critical theory for RE. At issue is what hermeneutical paradigm the subject should adopt. He is quite clear that 'critical realism' is to be defended against the rival claims of romanticism and postmodernism, which he identifies as uncritical approaches, insufficient for devising a curriculum rationale that will serve religious literacy.

Wright identifies the influence of romanticist hermeneutical theory as the shaping force in modern religious education, from Loukes and Goldman through to the phenomenological approaches. He sees this romanticism as emerging in the desire to engage children with the relevance of religion to their own lives, and in doing so to relativise religious (and more specifically Christian) truth claims.

He identifies postmodern hermeneutics as taking this further. Whereas romanticism believed that it could 'affirm a religious reality' and 'did not understand itself as mere subjectivity' (Wright 1997b:209), the postmodern understanding is that there is no knowledge of reality. Wright's concern is that 'the contemporary fascination of religious education with spirituality…embodies implicitly a post-modern hermeneutic' (ibid.:210). Wright turns to Gadamer to assert his own position. He is concerned to 'grapple with questions of realistic truth' (ibid.:204). In this the issue is to understand that 'our received linguistic traditions…constitute attempts to describe the actual order of things' (ibid.:60) and recognise that 'The only authentic criteria against which the truth claims embedded in language should be tested is that of reality itself' (ibid.:210). Gadamer's injunction that a text questions the understanding of the interpreter and thus has a transformative power that is realised in 'the experience of being pulled up short by the text' (Gadamer 1979:337) is the basis of Wright's idea that the interpreter can be confronted with such a reality.

Wright (1997b:63) cites Cooling and his process of 'concept cracking' (Cooling 1992, 1993, 1994) as an example of 'enabling pupils to fulfil their right of access to an understanding of orthodox Christianity' by developing 'a linguistic competency in which the child is enabled to listen to the realistic claims made by scripture and Christian doctrinal formulations and enter into conversation with them' (Wright 1997b:63). This, he claims, is illustrative of Gadamer's hermeneutical position. As a caveat, he questions whether Cooling's model sufficiently addresses how the child is to undertake the task of making an informed response to the Christian truth claims rather than simply being confronted by them (ibid.:63). This would seem to be precisely the problem with any absolute truth claim, and we shall return to this issue shortly.

In Wright's *Spiritual Pedagogy* (1998b) we find a fuller exposition of his argument and position in relation to spiritual education. His claim is that the loss of faith in 'ultimate spiritual truth' (ibid.:ix) as a result of the pursuit of rationalism and materialism in the Enlightenment gave rise to the Romantic ideal of an individualistic spirituality based on the inner experiences of the individual, 'dislocated from the wisdom of tradition and community' (ibid.:ix). This 'rootless romantic spirituality' we now find in the guise of postmodernism. As a result the postmodern child is 'deprived of spiritual roots and the skills of spiritual discernment . . . and prey to the cultural, political and economic powers operating in contemporary society' (ibid.:ix).

Wright criticises Christian liberalism and contemporary religious educators for failing to recognise that they have succumbed to the individualistic and relativistic models of knowledge and truth that pervade modern society and have eroded the consideration of religious truth claims as claims to absolute truth. At the heart of this argument is his specific concern for the claims of Trinitarian Christianity. It is his epistemological defence of this position that determines the sufficiency of his overall position.

Wright claims that 'True rationality lies…in understanding that accommodates itself to the objective claims of the actuality of divine revelation. Authentic faith is rooted in…a relationship with the Trinitarian God dependent on the mediation of revelation through scripture and ecclesiastical tradition' (ibid.:72), and asserts that 'If Christian spirituality, in its historical continuity, is incompatible with romantic and post-modern formulations, then the latter can claim universality only by deconstructing orthodox Christian discourse and colonising it within its own frame of reference' (ibid.:69).

In the first statement Wright presumes that 'divine revelation' can be understood as 'objective' and that 'authentic' faith is determined by its assent to Trinitarian doctrine. He also claims that this will be recognised in the ratification of scripture's and tradition's pronouncements. In other words faith is determined as authentic according to its assent to foundational claims, and these can be confirmed as authentic by appealing to 'objectivity', which is a scientific criterion. This satisfies most of the criteria claimed for knowledge in the modern period and prior to it. In the second quotation two further criteria are introduced: universality, which is the corollary of objectivity; and historical continuity, which is the criterion for affirming the authenticity of orthodoxy. In this series of assertions Wright seeks to ensure that 'faith' is bound within the criteria for knowledge that operate within religion and science in the modern era. Only by conforming to these does it gain any credence. This is a significant example of how religion seeks to ensure its own political purposes without sufficient justification or apologia.

What I wish to emphasise is that Wright's position, like any other, can only be justified by its own internal logic, not by its premises. The epistemological framework we adopt tends to be determined by the outcomes we wish to achieve. In Wright's case, however, what he wishes to achieve is the substantiation of Christian truth claims as absolute and objective, and thus inviolable. To do this he has to argue that such claims are not to be subjected to the same critical assessment as other claims, by virtue of their self-advertised, transcendent, ahistorical nature, and their universality, objectivity, rationality and historical continuity. I contend that such a claim puts the idea of spiritual education in great danger. The severity of Wright's condemnation of theological liberalism (ibid.:75) places his own argument in jeopardy. If we are to understand that theological liberalism begins and ends with the human spirit (ibid.:75), and that this position can only accommodate the Christian narrative within its framework by reconstructing it, we have to ask, what is this narrative and how was it constructed in the first place? Wright's answer to this is to assert the 'objective claims of the actuality of divine revelation' (ibid.:72), which expresses itself in the doctrine of the Trinity. This 'is not a culturally relative expression of the subjective religious experience of Christians' (ibid.:72). Here Wright draws a distinction between human sensibility and divine revelation. The latter acts as a critique of modernity in the light of Christian truth, rather than accommodating itself to the former (ibid.:72). Mediation of this truth is found only within the realms of scripture and ecclesiastical tradition.

This is an interesting God and he performs an interesting function. The truth that he reveals is separated from any other 'knowledge' by virtue of bypassing the historical/temporal process whereby knowledge is discovered or constructed. Wright is careful to side with science as long as science accords with this revealed truth. 'Such natural knowledge of God is immediately qualified within the

Christian tradition' (ibid.:73). Also qualified by means of the same strategy is 'negative theology'. Christian mysticism must be sanctioned by positive theology (ibid.:77), that is, the ecclesia. 'It is precisely through the aesthetic appreciation and scientific investigation of his creation that God is revealed' (ibid.:72). From this position of power, which is unquestionable and inviolable, those who make up the ecclesia can judge, censor and repress all other interpretations of 'God' and 'reality' since they have access to a truth that no others share. This metanarrological assumption defies credulity. It is also so patently politically conceived that it falls prey to all the deconstructive criticisms of Lyotard (1984), to whom we shall turn later.

When Wright (1998b:79) goes on to assert that the 'source of Christian spirituality is the Holy Spirit, not the human spirit', it becomes clear that God and the Holy Spirit are in thrall to the Church rather than its master since the distinction between the two spirits is a matter for the ecclesia to discern. Wright's position is not justified by argument alone but on an irrefutable premise as to who possesses the 'truth', which is why it is pedagogically repressive. His dismissal of the relationship between language and reality, which is so central to the present philosophical debate, is done on the basis that this 'truth' is not susceptible to such scrutiny. On what grounds? On the grounds of its own assertion that it is the truth.

When Wright moves on to the 'reconstruction of spiritual literacy' and considers the reality of spiritual diversity he places his discourse in the context of education and other religions. He states that 'a key issue remains that of our relationship with ourselves, with others, with the world we indwell, and with *the absence or presence of divinity*' (ibid.:89, emphasis added). Wright's concern is to ensure that a critical line is drawn according to this absence or presence. Consequently those traditions that assert the presence of divinity should be correctly theologically represented, according to their truth claims, and not according to a generic anthropological or theological framework that distorts them. What is then represented is their particular understanding of the nature of reality (ibid.:86).

I have no quarrel with Wright's desire for distinctiveness, however there are two corollaries to this. The first is that we are dealing with traditions as ideologies, within his characterisation. Insofar as specific religious truths advertise themselves as possessing *the* truth they are ideological in nature, since by implication they deny the truth of others, justified according to the basis of their own truth claims. In other words we have competing truths, each of which is seeking not only to voice its own 'representation of reality' but also to insist that 'reality' is only correctly understood according to its own doctrines. The second is that pedagogically we have to take this into account when being a representative of such claims as the teacher, whilst also occupying a specific personal position ourselves.

The problems arise when we acknowledge that, in relation to education and children's spiritual development, we must enable them to determine their own position on these claims. This does not mean asking which truth claim is correct, or even defending one's own, but asking whether such claims to ideological truth are appropriate in themselves. It is difficult to see how children can be offered this possibility if the aim is both to present children with distinctive truth claims, and to assert that these truth claims are not to be questioned at the deepest hermeneutical level. If the latter enquiry is deemed to conflict with the purposes of RE, it is RE that is called into question. What Wright is presenting is a defence of religious truth claims in general and the Christian truth claim in particular. Effectively, this is a defence of religious ideology against secularism.

Wright moves on to ask 'Are our spiritual lives attuned to the way things *actually are* in the world, or are they in dissonance with *reality*' (ibid.:92, emphasis added). How could we possibly answer this question, except by asserting, as if we know in advance, a doctrinal formula that pre-empts the question with an indisputable answer. Here the experience of living, with all its vicissitudes and complexity, as a progressive search for wholeness, is reduced to the imposition of a doctrinal formula that is meant to clarify and contextualise our problems such that they are resolved, or are at least seen as resolvable, only within the frame of reference offered by religion, with particular regard being given to Christian orthodoxy. Wright's attention to the issue of how religious education should be taught (Wright 1998a:69) can, in fact, only be resolved hermeneutically by questioning the epistemological framework within which he places it. In order to do this, greater attention has to be paid to Habermas' notion of contingent rationality (ibid.:66) and his communicative model of action, in which negotiation of common definitions of situations is suggested (ibid.:64; Habermas 1991:95); Habermas' criticism of Gadamer on the basis that his theory implies that the text is always right (Wright 1998a:64) and is not sufficiently open to 'the possibility of ideological distortion within the tradition's self-formulation' (ibid.:64; see also Warnke 1987:140ff); and the further possibilities offered by both relativist and postmodern writers. In other words Wright is seeking to close down the debate on, and enquiry into, the complexities involved in the construction of worldviews in order to favour religious orthodoxies and his presentation of Christian orthodoxy. Thus Wright uses critical realism, and interprets the views of its leading proponents, to justify a naive realist or foundationalist position.

By taking an ideological approach to spiritual education both Wright and Thatcher seek to ensure that RE serves the ends of religious, particularly Christian, ideology against secularity. Spiritual education is seen as a means to this end. This allows us to recognise the difficulties we face in continuing with a divided understanding of what RE seeks to achieve at the academic and political level as a curriculum subject. It also presents us with unresolvable differences in relation to the spiritual education of children and young people in state schooling. Implicit in these approaches is the assumption that content takes precedence over the pedagogical process, and that the two can be separated. Rather it is the case, as will be argued later, that the two are intimately related such that favouring the former over the latter imposes a certain type of pedagogical practice that favours certain restrictive outcomes. In fact this is Wright's criticism of what he calls the romantic, anthropological and postmodern approaches; thus he must acknowledge that the same is true of his own. His approach does not transcend or overcome this issue but is a particular stance within it.

Liberal investigations

Coming at the problem from a different perspective, Dennis Starkings (1993) argues the case for a broader approach than those of Thatcher and Wright. Starkings is concerned with the problematic divide between the religious and the secular in the definitions applied to spirituality, and he sees the arts as a mediating instrument. He raises the problem of how to take an overall view of spirituality whilst maintaining the distinctiveness of, for example, Christian spirituality. He suggests that 'while the religious kinds of spirituality find their focus and authentication in the distinctive experience of worship, secular spirituality is authenticated in a progressive integration of life's experience'. Despite this distinction he maintains that 'the religious and the secular are related to each other through the contemporary experience of living across essentially distinguishable frameworks of meaning' (ibid.:9). Starkings' position is that 'The challenge for anyone who wishes to form a view of the nature of spirituality that is sufficient for the comprehensive purposes of a national education system is...to draw such a map of spirituality's overall landscape as may relate spirituality's distinctively religious forms to its broader and secular manifestations' (ibid.:10).

Starkings charts the steps towards this relationship by identifying Christian faith as an experience of moving towards God through the disclosures of revelation. Revelation is to be grappled with in the progression from unknowing to knowing. This he understands as worship, in its broadest sense. Starkings wishes to retain the distinctiveness of the religious path but asserts the authenticity of the secular with reference to the spiritual value of music, ballet, painting or drama. He suggests that through these and other human activities we can reach out for some wisdom, some humanity, some integration of our life's experience (ibid.:14). Thus both the religious and the secular use of the term refer to moving beyond the purely material, and in neither case can spiritual development be gained solely on the basis of confessional attachment. The important issue, in Starkings' treatment, is to sustain the dynamics of the religious and secular options whilst discarding neither. The value of Starkings' view is that it seeks to be inclusivist whilst overtly acknowledging the various stances involved. He also identifies ways in which different understandings can be presented. However Starkings is not concerned with consensus as such, but an awareness of different conceptions of spirituality and their forms of expression. This falls short of what Thatcher requires in identifying religious faith as a necessary foundation, of what Tate requires in wedding spiritual development to moral ends, and of what the SCAA regards as essential—finding a consensus. It is also in conflict with Wright's desire to ensure that doctrine legitimises the aesthetic only when the latter is compatible with the former. Starkings is to be commended for his more culturally sophisticated approach, and yet it is characteristic of a liberal naiveté in supposing that religious ideology will allow itself to be challenged or competed with on grounds of creative expression in artistic endeavour. Starkings passes over the distinction between the idea of faith narratives as the communal sources of tradition, and religious ideologies as the repositories of truth.

Like Starkings, David Hay pursues the notion of common spiritual experience, but it is understood and expressed in a different way. Hay's research is grounded in the notion of experience as the source of the spiritual. In this respect he assumes a different starting point from the doctrinally articulated position of the theological approaches, but one that is not inclusive of secularity *per se*. He is also concerned with the spirituality of individuals rather than institutionalised expressions. This is reflected in his research with adults in *Exploring Inner Space* (Hay 1982), where he is keen to show that declining adherence to religious bodies, and in particular the Christian churches, is not evidence of increasing secularity. He shows that religious experience in the lives of individuals is as pervasive as ever, but is not doctrinally articulated. In this respect we might compare his work with William James' *Varieties of Religious Experience* (1902). Although this was written at the turn of the century it still makes pertinent reading. For both James and Hay, religious sentiment and the discovery of that in the articulated experiences of individuals is the major focus of their studies.

When Hay moved on to research the spiritual experience of children, presented in *The Spirit of the Child* (Hay with Nye 1998), he offered findings of particular relevance to us here. Hay is concerned with 'how ordinary children talk about their spirituality' (ibid.:vi), and this constitutes the empirical study of the research. He argues that 'children's spirituality is rooted in a universal human awareness; that it is "really there" and not just a culturally constructed illusion' (ibid.:4). He acknowledges that 'religion' and 'spirituality' can be understood as related or distinct terms, and that this dichotomy often creates confusion about the sense and application of the latter term when it is stripped of its religious terminology. There can also be indifference or even hostility towards it when it is accommodated within or even appropriated by religion. Hay's approach is based on the writings of Alister Hardy and the latter's use of the term 'religious experience', which Hay translates as 'spiritual awareness'. For Hardy (1966) this is biological in origin, 'it has evolved through the process of natural selection because it has survival value to the individual' (Hay, in and Nye 1998:9).

From this theoretical standpoint Hay argues that spiritual awareness will be found to be a universal phenomenon. Therefore it will have both religious and non-religious forms of expression. Religious and secular language can be understood as symbolic mediums for the expression of spiritual awareness. Whilst avoiding the issue of truth claims and yet still pointing to the articulation of the experience of something real, Hay seeks to give status to the spiritual as that which transcends both language and religion, both of which act as vehicles for its expression. Thus, he writes, 'it is at least conceivable that the things which different cultures have to say about spiritual awareness could at the logical level be utterly inconsistent with each other, though referring to the same human phenomenon' (ibid.:14–15). For Hay it is therefore possible to entertain the idea that spiritual awareness 'is much more like the perception of an objective reality' (ibid.:15) than a construction of a linguistic, cultural or religious kind. It can be neither explained away as 'subjective' nor reduced to a dispute over truth claims. The case marked out by Hay serves to question previous understandings of the relationship between religion and spirituality that seek to avoid critical or reductionist social-science understandings of religion being applied to spirituality, specifically those of Marx, Freud and Durkheim (ibid.:17).

The importance of setting out this case for the veracity of the spiritual lies not only in the benefit of spiritual awareness to the 'inner life' of individuals and their own particular concerns. Hay also wishes to show that it is of great political and social importance. He draws on Rahner's (1974) theological reflections and relates them to Hardy's (1966) biological approach, indicating a common understanding. Rahner asserts that even if religion and its vocabulary were to disappear from human culture we would 'still reach out towards that mystery which lies outside [our] control' (Hay ibid.:20). In response Hay notes that 'The problem that remains, if Rahner's vision should ever come to pass, is how to reconstruct a culture so that it gives proper social and political expression to spiritual insight' (Hay ibid.:20).

By implication, therefore, Hay considers that attending to and nurturing spiritual awareness in children is a fundamental aspect of education. For this reason the issue of secularisation is significant. Hay is concerned about our willingness to ignore or even to devalue children's innocence, which allows them to be open to experience (ibid.:21–2). In the values of contemporary culture he identifies its opposite as knowingness, 'to know the score' (ibid.:22) as that which is prized. He cites Rénan, Compte and Marx as examples of detractors of institutionalised, orthodox religion who in later life could find nothing to nurture their spiritual needs (ibid.:22–4). He criticises the churches as having failed in this respect: 'Like Rénan, people may choose to move away from a religious institution because they find it no longer sustains their spiritual roots' (ibid.:24).

Appropriately, Hay cites David Hume as a major influence in the movement towards secularisation. Hume opposes religion because it does not reflect universal human sentiment. This, for Hume, is expressed in such ideas as 'self-love', 'resentment of injuries' and 'the passion between the sexes' (Hume 1757; Hay:27). Hence religion is a problem because it neither does justice to nor appropriately serves our human needs and human nature. The significance of secularisation and the reason for its pervasiveness in the modern world is seen to be ironic. Religion is rejected as not appropriately serving humanity and yet modern civilisation, lacking a religiously influenced culture, has lost the capacity to attend to its spiritual nature.

Only in the arts does Hay find spirituality to be strongly expressed, but 'obliquely ... and easily missed' (ibid.:35). Thus we have a cultural crisis and the decay of social cohesion, which is why, for Hay, attending to children's spiritual education has such social and political significance. He approvingly cites the comments made by Sir Ron Dearing and Nicholas Tate at the SCAA conference on 'Education for Adult Life' (Tate 1996; Hay 1998:38), but recognises that the situation, and its remedy, is less straightforward than Tate appears to assume.

Hermeneutical difficulties

We can identify some of the difficulties that arise when seeking to address children's spiritual education by comparing the theological approaches of Thatcher and Wright with Hay's concern for spiritual awareness. There is a sense in which Wright and Thatcher wish to affirm what Hay identifies as the mistakes of religion in both limiting the spiritual to the expression of doctrine and failing sufficiently to address the spiritual as a result. Whilst Hay wishes to affirm religious spirituality he does so by inverting Wright's position. What Wright calls 'negative theology', which should serve orthodoxy, Hay recognises as the spiritual practice that underpins religious understanding, 'Thus prayer, meditation and contemplation become the foci of religious education because they are 'the heartland of faith' (Hay 1985:143).

Hay contends that religious education has distanced itself from a hermeneutic of faith, without which it is impossible for us to understand a believer's experience of the sacred. By understanding a believer's experience, rather than examining the truth claims of a religion, we can overcome what he calls a 'hermeneutic of suspicion' of the spiritual. According to Hay, 'We root science education in direct experience and I believe we should strive to do the same with religious education [otherwise] it will be impossible for them [children] to get a genuine grasp of the nature of religion' (ibid.:144).

In its relations with religion, secularity is also understood differently by Hay and the theological approaches cited. For Hay, secularity is the outcome of religion failing to attend to the spiritual, but its influence is not reflected in the accounts of individuals' spiritual experience, only in the decline in in-stitutionalised religious adherence. It follows, for Hay, that religious education should primarily attend to these experiences rather than institutional religious practice or religious truth claims. This does not mean failing to attend to religious language, but it should be related to experience as a means of articulation. Hence religious language is given a different role and a different status to that ascribed to it theologically. This can be formulated in the following way: the theologi-cal argument seeks to defend religion as rational, while Hay equates the predominance of the rational in modern society with the problem of not addressing the spiritual.

With regard to Copley's attitude towards the secular (cited in Chapter 2), Hay is situated differently and is more open to the debate between religion and its critics, seeing the spiritual as something of importance to the critics of religion and to wider society. Thus centrally addressing spirituality in RE is a means of overcoming this polarity. In comparison with Jackson and in opposition to Wright, Hay understands culture as more open, and it can be recognised in a more fluid way because of his focus on the individual's experience. Hay is concerned with the spiritual directly, while Jackson works at the level of the relationship between religion and culture, identifying faith practices in membership groups and questions of identity. This does not entertain any generic classification of the spiritual. Jackson is more concerned with the 'grammar' involved in the diverse self-representation of faith traditions and membership groups, and with the distinctiveness and complexity inherent in religious and cultural pluralism. Hay seeks to find an underlying common ground in spiritual experience that transcends its different articulations.

It is interesting to compare the positions adopted by the above writers with Nicholas Tate's views, in order to determine their attitudes towards the dominant political understanding of the relationship between spiritual and moral education and RE. The principal distinction lies in the connections made between education and nationhood. In this respect, whilst critical of the SCAA's approach in *Education for Adult Life*, Thatcher's position seems supportive of Tate, as does Wright's, insofar as they wish to endorse a closed understanding of culture; the need to enculturate children into normative values endorsed and underpinned by religious truth claims, and more specifically Christian truth claims consistent with orthodox pronouncements. They also have a concern for social cohesion wedded to the need to reassert tradition. Jackson (1997:78–82), in contrast, condemns Tate's cultural exclusivity as showing a partiality of view, being simplistic in design and lacking acknowledgement of more dynamic accounts of 'culture' and debate as to what culture means and how it can variously be represented. He does not equate the fluidity of cultural change with the breakdown of social cohesion or tradition. Indeed the idea of the decay of social cohesion might be understood as emanating from a particular view of what shape and aims a culture should have. What for Tate is decay, for others is simply change. Hay endorses Tate to some degree, but with a proviso. For Hay, morality arises out of spiritual insight, not religious adherence *per se*. He states the problem as follows: 'No obvious alternative to religion has emerged with sufficient power to act as a vehicle for the nurture of spiritual awareness. It is because of this that spiritual education has become such a salient issue in the school curriculum' (Hay in Hay with Nye 1998:39).

Priestley introduces a further dimension to this debate by attacking the notion of curriculum itself, in order to indicate how it represents a less than adequate way of attending to our educational responsibilities. Priestley is concerned with the way we talk about education. Drawing on the philosophers Ludwig Wittgenstein and Alfred North Whitehead he argues that the language we use to speak of education imprisons us in an impoverished conception of it. We have reduced it to a thing we call curriculum rather than understanding it as a process that is creative and dynamic. It is for this reason that we have such trouble with placing spirituality in education. Priestley suggests that:

To dwell on the spiritual is to emphasize the subjective, to dwell on the process of being and becoming. Discussion of the curriculum, however, centres around knowledge. Knowledge is seen as objective, something which exists outside of ourselves but which we can take in through learning and contain through memory. That is one of the key dangers of reducing education to curriculum and one of which we have suddenly become aware again. The documentation of the past decade has been depressing because of its limited vocabulary. It is dominated by the notions of teaching and learning. There has been precious little attention paid to thinking, creating, imagining, becoming.

(Priestley 1997:29–30)

The emphasis in Priestley's understanding of the spiritual is not related to a particular faith stance or the distinction between the religious and non-religious. Priestley even refutes the need for definition in an attempt to open up our understanding of the possibilities of education once it is understood in its fullest (spiritual) sense of being a life-giving process. In effect Priestley calls for a radical rethinking of our educational priorities in relation to addressing spirituality. This amounts to more than the reconfiguration of RE, it is substantially about what we are seeking to achieve in education as a whole in terms of pedagogy. Here Priestley introduces a critique of curriculum as static and concerned with bodies of knowledge, which equates with Jackson's critique of culture being conceived in a closed and static fashion.

Beyond religious education

It can be seen that this debate has a deep hermeneutical complexity that goes way beyond the guidelines previously offered by the SCAA in its model syllabuses for RE, with the attainment targets of learning about and learning from religion and the documentation on SMSC relating to *Education for Adult Life*. The most significant divisions in the present debate are as follows.

The first relates to attitudes towards cultural change and the representation of cultural plurality, as opposed to closed representations of religious and cultural tradition and truth claims. The second relates to the extent to which we are engaged with facilitating children's understanding and articulation of their own experience, as opposed to enculturating them into received wisdom. So far the latter has been insufficiently attended to in the above review but it is central to the concerns of both Priestley and Hay. We shall return to this below. What is clear is that those concerned with religious education and the direction it should take, regard one or other of these issues as paramount. As we shall see, they are not unrelated and together represent significant issues to be resolved. When Hay addresses his research with children he is keen to avoid cognitive assumptions concerning developmental theory proposed by those concerned earlier with the psychology of development and developmental stages, such as Piaget, Goldman and Kohlberg. This is not to dismiss them entirely but critically to assess their usefulness in relation to children's spirituality (Hay with Nye 1998:40–2). Hay is careful not to equate spirituality with Christian catechesis but rather relies on the approaches of Hardy (1966) and Robinson (1983), who attempted to represent the significance of childhood religious experiences related by adults. Influenced also by Coles (1990), Winnicott (1971) and Rizzuto (1979), Hay devises categories of spiritual sensitivity (Hay and Nye 1996:59–75), the openness of which are an attempt to ensure that a mapping of the 'geography of a novel spiritual terrain' (ibid.:58) is achieved. As Hay remarks:

> in post-Christian society we have very little idea of the ways in which children deal with their experiences in this area. How do they speak about it? What 'spiritual dialects' do they use? How do these languages relate, if at all, to religious language? We need to become at home in this landscape and used to the vocabulary and practices of the children in their own exploration if we are to help them to protect their spirituality.
>
> (ibid.:58–9)

Hay's categories are nonetheless rooted in ideas related to spiritual practice and awareness in religious contexts but conveyed in non-religious language, such as awareness-sensing, mystery-sensing and value-sensing (ibid.:59).

In relating the findings of the research and seeking the 'core' of children's spirituality (Hay with Nye 1998:92–141), Hay and Nye identify 'relational consciousness', an 'inclusive and all-pervading sense of relation to the spiritual which means for them [children] it is normally "everyday" rather than dramatic'. Relational consciousness is that which transcends 'materialist, secular, rationalist culture' (ibid.:129) in the responses of the children. For Hay this is evidence of an altruistic impulse that can provide further evidence of Hardy's biological theory (ibid.:146). In practical terms Hay lays out a classroom parallel with the undertaking of scientific activity to develop the spiritual. He suggests four responsibilities: helping children to keep an open mind; exploring ways of seeing; encouraging personal awareness, and becoming personally and socially aware of the social and political dimensions of spirituality (ibid.:163).

It is difficult not to be beguiled by Hay's analysis. What might be called its seamless holisticity, its concern to wed the spiritual to practical and altruistic purpose, and its lack of religious dogmatism (despite Hay's professed Roman Catholic affiliation) provide a sophisticated argument for educational and social purposiveness. However the question of what direction RE and spiritual education should take is riddled with problematic hermeneutical and epistemological issues that still require close attention. The most significant of these is the question of whether RE can offer sufficient epistemological justification for its curriculum presence. If it cannot we must ask what sort of influence the above debate can have on educational provision.

I would contend that addressing children's and young people's spirituality has weakened RE's claim to a curriculum site if we follow Priestley and Hay. This is partly because Priestley questions the efficacy of curriculum in relation to educational purpose and cites the need to address spirituality as a way of recognising this. In Hay's case it is a result of siting the spiritual in a larger context than RE, as a curriculum subject attending to a discrete body of knowledge and recognising the need to remove the secular/religious distinction when addressing the spiritual. This despite the fact that he draws on religious practices to do so.

Neither Priestley nor Hay are willing to offer an *epistemological* justification for RE, since their positions subvert the present epistemological justifications for a discipline. The present justification for RE is reliant on its opposition to secular knowledge; ironically it justifies itself by opposing the suppositions inherent in the rest of the curriculum. Hay's claim to root spirituality biologically is conjectural and unlikely to usurp current thinking, despite its universalist appeal. It also begs a number of questions that will receive attention later. Among the alternative perspectives, Thatcher and Wright are representatives of the desire to ensure that the representation and examination of truth claims is the principal object of RE. In this respect they are likely to receive support both from a policy perspective and from the mainline Christian churches. Politically they can be seen as supporting the academic integrity of the subject as a rigorous discipline, or at least as offering an apologia for being so. Also, they, or at least Wright, can be seen as defending different world religions as having the right to representation on the basis of their truth claims. On this basis RE could be understood as the province of interfaith dialogue. This in turn could be understood as a curriculum area where traditional values are defended against secularist influence. The preservation of a Christian right to hegemony in this respect could, in turn, be maintained by invoking the idea of cultural heritage and nationhood as founded on Christian truth claims.

Jackson's approach, being the most broadly informed in relation to the academic study of religion, respects the role of religious tradition and advertises the need to study it on academic and cultural grounds. Jackson's defence of 'new style phenomenology' against relativism ensures a pluralist approach to the subject's complexity, which is both academically defensible and concerned with social and cultural values. However it cannot accommodate spiritual education in a childcentred way to the same degree as Hay and Priestley.

When considering the above qualifications of the various approaches in relation to our political climate, particular issues become clear. The first is epistemological: an approach that relativises knowledge is liable to exclusion. The second, and related, issue is that any approach to RE that does not include the inculcation of traditional social and moral values as an aim is not able to satisfy the historical purposes of RE or the present desires of centralised policy. Identifying these issues allows us to realise the particular constraints placed upon the subject. In academic terms it becomes anachronistic. It preserves itself at the cost of failing to acknowledge the range of the debate on questions of epistemology, pedagogy and cultural change. Its strongest position, politically, is in resisting the importance of this debate and vilifying relativist and postmodern critiques, as Tate does, supported by Thatcher and Wright.

Pedagogically this places the subject in an invidious position, resisting cultural influences on young minds on the premise that they will be corrupting, unless they are derived from epistemologically accredited sources. This of course echoes the fears expressed in the quote from Henson at the beginning of this chapter, but placed in a later context. Most importantly it determines that young people's contributions to beliefs and values will only be positively received if they ascribe to an agenda that is already predetermined. It is this constraint, so pedagogically damaging, that we wish to question. In doing so it is necessary to present the case for a pedagogy based on relativism. In presenting this argument we are not seeking to undermine religious faith positions but to place them alongside non-religious alternatives as the appropriate range of enquiry that should be engaged with in an educational system that concerns itself with spirituality and values. What we are opposing is the idea that values can only be derived from religious truth claims in particular, or from epistemologies in general. In fact we can go further than that statement of opposition. The argument that will be presented in Chapter 4 proceeds from the conviction that an educational provision that is based on epistemologies and truth claims is pedagogically restrictive and damaging. The attempts to affirm spiritual education on the theological positions and centralised policies analysed above are insufficient for the spiritual empowerment of children and young people. The primary reasons why this is so are advertised by the liberals in this debate.

Priestley criticises the concern for curriculum rather than education. Jackson and Bauman criticise the political defence of monoculturalism and nationalism against cultural plurality. Hay speaks of the lack of attention to the spirituality of the child. However, as long as we defend religious education as a discrete subject with an epistemological validity the liberal argument is insufficient. That is why we must go beyond religious education and embrace relativism to establish an appropriate form of spiritual education that in turn embraces, rather than instructs, young people and the plurality of cultural experiences and values.

4 Relativism, postmodernism and the spirit of educational enquiry

Clive Erricker

Understanding relativism

In establishing the validity and value of a relativist position I shall draw in particular on the argument of John Smith that 'there no longer is a "contrary" to place in opposition to relativism' (Smith 1998:25). The aim is to provide evidence of the epistemological insufficiency of foundationalism and realism and, for Smith, the futility of postmodernism, due to the 'deep sense of a heterogeneity of [its] discourses', leading to the loss of a 'communal sense of "we" in favour of a strong individualistic sense of "me"' (ibid.:25). The significance of Smith's argument for us is that, if substantiated, it establishes that no progress can be made in attempting to ground the debate on morality, spirituality and values on positions that refer to 'objectivity' or 'truth'. At the least, if Smith's position is credible as a defence of relativism, there are no grounds for excluding relativists from a debate on spirituality and moral values.

At the outset Smith is concerned to rectify the belief that relativism espouses the notion that 'anything goes' (ibid.:33). This is precisely the definition of relativism that Tate employed in his speech (Tate 1996: point 15), by virtue of which he claimed that without recourse to truth in moral matters we will not see any point in arguing or reasoning about morality. This, in Tate's view, leads to morality being largely a matter of taste and opinion because there is no such thing as moral error. Tate's understanding is a wilful and almost universally prevalent misunderstanding of relativism. This movement from one proposition to another without justification deserves to be challenged because it is so influential and so misguided. This can best be done by presenting the relativist argument as an alternative model.

Smith draws attention to the encounter between Gadamer and Derrida in 1981, and its explication by Eisenstein (1989), in which Gadamer's dialogic paradigm is contrasted with the apocalyptic paradigm of Derrida. Gadamer argues for an 'hermeneutic of good faith ... [striving] for ever increasing honesty ... through dialogue' (Smith 1998:31; Eisenstein 1989:270), the goal being 'a shared understanding or at least the striving for the same' (Smith 1998:31). For Smith this can be understood as a relativist position (it is interesting to note here the difference between Smith's interpretation of Gadamer and that of Wright in

Chapter 3). Derrida invokes the notion of 'radical alterity', which identifies the 'radical incommensurability of different standpoints' (ibid.:31), which in turn presents 'fundamental obstacles to consensus and community' (ibid.:31). This can be seen as a particularly radical postmodernist position. Having separated the two, we can see that Tate simply misunderstands the usefulness and character of relativism by both radically misrepresenting it and aligning it with postmodernism. I shall be referring later to other writers who are labelled postmodern, but at this point it is necessary to say that it is misleading to presume that the two terms are utterly distinct, as Smith presumes. But it is also misleading to reject them as occupying the same position, as Tate does. It very much depends on the particular writings one chooses to draw upon. However it is clear from the varying interpretations and uses of the terms relativism and postmodernism discussed so far, that we must be wary of selective interpretation and political intention. Also, attention needs to be paid to one significant issue, to which Smith draws attention and on which relativists and postmodernists are divided: whether consensus is a possible or desirable goal. Whilst relativists and postmodernists adopt antagonistic theoretical positions on this matter, what will be addressed later in this chapter is that theory has no relevance once we recognise that epistemology is not a prerequisite for ontological action. In other words we do not have to agree about what to do in a situation by referring back to an epistemological position as the basis of action. That would make no sense in relation to either relativist or postmodern arguments. For a further exposition of this consult Newman and Holzman's (1977) argument, presented later in this chapter, and my discussion of this issue in relation to liberation theology and Anthony Swift's study (Erricker forthcoming; Swift 1997).

Returning to Smith's statement that there is no longer a contrary place in relation to relativism, we may ask on what basis this claim is advanced. Smith's answer is that it is now recognised 'that all observation is theory laden or that there is no possibility of theory-free knowledge' (Smith 1998:25). He offers this as a restatement of Heisenberg's postulation that 'the "knowing subject" is now recognised to be intimately a part of any claim to knowledge' (ibid.:25; Hazelrigg 1995:ix).

At this stage I shall not pursue this complex debate any further, but I shall return to it later in this chapter and elaborate on its significance for education. What needs to be made clear is that the influence of relativist and postmodern understandings is fully acknowledged as central to the epistemological debate in academic circles and yet is totally ignored, or rather discounted without sufficient refutation, by policy makers and executors in education. And yet pronouncements by the latter are riddled with logical inconsistency. What was advocated in the previous statements by Nicholas Tate, analysed in Chapter 3, was a foundationalist position dependent on recourse to and justification through objective knowledge or truth, supplied by science or a transcendent authority that self-evidences the claim to moral truth. Yet this truth is to be arrived at by consensus, a democratic process, as advertised in the Forum on Education for Adult Life. This, however, is not an avenue whereby objective knowledge or truth can be determined, because in itself agreement does not constitute knowledge, epistemologically, or validate truth claims. Consensus is precisely the alternative available when the latter is in doubt, therefore the pursuit of consensus is an acknowledgement of relativism, both epistemologically and socially. Refusing to acknowledge such contradictions suggests that the issues are more political than educational and, by virtue of this, cannot represent a way forward in addressing spiritual and moral development in a competent way. This critique also effectively exposes why the theological position can never act as the foundation of curriculum innovation in spiritual and moral development in a plural society.

This section seeks to defend the relativist position as that which has no 'contrary' and is therefore a position in which we seek 'to make and defend judgements when there can be no appeal to foundations or to something outside of the social processes of knowledge construction' (Smith 2000:14). In doing this I cannot escape the charge, and do not wish to, that my position is at odds with those in religious education who see their 'knowledge' as depending on such a foundation. This groups together most of those belonging to a religious tradition and some (a good majority possibly) of those who teach religious education. I am aware of the further charge that seeking to understand religion from this perspective is untenable because it distorts the understandings and utterances of the believer to fit with different methodological presuppositions. My defence against this depends on what is understood by 'knowledge' and the distinction that can be claimed between a believer's faith and knowledge as an epistemological claim or ideology. The term 'belief' sits fluidly between these two and, ambiguously, it can be wedded to either of the previous two terms. It is this very ambiguity in the meaning of these terms in relation to knowledge and truth claims that creates the problem. Here we are revisiting the debate that has informed the subject of the study of religion from its inception, but taking account of the current debate on epistemology that extends beyond the subject. Because of the concern—and it was a justified concern given the critical attacks upon it—that it lacked credibility as a social science, the study of religion has always sought to maintain its epistemological credibility. This has resulted in a number of problematic issues that still await resolution, if that is possible. Perhaps the most significant of these has been whether apologists for the subject actually wish to assert and demonstrate the existence of the transcendent or, less militantly, argue that religion as a phenomenon is worthy of study because of its continuing importance in human affairs. As noted in Chapters 2 and 3, this distinction is also characteristic of those supporting religious education. We often find individuals in this debate working to establish both positions, not always systematically or coherently. The significance of this division of labour is paramount since, professionally speaking, both the presuppositions and the method of enquiry are distinct in each case. Furthermore the manner of engagement with others involved in the fields of epistemology, ontology and social enquiry are different in each case. Coming from the first position the manner of engagement is likely to be polemical; from the second it will be more conciliatory—a matter of finding common ground. Taking up a relativist position substantially affects presupposition, method and manner of engagement. Relativism posits that we are not engaged in epistemological enquiry at all. Drawing on Smith, relativism is 'a recognition and acceptance of our human finitude' (ibid.:17), the result of which is that we understand the world as that which we construct rather than discover (ibid.:16–18). This construction is inevitably always incomplete and provisional, and, by virtue of being a construction, can never claim any epistemological foundation outside itself. There are no 'epistemological guarantees' (ibid.:14; Schwandt 1996:59). The aim of enquiry thus turns from seeking to make epistemological judgements to making practical and moral ones. Smith conceives this 'as a social process in which we construct reality as we go along and as a social process in which we, at one and the same time, construct our criteria for judging inquiries as we go along' (Smith 2000:18).

If we revisit the debate on the study of religion on this basis we find significant changes in the issues to be addressed and how we address them. First, it would follow that secular constructions of reality have no greater or lesser plausibility than religious faith narratives, since neither can claim to have any epistemological foundation. Second, faith narratives have to be distinguished from religious ideologies, which do claim absolute epistemological status. The latter, from a relativist or postmodern position, are as fraudulent in their claims as any other grand narrative; for example secular, scientific or nationalistic. It is also significant that all these terms are often invoked when claiming the veracity of particular grand narratives. They are not different species but part and parcel of the imperial complexities of the grand narrative language game, as Lyotard (1984) has argued. We shall come to the substance of this argument later. Third, if faith narratives are different from religious ideologies we must establish the criteria for differentiation. This must entail asking whether the term 'faith' is exclusively related to religion. I maintain that 'faith' has been given exclusivist definitions by religious ideologies, and that this is no longer tenable. The reason for these exclusivist definitions is to attempt to wed faith to knowledge claims, most often via the bridging concept of belief. The problem is that faith is an ontological category, not an epistemological one.

Fourth, we now arrive at a point where the construction of a discrete subject, religion, with a clear definition is inappropriate to the purposes of enquiry. Rather we are engaged in, and are seeking to engage with, as insiders, the processes of world construction for practical and moral purposes. This involves attempting to understand 'faith' and ideological stances of various kinds, and making judgements as to our relationship with each as part of the process of our own world construction. This can be recognised as a spiritual activity as much as a political and social one, indeed it would be distortive to treat the three terms as entirely distinct from one another.

When we turn to the purpose of religious education we must accomplish the same transformation as undertaken above. In short the presuppositions of religious education, its methods, its title and its subject matter need radical revision in order to satisfy our educational aims. It may seem that the above analysis destroys what is to be gained from the study of religion. I would argue that this is not the case. Rather it frees up the possibilities of enrichment that can follow from including the 'religious' with the 'secular'. What I am proposing is that this rigid demarcation of the two realms is fictitious and unhelpful. The reason for the distinction is ideological and a result of the historical animosity they have for each other. Since I am proposing that ideological distinctions based on epistemological claims should not be the basis of the study of anything, it follows that faith narratives are as important to our educational enquiry as any other narratives, and that the matter of definition in this respect is part of the enquiry, not assumed at the outset.

To summarise, the aim of this educational endeavour is to enable learners to engage in making informed 'practical and moral judgements' (Smith 2000:18). To this end we must understand learners to be players in this endeavour, being members of social groups and democratic citizens from the outset. Recognition of diversity and difference plays a significant part in this process since judgements are made in relation to the judgements, needs and claims of others. It is in this context that the spiritual and moral development of the learner occurs. To put it more aptly, our spiritual, moral, cultural and social environments are both inherited and constructed in the context of this development, they are not separate things.

We must not confuse this venture with the oft-quoted underlying values attached to religious education: respect, tolerance and empathy. I have no problem with the sentiments behind these terms, but they are often used as a liberal gloss to justify the subject as a form of values education. Indeed they also operate as an implicit form of vague, uncontextualised moral instruction, often preventing rather than enabling the investigation of value judgements, political structures and ideological stances. Apart from such terms being interpreted quite differently by different parties, in relation to the accommodation of ethnic difference, for example, it is quite preposterous to suggest that we should attempt to generate such sentiments specifically towards particular religious groups in a curriculum that has been designed, through legislation, to rule out other non-religious groups. It is even more preposterous that we should recognise religious ideologies in this way, despite the obvious lack of respect they have often shown towards others and each other at different times. It also overlooks the extreme conservatism and bigotry often directed towards other specific groups in society by some of the ideologies' followers, justified on dubious ideological grounds; such as attitudes towards women and homosexuals.

However, to characterise religious faith in a wholly negative way would be as unsatisfactory as indiscriminately representing religious ideologies in an un-blemished light, but this merely serves to identify one aspect of the complexity of the representational issue that is not well served by the current provision. What we need is a radical reconstruction of the way in which we define our educational purposes such that the complexity of purpose can be addressed most effectively. The following section presents the case for re-envisaging this educational purpose by examining the distinction to be made between faith and religion, with reference to Kierkegaard; the distinction to be made between narrative knowledge and grand or metanarrative, with reference to Lyotard; and Hayden White's understanding of poetics as a means of enquiry and communication.

Kierkegaard and the problem of faith

On the title page of Kierkegaard's *Philosophical Fragments* or *A Fragment of Philosophy* (1962), pseudonymously attributed to Johannes Climacus we find a question that underpins the whole work: 'Is an historical point of departure possible for an eternal consciousness; how can such a point of departure have any other than a merely historical interest; is it possible to base an eternal happiness upon historical knowledge?' (Kierkegaard 1962). We can pursue the import of this question by considering his analogy of the King and the Humble Maiden (ibid.:xxiii).

The problem posed by Kierkegaard is that, in order to enter into a relationship with the maiden, the King cannot present himself as he is. He must humble himself and appear otherwise. Equally it is the case that God must do likewise in order to reveal himself to his creatures, otherwise he cannot be known by them. Here, therefore, we have a paradox: by entering into disguise God can reveal himself, but he will not be revealed as he is. In other words God cannot be known in the conventional sense: objectively. Nor can he be known in any systematic sense, according to dogma and doctrine. He can be known only insofar as he reveals himself to the individual and is apprehended by him or her.

In posing the hiddenness of God—which means that human eyes can only be opened by the immediacy of faith, bestowed by God within the contingency of experience—Kierkegaard questions the whole conceptual construction of God that theology offers. He attacks the claims of metaphysics and systematic theology whilst also rejecting the possibility of any idea of objective knowledge. In effect God is dead, as Nietszche claimed. In this a/proposition Kierkegaard answers the question he posed at the beginning of his work and offers us a way of addressing the spiritual as radically subjective, unsystematic and opposed to constructions of a formulaic kind. My contention is that in doing this Kierkegaard allows us to consider the notion of faith beyond the confines of Christianity or religion, and beyond the idea that faith is that which delivers salvation.

In contrast modernism (based on the idea that we can make rational, objective and systematic statements about knowledge), which is the antithesis of Kierkegaard's position and does not consider the question he posed, is a project that calls for faith in a system. The basis of its logic is that the system will deliver progress. Faith here is something that will be justified by the achievement of certain demonstrable ends. Of course in practice it doesn't work quite like that and faith turns out to be faith in the promise that the system will achieve those ends, which inevitably recede into the future—an historical future, of course, in contrast to faith related to transcendence, which is located in a post-historical future. Here we find three different usages and three different conceptualisations of the term faith.

The question posed by Kierkegaard and the way in which he answered it subverts the promises of modernity. Today we find the legacy of Kierkegaard carried by thinkers who are critics of modernity in the same way as Kierkegaard was a critic of the Christianity of his day. This legacy includes the use of the same stylistic weapons of paradox and irony to subvert the foundational principles and practices of order that Kierkegaard demonstrates in the extract below:

> Whoever you are, my friend, and whatever your life may have been, by refusing any longer (if you have hitherto done so) to participate in the public worship as now conducted, with the pretence of being the Christianity of the New Testament, you will have one less crime on your conscience, and that a heavy one; for you will no longer take part in making a mockery of God.
>
> (ibid.:xli)

It is at this point that commentators have taken to analysing the pathology of Kierkegaard rather than pursuing the epistemological implications of his attack on the church (ibid.:xli). He is dismissed as Nietszche's madman. Equally, conservative (modernist) critics did the same with Roland Barthes, who is regarded by Philip Thody, in his (Barthes') ' "waywardness", as one whose subversive tactics come down to an inordinate fondness for paradox disguising a commitment to order and method' (Norris 1982:12).

Also, those who 'discovered' Kierkegaard, in a theological sense, actually used his existential ideas to reconstruct a theological understanding that was often exclusivist in character. Foremost and most influential amongst these was Karl Barth, who sought to show how God's transcendence was legitimated by Kierkegaard against the idea that humans could find a way to reach God through their own religious constructions or systems. Thus Kierkegaard's influence was consigned to a neo-orthodox theology that sought to oppose interpretations rather than investigate the radical implications of his observations in relation to dogmas and creeds. In this way the radicalness of Kierkegaard's position is passed over.

I am not concerned here with Kierkegaard's question as to whether we can take the 'leap of faith' in order to transcend our historical consciousness, but with the way in which the question he posed and the critique he advanced gives us insight into the idea that constructing a systematic and rational understanding of reality, which is conveyed by institutions as true or commensurable with reality, is an impossible and fallacious endeavour. Rather, Kierkegaard's investigation of faith allows us to see that any attempt to place spirituality within a closed system constructed according to the formulations of doctrine or ideology is false; whatever form or character that system may have and on whatever premises it may be based.

Kierkegaard's critique and its implications can be applied to our construct of education and spiritual development within education. It highlights the problem of the development of children's spirituality being driven by modernism and thus actually being some sort of ornamentation on a moral(ist) base, such as we find in the SCAA discussion papers (SCAA 1995, 1996). What I wish to explore is the facilitation of the metaphorical constructs of children for providing meaning, or being the basis of a notion of faith, without resorting to a modernist construct of truth; and the possibility of collapsing the division of religious and secular, constructed on the basis of doctrines that are antithetical to one another, in favour of metaphorical narratives that are always provisional. In short, seeking, in Derrida's words, 'to release a multiplicity of meaning' (Derrida 1977:292).

The legitimation of narrative and the delegitimation of metanarrative

In this section we turn to Lyotard's understanding of narrative pragmatics, Kermode's deconstructive analysis of biblical text, and Hayden White's removal of the customary distinction between fact and fiction in order epistemologically to underpin the validity of narrative theory.

David Carroll, in *The Aims of Representation* (1987:76) observes that pragmatics is opposed to metaphysics and the 'entire theoretical, speculative, dogmatic genre. Lyotard identifies pragmatics as 'a word that designates the set of very complicated relations that exist between the person who narrates and what he is narrating, between the person who narrates and the one who listens to him, between the latter and the story told by the former' (Lyotard 1984:16; Carroll 1987:76). As a result, Carroll observes that

> Critical pragmatics admits that one can only analyse, respond to, and counter narratives with other narratives, . . . One is always already situated within narrative . . . and that one acts by countering and responding to these narratives and by occupying differing places within differing narratives. . . . The possibility of responding is thus crucial to all narrative; it is an opening in narrative to other narratives, an opening that is fundamental to the very structure or form of narrative.
>
> (Carroll 1987:77)

Thus Lyotard offers us a way of understanding the means of addressing what Benjamin (1970:83) had previously called the role of storytelling and the facilitation of the exchange of experiences. What, in principle, we must and must not do. Contrastingly, what we often do is determine the veracity of one narrative over another and teach from that assumption. Such assumptions tend to be validated by notions of what is factual as opposed to fictional, and what is true as opposed to false. As an example of how this occurs we can cite Frank Kermode's (1979) deconstructive analysis of the text of John's gospel. Kermode cites John 19:31–7 (ibid.:101–2):

> Since it was the day of Preparation, in order to prevent the bodies from remaining on the cross on the sabbath (for that sabbath was a high day), the

Jews asked Pilate that their legs might be broken, and that they might be taken away. So the soldiers came and broke the legs of the first, and of the other who had been crucified with him, but when they came to Jesus and saw that he was already dead, they did not break his legs. But one of the soldiers pierced his side with a spear, and at once there came out blood and water. He who saw it has borne witness—and his testimony is true, and he knows that he tells the truth—that you also may believe. For these things took place that the scriptures might be fulfilled, 'Not a bone of him shall be broken.' And again another scripture says, 'They shall look on him whom they have pierced'.

Kermode's point is that theological interest always fashions the account through emplotment, whilst explicitly (as in this case) or implicitly making a naive realist appeal to the witness of events, thus claiming factual accuracy as the means of their verification ('He who saw it has borne witness—his testimony is true, and he knows that he tells the truth—that you also may believe'). But what is actually being asserted is a metanarrical/metaphysical affirmation of truth. For this to be defended the writer has to show how events comply with prophecy ('not a bone of him shall be broken', and 'they shall look on him whom they have pierced'), derived in this case from the Hebrew bible, which has already been affirmed as a source of authority for the intended reader. The hermeneutical twist in this is interesting because, ironically, the reinterpretation of past utterance to conform to the interpretation of later events, in order to affirm the veracity of the latter, is a theological shift within an ongoing tradition, or metahistorical plot, whereby the conjunction of witness (eye-witness account) and previous prophecy coaffirm each other. The internal logic is complete, but the claim is not to logical consistency—which is what a novel or fictional account must achieve in order to captivate its reader—but to something far greater; that a transcendent truth has been affirmed that counters any other claims to truth on the basis (bias) that no other account conforms with history, that is, events as they happened. This unwarranted claim is precisely the means of the denial of narrative response and its assumed metanarrical status is thus oppressive rather than liberating because no other text can be legitimately voiced. This is not to say that such a narrative cannot operate as an empowering story for a community but that it cannot make claims beyond that context. However we should note that it is in direct opposition to Kierkegaard's notion of faith.

Significantly the above is only one example from one genre of a system of operation that underpins all our modernist practices. Thus Lyotard shows how the same operation is used by science to affirm its objectivity against rival claims to truth or knowledge (Lyotard 1984:23ff). Uncovering this we come to understand how legitimation occurs (ibid.:27f, 31f) and how this is underpinned by language games as the method of legitimation (ibid.:10). Following Wittgenstein, Lyotard makes three observations about language games (ibid.:10):

1. their rules do not carry within themselves their own legitimation, but are the object of a contract [between players]

2. that if there are no rules there is no game
3. that every utterance should be thought of as a move in a game ... [in which] success is won at the expense of an adversary.

The game we are involved in here we can call the 'Truth Game'. The important observation is that the rules of legitimation are always self-referential, and cannot despite claims to the contrary, achieve a status or authority beyond their *claim* to status and authority, i.e. from a transcendent source (a source or reality *beyond* the game itself).

This leads Lyotard into a discussion of narrative pragmatics and the denial of metanarrical claims because they are always power moves (that is, political rather than academic in nature, despite their form, which is academic discourse). This understanding is relevant to all institutional structures and processes, especially those of curriculum and education in relation to spirituality. How do we go beyond the agonistics of the above situation in our consideration of spirituality in education and the notion of spiritual development? In other words, how do we ensure that we facilitate children's narratives in the context of the school community rather than imposing narratives upon them, to which they are expected to consent? Lyotard posits that:

A postmodern artist or writer is in the position of a philosopher: the text he writes, the work he produces are not in principle governed by pre-established rules, and they cannot be judged according to a determined judgement, by applying familiar categories to the text or to the work. Those rules and categories are what the work of art itself is looking for. The artist and the writer, then, are working without rules in order to formulate the rules of what *will have been done*.

(ibid.:81)

When we attempt to apply this understanding to education we can think of children working in the same way. In order creatively to affirm their own narratives they have to work out the rules as they do so, retrospectively. From any given present they work with a memory of events and the issues arising from them. Events must be given and regiven form and meaning in an ongoing hermeneutical process of understanding, which provides for formulations and projections for the future. There are rules, but they are always in the process of becoming, being reaffirmed or revised in the light of experiences. It is this shaping that the child (like ourselves) has to have a critical confidence in. These constructions are never a full representation of reality because they cannot be matched against anything fully finished or disclosed. It is a reminder of Foucault's statement that what matters is 'to be artists of our own lives' and Nietszche's comment that 'The world is a work of art that gives birth to itself' (Cupitt 1998:18). It is also the basis of what we might call children's poetics, which is what I understand the term spirituality, in the educational context, to refer to. For the meaning of poetics we can refer to Hayden White's description: 'the process of fusing events, whether imaginary or real, into a comprehensible totality capable as serving as the object of a representation is a poetic process' (White 1985:125).

In summary, then, I am arguing for the reconstruction of our understanding of spiritual development as an artistic endeavour that is creatively ongoing and of which the rational is but one aspect, alongside the intuitive and emotional. Addressing the integration of these capacities in what we might call the construct of autobiography, by means of the process of narrative pragmatics; this we can call a pedagogy based on poetics or narrative construction. However this is not a 'romantic' venture, in that I am not suggesting a prescribed outcome in the form of well-being or happiness. Current pronouncements on spiritual development in education seem contrived to achieve these ends. I am not saying they are bad ends, just that you cannot set out to ensure their achievement. That would undermine the process itself. In other words these desired outcomes act as a protective device in terms of what can and cannot be heard or voiced, and they assume a lack of sufficiency in children.

Knowledge and method: the search for a new paradigm

We have referred throughout this work to three different ways of conceiving knowledge or enquiry: the absolutist or objective paradigm; the interpretive paradigm; and the relativist or postmodern paradigm (as indicated previously, I make no hard and fast distinction between these last two terms since there is considerable overlap between and significant diversity among the writers in these categories). The aim of this chapter is to argue in favour of the third of these as the preferred option and to delineate its specific characteristics with regard to method, rather than epistemology. This in turn emphasises the importance of the process of pedagogy rather than the inculcation of knowledge. The terms used above are, of course, open to varying interpretations in relation to one another. Why should we oppose method and epistemology, pedagogy and knowledge? We hope the answer to this question will become clear in what follows.

An important text in the context of this argument is Newman and Holzman's *The End of Knowing: a new developmental way of learning* (1997). The authors' starting point is to uncover the radical difference between knowledge and method. In doing this they take the writings of the early Marx (in the *Theses on Feuerbach*), Lev Vygotsky (the educationalist and psychologist) and the later Wittgenstein and subject these to a rereading outside and beyond that of other contemporary theorists. They describe this as 'moving beyond the rational towards the "performative" which is a political activity of bringing about change that is dependent on method rather than the theorising character of "knowing" ' (ibid.:63).

It is an axiom of modernist thought that nothing can be achieved without knowledge or theory as the starting point. Thus such phrases as 'to know what we are talking about' become a way (within the rational rules of modernism) of establishing definition as determining rational knowing or having a purposive debate on how we arrive at 'knowledge' (no matter that the process is tautological in its design). Newman and Holzman's point is that this becomes 'the typical dualistic reduction of ontology to epistemology—the insistence that everything (worthy or not worthy of a name or a description) must be knowable. But if a challenge to that claim is successful, it will not be *known*, we think. It will "merely" be performed' (ibid.:31). In this statement they revisit a long-standing battle between existentialist philosophy and systematic philosophy in respect of the relationship between ontology and epistemology. They do not rehearse this history, but it can be identified in the polemics of Kierkegaard on the matter of faith and choice and the necessity to choose without knowing. In Sartre it centres on the matter of choice, of freedom to choose on the basis of existing, and the argument that experience precedes essence. The dualism that is referred to is posited as a false dualism because it asserts that there is a point of knowing upon which action is predicated, whereas, ontologically speaking, there is no point at which action occurs that presumes a prior point of knowing. In other words the point of acting is to move beyond one's present situation *despite* not knowing. We might suggest that this opposition is overcome by recognising that action will result in knowing, that is, that by reversing the equation we still necessarily end up with knowledge (in this case on the basis of experience rather than theorising or rationality alone).

However, note the shift in the conceptualisation of 'knowledge'. Knowledge based on experiencing is necessarily 'subjectivised', it can make no universal claims, thus, in a rational or objective sense it (what we claim to know) cannot claim to be knowledge at all. In other words the modernist language game of epistemology cannot entertain the ontological variant on its own conceptualisation. Newman and Holzman's point is that there is nothing productive in entering into an argument with modernism over this issue, for example in Lyotard's contention that there is only 'narrative knowledge'. Lyotard's insights in this respect and his deconstruction of the claims of science and religion as being only narrative rather than capable of a universalised objective or absolute norm are exceedingly perspicacious and act as a viable starting point, but it is fruitless, once the point is made, to continue to debate epistemologies. Now the issue is to recognise the irrelevance of epistemological stances, since they are recognisable only as power moves of a political nature. According to Marx the enterprise of 'knowing' is entirely unproductive, 'The philosophers have only *interpreted* the world, in various ways; the point is to *change* it' (Marx 1973:123). This can be translated into Wittgenstein's understanding that 'the speaking of language is part of an activity, or a form of life' (Wittgenstein 1967:11). In other words language is part of the process of action, not a means for theorising on what is necessary (epistemologically) before action can take place.

The significance of the above analysis is the shift in the understanding of the relationship between process and product from a dual but complementary movement towards progressive epistemological understanding (that is, knowledge or truth), to the recognition that the idea of product or theory is nothing more than an extrapolation from the process or the ontological activity of living. This shift of status from process to theory confers a doctrinal status which, in turn controls subsequent activity in a political fashion without sufficient (indeed illegitimate) justification. Realisation of this provides the basis for a new pedagogical purpose emerging from Vygotsky's observation that:

> The relationship of thought to word is not a thing but a process, a movement from thought to word and from word to thought. . . . Thought is not expressed but completed in the word. We can, therefore, speak of the establishment . . . of thought in the word. Any thought strives to unify, to establish a relationship between one thing and another. Any thought has movement. It unfolds.
>
> (Vygotsky 1987:250)

In this unfolding, which is what we are now invited to attend to as our educational task, we cannot speak of a final product, that is, a point at which 'knowledge' is established. Rather we must speak of an utterance (a performative action) that makes us aware of the point or site of understanding—the location—in the process. This is not to be confused with a 'knowledge' or epistemological statement. In other words it is a communication to be responded to, not an edict that defines and judges the plausibility of responses (that is, acts as a site of power). Rather it occupies a particular location but always a provisional, temporal one.

The value of Newman and Holzman's observations lie in freeing the postmodern understanding from what Foucault (1971) describes as 'the prison-house of concepts'. Epistemological debate is undertaken using the tool of rationality, thus it can never escape the designs of modernism, indeed it is *the* characteristic feature of modernist design and the criterion by which all design is judged. If conceptualisation is itself understood as part of a larger activity of living and we ask 'how can it best contribute to that (ontological) activity?', we do not end up saying 'by replacing it with theorising'; rather we ask a relational question such as 'what use can we put conceptualisation to, in order to serve our (existential) needs?' In doing this we implicitly acknowledge that thoughts and their creation and expression in language are part of that activity and do not represent a fixed point (objective or absolute) which we can depart from, return to or map our position.

It is clear that the activity of conceptualisation moves contemporaneously with other activities, such as emotions, contingency of circumstance and so on. There is no 'chart', no fixed map to journey by. There is only activity itself, of which conceptualisation within conversation is a part. This leads us to recognise the unfoundedness of scientific and religious claims to knowledge as fixed points to which return can be made. It makes clear why there are always rival claims to knowledge and the uselessness of setting up epistemological variants that claim not to be variants at all, but the only basis upon which human 'progress' (according to the definition in each claim) can be accomplished. This whole game would be laughable if it did not result in such endless human tragedy. The sale of epistemologies always goes hand in hand with the sale of arms. In Cioran's words, 'knowledge is a "leprosy of the mind"', and 'every recipe for salvation erects a guillotine' (Cioran 1975:88–9).

Educationally, Cioran's observation is particularly apt since the guillotine cuts off the possibility of the learner's own development beyond the acceptance of the recipe of knowledge and the values already put in place. Underpinning this are often dubious political motives dressed up as high-minded ideals. Consider for example the concept of charity (not as love but as it is conventionally used, taught and practised). Charity is what we give to others who are not one of us. We give it from a position of comparative privilege and power, gained by virtue of political and economic ascendancy. Charity is made possible by the existence of wealth and power. It is not a way of addressing inadequacy, but of assuring that the system that brings about inadequacy and those who create and maintain that system cannot be subjected to moral vilification. In effect, if we ask 'what is charity for?', the answer is not 'to help the poor' but 'to protect the powerful'. To protect the powerful is to protect their epistemological structure, for example capitalism, by giving it a moral sanction. The plight of those who receive charity is the result of the guillotine (of economic measures) erected by those who put into practice a recipe for their own salvation. This is not what we teach in schools. Schools are run according to capitalist designs, for future wealth production. Schools are advertised as places where individuals are given the opportunity to succeed in life.

Returning to Newman and Holzman, this recipe is diagnosed in their discussion of Rosa Luxemburg's thesis on why capitalism needs precapitalist societies to exploit; that is, wealth cannot be produced within the capitalist society itself, but has to be imported and exported. This is not just a matter of 'economic imperialism'—forcing labour to work for less and forcing buyers to pay more—but of forcing non-capitalist societies to buy into capitalism. Again, what is being sold is epistemology to ensure the increase in added value (profit) that the capitalist system demands (Newman and Holzman 1997:85–6). It is such thinking that lies behind Third World debt. The argument in this chapter and throughout this book is that feeding children a diet of epistemology (in the form of curriculum) in order to ensure economic profit (or wealth) from their future activity as an intellectually and practically skilled but politically and socially compliant workforce does not constitute a sufficient (or even justifiable) education. The significant issues that Newman and Holzman take up relate to what should replace an education based on epistemology. They reject 'knowing' in favour of a 'performed activity' or 'practical-critical revolutionary activity' to create a 'development community' (ibid.:60).

Following Shotter (1993b), but not uncritically, Newman and Holzman (1997:60) identify his 'knowing of the third kind' or 'practical-moral' knowledge. Shotter (1993a:19) explains: 'Knowing of the third kind is "knowing *from within* a situation, a group, social institution or society" rather than knowing-what or knowing-how; it is "knowledge in-practice" or "knowledge-held-in-common with others".' This knowledge is inseparable from our constitution of it in the conversational activity that Shotter refers to as the 'disorderliness of everyday social life'. Whether we object, as Newman and Holzman do, to the use of the term 'knowledge' by Shotter and Lyotard, as a misnomer, is not the most significant point. By moving on from the explication of this ontologically based understanding we can understand education quite differently. What is being proposed here is a new conception of the classroom: a place of conversational activity within the disorderliness of everyday social life; a place of unfolding thought and performance that will have political effect. This can be understood as attending to a spiritual process.

Non-epistemological education

Once we understand our task in non-epistemological terms the criticisms directed at relativist and postmodern standpoints by realists and critical realists become superfluous. For example, we may take the idea that religious believers have conviction in their belief and therefore must regard it as true in an objective and absolute sense. They cannot be represented as believing in something that they can also accept to be relative or even fictional in relation to reality, or in relation to the impossibility of knowing a reality. The point is precisely this: people act on a knowing within a situation. They act within an ontological process. To affirm a particular epistemology is part of that activity. Metaphorically, it is akin to 'interior design', that is the design of our reality takes place on the inside. This conceptual construction is an act of making within which the psychological confirmation of it as absolute or real is part of the construction that we choose to make, if we wish. There is no contradiction here between it being fabricated or real. We can choose to regard it as either without breaking any logical rules, because the logical possibilities of the design allow either. We can inhabit whatever world we choose to construct and justify it accordingly because there are no rules to say that we cannot, except the rules we choose to make. This is possible because there is no 'outside' to this reality, unless we choose to construct one. In which case the outside becomes part of the design. If we choose to confer upon it an absolute status, that is no problem. If we choose to say it is therefore not of our making, that is possible too. Epistemological design has no limitations within the ontological process precisely because there is nothing with which it has to be compared and found wanting, except our own interpretations of our own experiences. Thus all epistemologies are inherently ironic in character despite or because of (ironically) the fact that they are truth claims—attempts to overcome the ironic. This is the significance of the earlier reference to the 'linguistic net' (Chapter 2), as used by Bauman.

We can substantiate this argument using a different form of analysis. Outside and inside are related terms that operate within a dualistic mode of conceptual and linguistic design. There is no other way of formulating or communicating the ordering of the world. However this classificatory system is constructed within our mortal captivity—we cannot appeal to experience that is beyond it with any objective or rational validity. This is not a problem if we do not wish to invoke such justificatory principles of knowing, but we cannot use them to justify constructions that apply neither to the frame of reference within which their validity is recognised, nor to the epistemological issues they are capable of resolving. This leaves us with two insoluble problems, two domains in which we cannot say we know, in the sense of rational and objective knowing. The first is that of absolute knowledge—final and complete answers. The second, and related, is a form of knowing that is not based on dualistic thinking. In effect this means that the ideas of rational and objective knowledge are fraudulent claims if the claim is to knowledge that is more than that related to a dualistic paradigm. It also means that claims to knowledge beyond the transition from birth to death are fraudulent if they use rationality and objectivity as their justification. Either way knowledge is relative.

'Inside' and 'outside' work as linguistic and conceptual constructions within the spatial and temporal terrain we inhabit. As such they do not apply to that which exists beyond the terrain we are capable of mapping, even though the terms, when used in relation to the possibility of such a terrain, seem logically but spuriously to justify its linguistic and conceptual existence. What we create by thinking that our conceptual cognisance equals the necessary existence of that which we are cognisant of is a conceptual mirage. We do not live in an inside, because we do not know if there is an outside to the inside within which we live. The point I am making is simple: conceptual and linguistic constructions have no relationship to a reality that is not cognisable. It follows that the use of language to describe such a reality—true, real, absolute, objective and so on—is mythical or fictional. This does not mean it is not helpful, functional or necessary in its application and value, in relative, pragmatic and affectual terms. But we must recognise it for what it is. Even the term fictional is not appropriate because, in a strictly epistemological sense, it presumes a factual opposite, which again falls into our dualistic classificatory mode of representation.

To put all this in a more prosaic manner, epistemologically we do not know and cannot know where we are, but it does not actually matter. It can be welcomed as a release from a burdensome conceptual captivity. This, of course, is to state no more than the conclusions of Buddhist Madhyamika philosophy, Sufi mysticism and much that has been written in the tradition of the Christian Desert Fathers, as well as in Wittgenstein and postmodern writings.

This leads us to consider a second charge often levelled at the ironic position presented by postmodernism: that it is pessimistic and therefore offers only futility rather than possibilities for action. This was a charge previously brought against existentialism, and specifically Sartre's writings on existentialist humanism. It is worth revisiting his response:

> But there is another meaning of humanism. Fundamentally it is this: man [sic] is constantly outside of himself; in projecting himself, in losing himself outside of himself, he makes for man's existing; and, on the other hand, it is

by pursuing transcendent goals that he is able to exist; man being this state of passing beyond, and seizing on things only as they bear on this passing beyond, is at the heart, at the centre of this passing beyond. There is no universe other than a human universe, the universe of human subjectivity. This connection between transcendency, as a constituent element of man—not in the sense that God is transcendent, but in the sense of passing beyond—and subjectivity, in the sense that man is not closed in upon himself but is always present in a human universe, is what we call 'Existentialist humanism'.

Existentialism . . . isn't trying to plunge man into despair at all. But if one calls every attitude of unbelief despair, like the Christians, then the word is not being used in its original sense. . . . Existentialism declares that even if God did exist nothing would change. . . . In this sense Existentialism is optimistic, a doctrine of action and it is plain dishonesty for Christians to make no distinction between their own despair and ours and then to call us despairing.

(Sartre 1948)

What Sartre underlines, in relation to what has been said above on interior design, is the way in which positions that seek to establish specific truth claims, and most obviously theistic traditions that are missionary in purpose, regard their epistemologies as necessary for human spiritual purpose. It is therefore in their interests to characterise positions that oppose such truth claims as having a deleterious ontological effect. We have witnessed this in relation to the comments of Wright and Tate, for example. Sartre, rightly points out that this is not the case and may in fact be seen as a form of projection that emanates from within the characteristics and conceptions of, for example, Christianity itself, with its doctrine of sin and fallenness. In other words, if you start with sin you are going to get despair unless you introduce salvation. This does not mean that if you do not start with sin you are going to get despair, because there is no salvation.

Interestingly, the charge levelled against Sartre and postmodern writers has often been similarly levelled against Buddhist teachings. Their similarity to Sartre's existentialism lies in the refusal to privilege epistemological claims over ontological enquiry. In other words the process of discernment is a result of reflecting on experience rather than interpreting it according to a pre-established salvific design. There are tensions, of course, in relation to the status of Buddha as accorded to Siddhartha, and how that influenced the development of Buddhist tradition. In other words we can find forms of Buddhism that display 'ism-like' ideological tendencies. The history of the Buddhist tradition reveals these tensions. My point is that ideologies criticise process-oriented ontological perspectives and pedagogies because they do not offer certified happy endings or outcomes, and because they are open to the importance of individual difference and subjectivity. The debates on religious, moral and spiritual education reflect the same tensions, as we have noted.

From objectivity to subjectivity

We can illustrate the issues that arise in the classroom and school by using Sartre's analogy of the bus, by which he seeks to show the way in which 'serial unity' is constructed (Sartre 1964:310–12; Cumming 1968:456–61). The passengers on the bus, regular commuters, come to see themselves as having a shared identity that negates the importance of their individuality. As such they become objectified, that is, they identify themselves as objects (in this case passengers) and thus come to understand themselves primarily as such. This is their identity, dependent on their serial unity, their group recognition. Sartre's point is that the metaphor of the bus illustrates how the notion of objectivity operates on the individual's self-perception, not just as a way of objectifying the world in which he or she finds him or herself. This is an example of Sartre's central idea of bad faith or inauthentic existence. Other existentialist writers made similar observations about this objectivisation, notably Jaspers and Heidegger (Gaidenko 1966:259–76).

Sartre's polemic was principally directed against Marx and orthodox Marxists who pursued a Stalinist line, but it is similarly applicable to all ideologically and epistemologically inclined traditions. Whether religious, political or scientific, the fault, and false consciousness, lies in the objectification of the world and the individual within the world. The bus is a metaphor we can use for such traditions and those who defend truth claims on such premises. Thus we can apply it to Wright's (1997, 1998) argument considered in Chapter 3. In this respect traditions are not benign, so that even diverting our aim from the study of religious truth claims to the study of religious traditions, and even membership groups, as Jackson does, still leaves the issue untouched and perhaps even conceals it. However the bus is also a metaphor for the school, and its effect on pupils rather than passengers, if it follows an educational system according to these principles.

Sartre also made a distinction between 'seriousness' and 'sincerity' to indicate their antithesis. Seriousness prioritises the object over the subject and 'Man is serious when he takes himself for an object'. In this position the denial of his freedom means he cannot act with sincerity, which is to act with the consciousness of his freedom as a subject (Sartre 1957; Novak 1966:17). Historically, within the major religious traditions we can find many figures who taught and practised against this objectivisation of faith or consciousness, reacting similarly to Sartre. Ironically, we teach about them as saints, martyrs, prophets and reformers but miss the point they were trying to make because they are represented within the historical continuity of the tradition, which is placed within the historical continuity of religion, which we teach within the historical continuity of education. All three historical continuities are wedded by their interest in objectifying faith, the world and the individual to create a serial unity or unified, rationalised conception of reality. This is the opposite of the realities of children and young people's lives (see Erricker *et al.* 1997).

For faith to be faith it can have no object. The same is true of values. They both have subjects: subjects with faith and subjects of faith; subjects with values and subjects who are valued. Such an understanding suffices as the basis of spiritual and moral education because it is the basis of community.

Relating this to our pedagogical purposes indicates why children and young people often relate negatively to religious and moral education. It is not because the issues involved do not have an intrinsic interest for them, but because the issues are not the open focus of enquiry. There is an agenda, devised through curriculum circumscription and desirable outcomes in both cases. This agenda seeks to ensure that certain types of citizen are formed, valuing religious constructions of human purpose, even if not subscribing to them, and agreeing to a consensus of normative morality. The problem is not whether these are good aims, it is that they are imposed aims. Pupils and students know they are expected to buy into them. This limits the possibilities of response and involvement in the process of development. Put simply: what if we disagree not only with what we have to learn and respond to but also with the pattern of learning that is being provided? If we respond like Sartre (and young people do, but usually with less sophistication), will we be listened to? How will our response be evaluated? What will the effect of that evaluation be on our own motivation and the value we accord to learning, the dynamics of classroom activity and curriculum aims? In this respect religious and moral education, as they stand, largely defeat their own purposes.

Section II

Narrative, morality and community

5 Moral education as relationship in community

Jane Erricker

Introduction

> Dear Teacher,
>
> I am a survivor of a concentration camp. My eyes saw what no man should witness: Gas chambers built by learned engineers. Infants killed by trained nurses. Women and babies shot and burned by high school and college graduates. So, I am suspicious of education. My request is: help your students to become human. Your efforts must never produce learned monsters, skilled psychopaths, educated Eichmanns. Reading, writing and arithmetic are important only if they serve to make our children more human.
>
> (Author unknown, quoted by Bardige in Gilligan 1982:87)

The above quotation sets the scene for what we wish to accomplish in the following chapters. At the time of writing the media are full of accounts of atrocities: Nato planes are bombing the Serbs (the 1999 war in Yugoslavia caused by Slobodan Milosovic's ethnic cleansing of Kosovo); students from Columbine High School in Colorado, are being buried (two pupils shot a number of their classmates before killing themselves in April 1999); and the surviving victims of the latest extremist bombing in Soho, London, are still recovering in hospital (this was the third in a series of nail bomb attacks on minority groups in London in April 1999).

The question we have to ask ourselves, as each generation has asked in the face of such events, is if our society is producing people who can perpetrate such things is there any way in which the education of our young people is lacking, and is there any way in which we can educate them to reduce the likelihood of such events? To summarise the argument to be put forward in the following chapters, we believe that the education we offer our young people today has become altered, mutated by the demands and influences of modernism and capitalist culture, such that the skills necessary for living a 'good life' are no longer allowed to develop. We, the teachers and the policy makers, do not encourage these skills in our schools, and sometimes we even stifle whatever development might naturally occur. The school curriculum in Britain today demands that a particular form of knowledge is pursued, and, given that the time available to 'deliver' the curriculum is necessarily limited, the time available for other forms of knowledge, and for other skills apart from rote learning and logical argument, is severely curtailed. This restriction of space in the curriculum gives a particular message to teachers and their pupils about the value that we, as a society, place on this different knowledge and these different skills, the knowledge and skills needed to live a good life. What I mean by different 'knowledge' and different skills will become obvious as this chapter progresses.

It seems plain that what is required is moral education, and our present government, and the previous one, would claim that they have tried to address this. The overarching aim of the national curriculum for England and Wales includes a commitment to 'promote the spiritual, moral, cultural, mental and physical development of pupils and society'. The QCA and its predecessor the SCAA have published discussion documents (SCAA 1995, 1996) and matrices to help schools with their planning, and reports are currently being presented by assorted groups in order to develop a curriculum for citizenship education that will include spiritual and moral education, health education, political education and preparation for adult life.

However I argue that all this activity has resulted in very little actually being done in schools in the way of explicit moral education, and that what is being done is rooted in an epistemology and a notion of the self that are less than useful in today's pluralistic society. I shall explore what it might mean to have a moral education in schools that is based on a different theory from the abstract logical theory upon which moral theorising has been based since the Enlightenment. The discussion will draw on feminist and postmodern notions (it is not suggested that these two necessarily represent distinct categories) and involve a redefinition of subjectivity and agency. In the light of these redefinitions, a different epistemology will mean that in the process of education, knowledge content will be replaced with narrative construction. I shall illustrate and support my claims for this process using narrative data collected in the classroom.

The present situation

This section will investigate the state of moral education in schools today by examining published materials, agreed syllabuses and government documents, and relating conversations with teachers. The aim is to reveal what is happening in schools and to expose some of the epistemological and psychological assumptions behind common practice.

I shall consider the following questions. How do schools approach the 'subject'? Where in the curriculum is it found? Is moral education always part of religious education? Is religious education all of moral education, or does it take place elsewhere? What do schools think they are doing in this area? What assumptions do both teachers and policy makers make about the nature of the 'subject', and how might these assumptions be challenged in order to suggest a new way of morally educating?

As examples of suggested practice in schools I shall look at an agreed syllabus for religious education, the School Curriculum and Assessment Authority's document on spiritual, moral, social and cultural education (SCAA 1995) and the guidance to schools on spiritual, moral, social and cultural development (SCMS 1997).

An agreed syllabus for religious education—Hampshire County Council, Portsmouth City Council, Southampton City Council: Vision and Insight 1998

In the UK religious education lies outside the national curriculum, but is still statutory. Instead of a national curriculum, regional curricula are used, albeit structured around recommendations from the government. Model syllabuses are supplied to and used by each education authority to construct their own syllabuses, which are then agreed. I shall look at one particular syllabus, 'Vision and Insight', produced by Hampshire County Council, Portsmouth City Council and Southampton City Council, and take it to be typical of the various syllabuses in use around the UK. The general thrust, if not the specifics, of my critique can be applied to other agreed syllabuses.

On the first page the writers of this syllabus acknowledge the place of RE in realising the commitment of their school to SCMS: 'The strong emphasis placed on the responsibility of schools in the area of the spiritual, moral, social and cultural development of pupils has also recognised the distinctive and important contribution of Religious Education' (Hampshire County Council *et al.* 1998:1). The stated aim is to 'foster in pupils a reflective approach to life' (ibid.:3).

The syllabus is divided into two attainment targets, one concerned with 'Exploring and responding to human experience' and the other with 'Investigating the religious traditions' (ibid.:6–7). Both these targets contain aspects that can be said to encompass moral education. The first is concerned with the ability of the pupil to 'engage with, and respond imaginatively to, evocative, inspirational or thought-provoking aspects of human experience and expression', and 'explore the more profound questions raised by human life and develop their capacity for, and understanding of, reflection'. The second target is concerned with the ability of the pupil to understand the central beliefs and values of those religions.

All of these abilities could be considered to be part of moral education. Later on in the syllabus the skills in religious education are listed. These include reflection—the ability to reflect on feelings, relationships, experiences, ideas, ultimate questions, beliefs and practices—and empathy—the ability to consider the thoughts, feelings, experiences, attitudes, beliefs and values of others, and the ability to glimpse a little of how others see the world and to see issues from different points of view (ibid.:15).

Also included are weighing the respective claims of self-interest, consideration for others, religious teaching and individual conscience, and recognising and critically evaluating one's own standpoint and presuppositions and recognising bias, caricature, prejudice and stereotyping (ibid.:16).

A section on attitudes starts with the statement that 'Attitudes such as respect, open-mindedness and tolerance will be promoted throughout all areas of school life (ibid.:17), and then goes on to list the particular attitudes at the heart of religious education. These include the following which can be classed as part of moral education.

Curiosity:

*   A desire to seek meaning in life.
*   A wish to seek truth and explore ultimate questions.

Open-mindedness:

*   Listening to other people's views.
*   Avoiding bias and prejudice in discussion.

Self-understanding:

*   Developing a mature sense of self-worth and personal value. Respect.
*   Recognising the human rights of people to hold and practise their beliefs.
*   Respecting those with different opinions from one's own.
*   Discerning what is worthy of respect.
*   Appreciating similarities and differences.

At first glance this syllabus appears entirely worthy. For example who could argue with the aim of inculcating open-mindedness in children? However it merits deeper examination.

First of all, this is not a syllabus for moral education, it is a syllabus for religious education. Nonetheless, many of the aims are moral, and the language used is the language of moral development and moral education, as identified above. This is not really surprising as religious teaching has always included injunctions about how to behave, but if moral education is only taught in combination with religious education, then the juxtaposition of professed values with religious ideas legitimates the moral ideas. The children are morally educated without any discussion of the ideas as moral education *per se*. The children are morally indoctrinated as they are religiously educated and the values are implicit.

The fact that an RE syllabus contains such things as respecting those with different opinions from one's own and discerning what is worthy of respect (which are moral attitudes, not religious ones), alongside being open and exploratory when investigating religion (which is an attitude to do with religious education) illustrates my point. I do not deny that this kind of moral indoctrination goes on elsewhere in the curriculum. Of course it does. The school curriculum and the stance of teachers are both part of the 'habits' of moral life that we all learn as we learn our native language (Oakeshott 1962).

However, what is happening in RE is more invidious because it sets out to morally educate, but it does not call itself moral education, and the syllabus is not written as moral education, it is written and legitimated as religious education. It is moral education, but with only one particular slant on it, and by default that slant can be interpreted as the only valid one. There is no other part of the curriculum where this moral stance is explicitly questioned or different bases for moral decision making examined.

The approach to moral education within religious education illustrated here has the bias and the omissions identified by the psychologist Carol Gilligan (1982) in her challenge to conventional theories of moral development, because underpinning it are Kantian, Kohlbergian and Piagetian ideas of a rational, detached, abstracting, morally mature subject (Kohlberg 1984; Piaget 1932). This person seeks truth and discerns what is worthy of respect, she or he does not build relationships and communities, care for others or seek solutions to moral problems which involve the least harm to the most people. The differences between the two approaches or attitudes towards moral development are examined in greater detail later on in this book.

This deficiency in scope of the moral education offered within religious education would not be so much of a problem if this type of moral education was not often all that is offered in schools, particularly in primary schools, and if this type of moral education was identified for what it was, legitimated by particular religious traditions.

SCAA Discussion Paper 3: Spiritual and Moral Development (1995)

This discussion paper was first published by the National Curriculum Council in the UK in 1993 and then republished in 1995 on the recommendation of Ron Dearing, prior to the values consultation exercise that took place in 1996. It was written for schools without a religious foundation, though it was suggested that denominational schools would also find it useful.

The document was intended 'to guide schools in their understanding of spiritual and moral development and to demonstrate that these dimensions apply not only to religious education and collective worship but to every area of the curriculum and all aspects of school life'. It did not suggest that the promotion of spiritual and moral development should have a particular slot in the curriculum apart from RE and collective worship, but that opportunities should arise in the aforementioned areas and also in the ethos of the school. It was an attempt to widen schools' perceptions of spiritual and moral education, and to show how, as they are partially removed from the context of a particular religion, these aspects of education can be addressed in a culturally and religiously varied classroom.

The document separated spiritual and moral development and gave working definitions of the terms. Rather than limit the definitions to simple statements, the document acknowledged the complexity of the terms by listing aspects of spiritual development and elements of moral development. The aspects of spiritual development included:

- Beliefs.
- A sense of awe, wonder and mystery.
- Experiencing feelings of transcendence.
- Search for meaning and purpose.
- Self-knowledge.
- Relationships.
- Creativity.
- Feelings and emotions.

It went on to explain that these things could be attributed to God, or to physical, sociological or psychological causes, by different people.

Moral development is said to involve several elements:

- The will to behave morally as a point of principle.
- Knowledge of the codes and conventions of conduct agreed by society.
- Knowledge and understanding of the criteria put forward as a basis for making responsible judgements on moral issues.
- The ability to make judgements on moral issues as they arise by applying moral principles, insights and reasoning.

The document goes on to say that 'Children need to *know* the difference between right and wrong' and that 'children need to be introduced from an early age to *concepts* of right and wrong' (emphasis added). 'Personal morality combines the beliefs and values of individuals, those of social, cultural and religious groups to which they belong, and the laws and customs of the wider society. Schools should be expected to uphold those values that contain *moral absolutes*' (emphasis added).

School values should include:

- Telling the truth.
- Keeping promises.
- Respecting the rights and property of others.
- Acting considerately towards others.
- Helping those less fortunate and weaker than oneself.
- Taking personal responsibility for one's actions.
- Self-discipline.

School values should reject:

- Bullying.
- Cheating.
- Deceit.

- Cruelty.
- Irresponsibility.
- Dishonesty.

The document reads like common sense; it is difficult to find anything in it with which one could reasonably disagree. It lists every mode of behaviour that nice, middle-class, British parents would want their children to conform to. But once again the epistemology behind the assumptions, and the notion of the self, can and should be challenged. Children are expected to come to *know* particular *concepts*. Teachers are expected to teach them what is right and what is wrong. There is no sense that these concepts are anything but unchanging and constant: once learned never forgotten and never altered. This knowledge has nothing to do with the child as a person but exists in the ether, in its 'rightness' or 'wrongness'. It has nothing to do with the way the child is feeling at any particular time, nothing to do with relationships that exist with any other people who might be involved. In fact this 'rightness' and 'wrongness' exists outside any concrete situation, but is there to be plucked out of the void and applied, like sticking plaster, to the problem area. It is also intimately involved, in a Kohlbergian or Piagetian manner, with the child's cognitive development. The child must be able to apply reasoning, and must be able to abstract and universalise a situation in order to apply moral principles. Is this really what we want to imply? That children cannot be moral until they reach some preconceived standard of cognitive attainment? I would suggest that such a notion, apart from being positively insulting to our children, is very dangerous in that it excuses a disempowerment of young children that runs contrary to their abilities and devalues their experiences.

The document walks a thin line between moral absolutism and moral relativism as it attempts to be acceptable to a plural society. It claims that 'personal morality combines the beliefs and values of individuals, those of the social, cultural and religious groups to which they belong, and the laws and customs of the wider society.' Having thus given pupils the right to have a personal morality, it then says that 'schools should be expected to uphold those values which contain moral absolutes.' So how does a school decide which those 'moral absolutes' are? And how does it deal with possible conflict between personal moralities and the morality of the school?

The document lists values, as shown above, but I would like to question the presentation of such a list as explicitly identified values for a school to uphold. Of course if you were to ask anyone if they thought that schools should support truth-telling then the answer would certainly be yes. However we are asked to support these as *moral absolutes*. In other words there is no situation where the truth must not be told, likewise with keeping promises. Now ask any child whether adults tell the truth, ask them if they keep their promises, ask them if newspapers tell the truth, if the television tells the truth, ask them if politicians take personal responsibility for their actions, if sports and pop stars show self-discipline. Do we really think that children do not know about the world they live in? These might be worthy aspirations, but are they moral absolutes? Children are not fools, many of them have had experiences, even by the age of six, that their teachers will never have and would never want to have. If we try to impose such moral absolutes on them, then they will either feel as though they are being treated as fools, or they will consider their teachers to be fools for being so ignorant of their experienced world. Of course we would like to reject cheating, deceit and dishonesty. But in our consumerist world they are often rewarded, and their perpetrators held up as role models.

As a wish list this SCAA discussion paper is unexceptional. Any one of us in education could have written it. But as advice to schools on a notoriously difficult area, in terms of both the curriculum and society, it is sadly lacking. We can identify several serious omissions:

- It does not sufficiently address the issue of a plural society.
- It does not admit to or deal with the basic dishonesty of a capitalist society.
- It does not address the issue of disaffected young people who have to deal with a consumerist society.
- It does not sufficiently value community.
- It does not sufficiently value relationship.
- It does not sufficiently value young people.

The SCAA guidance for schools on their promotion of SMSC development (1997)

This guidance was based on an exercise in consultation that was carried out by the government in 1996. Called the National Forum for Values in Education, it was set up by the SCAA to (1) discover whether there are any values upon which there is common agreement within society; and (2) decide how schools might be supported in the important task of contributing to pupils' SMSC development.

A group of consultants formed the forum, with representatives being gathered from various religious traditions, education, government and society in general. The selection of these representatives was not a transparent procedure. The forum met, heard prepared contributions from members and discussed the issue of common values: the importance of 'common values' was predetermined and assumed.

The forum identified a number of values (see box) on which members believed society as a whole would agree. 'Extensive consultation' showed there to be overwhelming agreement on these values. However the nature of that consulta-tion—that is, the actual nature of the questions asked—made it difficult to disagree with the forum's conclusions in that the questions were vague and general. The remit of the forum was to decide whether there are any values that are commonly agreed upon across society, not whether there are any values that should be agreed upon across society. Accordingly the only authority claimed for these values is the authority of consensus.

This remit shows an interesting approach. On the face of it, it conforms with the notion of socially constructed morality, that is, there is no authority claimed for these values except consensus. However this is not the process of the construction of morality, but an attempt to get people whose moralities have been constructed in different communities to agree that their moralities are the same. Each of these separate moral systems are based on and legitimated by different authorities: the various religious traditions, humanism and so on. The varying philosophies behind the values were ignored and only the discrete, identifiable, common bits were deemed important. There was no suggestion that difference was to be appreciated, lived with and celebrated, but that everything that could not be identified as 'the same' was to be ignored. Thus if we can all agree on a particular value it can be included, but if we do not, however important that value is to our community, it will not be included. The possibility of 'consensus' is obviously remote, and even if it is achieved the value of the agreed values is debatable.

The following quotation shows how the authors of this exercise attempted to address some of the above points:

> These values are not exhaustive. They do not, for example, include religious beliefs, principles or teachings, though these are often the source from which commonly-held values derive. The statement neither implies nor entails that these are the only values that should be taught in schools. There is no suggestion, in particular, that schools should confine themselves to these values.

It is difficult to see which values will remain 'common' after this disclaimer and difficult to see the point of identifying these putative common values. Will the common values be given more emphasis in school? Will they be taught as having more value because they are common? If so, what will be the status of other values that are associated with the traditions?

The next quotation disclaims even more: 'Agreement on the values is also compatible with different interpretations and applications of these values. It is for schools to decide, reflecting the range of views in the wider community, how these values should be interpreted and applied'. Here schools are permitted to interpret and apply the common values as they wish, presumably by putting them back into the context of the traditions and philosophies from whence they came, and from which they were extracted by the processes of the forum. What, therefore, is the point of identifying their commonality?

The document goes on: 'The ordering of these values does not imply any priority or necessary preference. The ordering reflects the belief of many that values in the context of the self must precede the development of other values'. I think this too is problematic. To state that the ordering does not imply priority but 'reflects the belief of many' is to sit on the fence. Either there is no priority, or values in the context of the self are to precede others. The latter statement certainly reflects the standard Kohlbergian theories of moral development.

These values are so fundamental that they may appear unexceptional. Their demanding nature is, however, demonstrated both by our collective failure consistently to live up to them, and the moral challenge that acting on them in practice entails. The values identified by this process of 'consensus' are certainly unexceptional, but this is not because they are fundamental. Our behaviour as a society cannot be said to live up to them, as they are stated here, but this is not because we are moral failures, it is because these values, as stated here, have been reduced by the process of consensus to simplistic, generalised clichés that have no more power or meaning than the stricture 'be good'. Life is so much more complicated than these values give it credit for, and by reducing moral guidance to this level we do our children a great disservice. We run the risk of, once again, having an aspect of education dismissed by pupils because their thinking is at a much more sophisticated level than the curriculum we offer them.

All that this exercise has done is to identify what schools should tell children to do. It does not offer any help in the difficult task of justifying this prescription to the children, explaining why they should hold the values that have been identified or help in developing the emotional skills that the children will need in order to live by these values.

It will be argued later in this chapter that without personal engagement in actual moral situations, as they appear in real life with real participants, children will not be able to decide how to behave. No amount of prescription of the values they should hold, or the way they should behave, will change what they do or what they believe. But personal and emotional involvement in their own experiences and those of their peers will allow them to develop their own moral positions.

The statement of values

The self

We value ourselves as unique human beings capable of spiritual, moral, intellectual and physical growth and development. On the basis of these values, we should:

- develop an understanding of our own characters, strengths and weaknesses;
- develop self-respect and self-discipline;
- clarify the meaning and purpose in our lives and decide, on the basis of this, how we believe that our lives should be lived;
- make responsible use of our talents, rights and opportunities;
- strive, throughout life, for knowledge, wisdom and understanding;
- take responsibility, within our capabilities, for our own lives.

Relationships

We value others for themselves, not only for what they have or what they can do for us. We value relationships as fundamental to the development and fulfilment of ourselves and others, and to the good of community. On the basis of these values, we should:

- respect others, including children;
- care for others and exercise goodwill in our dealings with them;
- show others they are valued;
- earn loyalty, trust and confidence;
- work cooperatively with others;
- respect the privacy and property of others;
- resolve disputes peacefully.

Society

We value truth, freedom, justice, human rights, the rule of law and collective effort for the common good. In particular, we value families as sources of love and support for all their members, and as the basis of a society in which people care for others. On the basis of these values, we should:

- understand and carry out our responsibilities as citizens;
- refuse to support values or actions that may be harmful to individuals or communities;
- support families in raising children and caring for dependants;
- support the institution of marriage;
- recognise that the love and commitment required for a secure and happy childhood can also be found in families of different kinds;
- help people to know about the law and legal processes;
- respect the rule of law and encourage others to do so;
- respect religious and cultural diversity;
- promote opportunities for all;
- support those who cannot, by themselves, sustain a dignified life-style;
- promote participation in the democratic process by all sectors of the community;
- contribute to, as well as benefit from, economic and cultural resources;
- make truth, integrity, honesty and goodwill priorities in public and private life.

The environment

We value the environment, both natural and shaped by humanity, as the basis of life and a source of wonder and inspiration. On the basis of these values, we should:

- accept our responsibility to maintain a sustainable environment for future generations;
- understand the place of human beings within nature;
- understand our responsibilities for other species;
- ensure that development can be justified;
- preserve balance and diversity in nature wherever possible;
- preserve areas of beauty and interest for future generations;
- repair, wherever possible, habitats damaged by human development and other means.

Different approaches to moral education

In this section I shall look at different approaches to moral education—some very recent, some not—that would allow us to remove moral education from the constraints of religious education and thus from a moral code prescribed by specific religious bodies. Elsewhere in this book we shall examine how these types of approach can also be responses to different visions of the self and different attitudes towards knowledge, and we shall develop some of these ideas further.

The approaches we shall examine have been suggested by the following research group and authors: the Children and Worldviews Project, Michael Oakeshott and Gavin Baldwin. We shall also look at some of the implications of the proposed new citizenship curriculum for moral education.

The Children and Worldviews Project

This research project has been working in primary schools since 1994, interviewing children about their attitudes towards and opinions on their schooling, culture, environment and beliefs. The stories that children tell about their lives often reveal their attitudes towards right and wrong action, and thus the moral codes they live by and expect others to live by, and these have been identified by the research team.

Moral education can be positively identified in the primary school curriculum, the RE curriculum, stories told in the literacy hour, circle time and behaviour management. It is in these contexts that moral issues are discussed with children. The policy of teachers towards moral education is likely to be influenced by the RE syllabus, the guidance for SCMS, possibly the above statement of values and the behaviour policies of the school.

When moral issues arise in any of the above contexts, teachers generally use the opportunity to remind and encourage children to behave as they should, in a way that the teachers have already decided is 'moral' on the basis of any or all of the above guidance documents or on the basis of their own personal beliefs. Even if discussion is allowed, the consequence of that discussion is predetermined as teachers are unlikely to change their moral stance because of a child's argument.

This raises several issues in respect of power and teaching objectives. The assumption is made that teachers know better than children how to behave because they are assumed to have more experience, if only because they are adults, and they are assumed to be 'cleverer' than the child. The first assumption, that teachers have more experience because they are adults, has been shown to be unwarranted. In the research of the Children and Worldviews Project, and indeed in informal communication with teachers generally, we have found that some young children have had a great deal of experience that many protected, middle-class teachers have not. This is because their family situations can be complicated, unstable and possibly abusive, and the children might be expected to take on emotional and practical responsibilities at a comparatively young age. It can sometimes be assumed that they have not reflected on their experiences in a 'moral' way, and that all these experiences have done is to traumatise them to a greater or lesser degree. However we have found that even very young children are capable of mature and sophisticated reflection on their experiences and that they can make considered moral decisions based on those reflections, as the following quotations show.

Nelson, a six-year-old boy, explained why he thought it was wrong to kill animals. He said that God had told us that we should not kill animals, and he enlarged on this as follows: 'It's like if you kill God's animals then he'll be very sad and upset. It's just like you've just bought a very nice toy and then the next day somebody comes and breaks it all up.'

Alaric, who was being interviewed with Nelson and was the same age, came to the very carefully considered conclusion that 'People love killing. They kill things because they like it', a position that Nelson argued with, eventually suggesting that animals should not be killed for human gain, but only when they were ill.

Ten-year-old Lee and Glen also had a lengthy discussion, but this was about their family experiences. There was an interviewer present and his comments are prefaced below by Q. The children had previously put it in writing that they would like to be interviewed.

GLEN: Hi, I'm Glen, I go to . . . Junior School and I've learnt to play football.
LEE: I'm Lee and I play for . . . Rangers, um, I go to . . . Junior School, my parents are divorced, I've got a step-dad, my dad's got a girlfriend and we get on really well.
Q: That's lovely, thank you . . . so, talk to me then about why you wrote down on your paper what you wrote down.

GLEN: I'd like to discuss it, its really hard for me, my mum split up with my dad and I don't know what its really like to have a mum cos I wasn't old enough to know when they split up and I'd just like to go and see her more often cos all I hear of her are like phone calls or I go and see her about once every year.

Q: So how old were you then?

GLEN: I was three, all I remember was my mum and dad having a row.

Q: But you remember that do you Glen?

GLEN: Yeh, that's all I remember of it.

Q: Can you say how you remember that? Have you got a picture in your mind of how it happened?

GLEN: Yeh, very clearly.

Q: And what was it like? How did that feel at the time?

GLEN: It felt really scary, cos I didn't know what was going on where I was so young.

Q: Right, and how old were you at that time?

GLEN: Three.

Q: And the situation now?

GLEN: Well, it's really hard for my dad and he gets a bit stressed up because he's got to look after all four of us, he used to have four kids, but now he's only got three, cos one's moved out.

Lee gets on pretty well with his dad cos he trains us in football, he's a manager.

Q: Your dad trains . . . Rangers?

LEE: Yeh.

GLEN: Yeh, my dad works a lot out of hours, he gives up Sundays and Saturday mornings and works then as well.

LEE: He looks really tired every time we see him.

Q: So what did you say? You thought he was a bit stressed?

LEE: Yeh, he's like my dad . . . my mum and dad split up cos my dad had other girlfriends in other countries and he was hitting my mum and my sisters and I was about seven and they split up and a couple of years ago I went to a social worker cos I was really in distress and my mum's remarried and they've had another baby, his name's Ashley, he's my brother, and my dad's, my dad isn't married yet but he's got a girlfriend and she's got two kids, there's one, a boy about my age, so I get on very well with him, but um, when they first split up I thought, I felt really alone cos there was no one person, um man in my life who I could mess around with and things.

Q: Really?

LEE: Yeh, and it was a bit distressing for me. I only see my dad every other week now, but its better than then.

Q: Better than then?

LEE: Yeh.

Q: And do you live with your mum?

LEE: Yeh.

Q: And do you remember that very well, that happening, when they split up?

LEE: Yeh, I remember the exact night it happened, cos I was coming down the stairs and my dad was slapping my mum and it was really horrible.

Q: It was horrible?

LEE: Yeh.

Q: So what do you think would help you in your situation? Is your situation better than it was? Are there things that you think need to be sorted out?

GLEN: Yeh, I reckon I should go and see my mum about every other week or stay there at weekends and stuff to get things sorted out, cos I always ask my dad 'why did we, why did you get divorced and that?' but he hardly ever explains it to me, he just says 'cos we had a row'.

LEE: That's like, just like really shouting at each other and things cos my sisters, well they're both older than me, and they know a lot more about it, cos I remember when my sister almost got stabbed by my dad and we had to go to my next door neighbour's house and the police came round and . . . he used to say he was going abroad for his work, but he didn't, he has girlfriends like in Sweden and Malta and places and we found out that for sure.

Q: Right, and that's what forced the split?

LEE: Yeh, I just wish things would change but they won't, I know they can't.

Q: So what could you do about this situation, you were saying Glen that you could see your mum more?

GLEN: Yeh.

Q: What would you say to your mum?

GLEN: I'd just say like 'I'd like to like stay here', and when I'm older I'd like to move in with my mum because me and my mum, when I go and see her, just on my own, she like starts to cry and that.

LEE: Don't you go with your sisters?

GLEN: No, I just go on my own cos my sisters don't like my mum that much and I really love my mum and she . . . when I go there she cries and normally we have to . . . we always go out for like a MacDonalds or go down town because she can't get her mind off it.

LEE: Yeh, its exactly the same as what I do with my dad, he doesn't cry like cos he doesn't like expressing his feelings, he likes to express his anger a lot cos once I got punched in the eye by him. I had a great big bruise but he didn't get anything done about it.

Q: What does that mean? You didn't go to the doctor or . . . ?

LEE: Yeh, I went to the doctors and we got the police as well but they didn't do anything about it, he doesn't really do it to me, well, he's bruised me once but he's knocked my sisters a lot.

Q: But you still see him?

LEE: Yeh, cos that was a few years ago now and now he's found a girlfriend he's a bit more lightly tempered so . . . he's a bit more even because she's got kids and she says to him that she doesn't want him hitting them.

Q: Right, and what do you think you could do, or someone could do about this situation that would make it better?

LEE: I don't know.

Q: That's difficult is it?

LEE: Yeh, I enjoy seeing my dad a lot, a lot yeh, cos he likes all the things I like to do as well, because he's not that violent any more round me, well, my older sister doesn't like him, she goes, but she usually gets in one of her moods, she has one of her moody days before we go to my dad's cos every other week we either go for a weekend or we go for a Sunday.

Q: And you always go together?

LEE: Yeh, or sometimes my older sister doesn't . . . but my other one does, I've got two sisters.

GLEN: That's another thing about my mum as well, another reason why she's distressed, she found another man, she had another baby, but where she couldn't cope, where she had no money and everything, that baby had to go into foster care, and I only saw him once, he's my only like step brother.

Q: And you don't see him now?

GLEN: No, cos my mum hardly sees him now . . . I don't even know where he is or anything.

Q: And you hardly see her?

GLEN: Yeh.

Q: And does she live very far away?

GLEN: She just lives in . . . but . . .

LEE: That's where my dad lives.

GLEN: But when we don't hear from her we think maybe she doesn't live there anymore so we don't know where to go if we want to go and see her. Once we didn't know but she was in hospital cos she had very bad things, she forgot our phone number and we went up there and she wasn't in and we, I got really worried cos my mum wasn't there and found out that night, my nan phoned up and said she's in hospital.

Q: Right, and you didn't know and you couldn't contact her?

GLEN: No.

Q: And do you have her telephone number now?

GLEN: I'm not sure, I don't know it. My dad might, but I don't.

Q: Right, and you're not sure if your dad does?

GLEN: No.

LEE: A lot of things are kept secret aren't they?

GLEN: Yeh.

Q: A lot of things are kept secret?

LEE: Yeh, it happens all the time. My mum . . . cos sometimes I get like my dad and I get really angry and sometimes I hit people too, like my sisters, and I know . . . and I don't do that any more, I take it out on like sports and stuff.

Q: Does sport help?

LEE: Yeh, a lot.

GLEN: Yeh, a lot.

A detailed analysis of this transcript is provided in Chapter 9 of this book. The conversation has been used here to demonstrate the empathy and understanding that children of this age can show towards their parents and friends when they are allowed to work from their own experiences.

In the history curriculum—Gavin Baldwin's approach

The work of the Children and Worldviews Project, discussed above, relies on children narrating their own life experiences, listening to others narrating theirs, and developing empathy and moral judgement as a result of sharing their stories. Gavin Baldwin's (1996) approach to moral education is in some ways similar to that of the Children and Worldviews Project, but he uses historical stories instead of present-day, personally narrated life stories.

Baldwin has his own definitions of spirituality and morality. According to Baldwin, spirituality 'grow[s] from the individual and [is] not modelled/trained/conformed from without. In that sense it may be both relative and rational' (ibid.:210). When discussing modern morality he

> follows Ross Poole [1991:51–2] in identifying a split ethic in modern society. Accumulative capitalism makes a virtue of acquisition at all costs and rapid consumption. This suits the fragmented nature of modernity suggested above. In contrast to this is the virtue of caring for family and friends in the small community with which we still identify, the home. Here we may develop the intersubjective notion of good justice as a solution to Liberal failure. When linked to individualized spirituality this discovers the individual, as the source of spiritual and ethical concern, faced with greed as a virtue on the one hand and love on the other. Where does this leave moral education? . . . [M]oral education must nurture the individual's ability to understand his or her own moral position and that of others and to become critically aware of the assumptions which underlie such principles . . . and which might help to make sense of seemingly incompatible moral positions in a rapidly changing society.
>
> (Baldwin 1996:210–11)

He then asks how moral education can be realised and uses the subject of history as an example of how it might be done. He quotes Cooper (1992:12) as defining historical empathy as 'the achievement of understanding the ways in which people in the past have thought, felt and behaved differently from us because of their different knowledge bases and because of the different social, political and economic constraints of the society in which they lived'. Baldwin claims that the three areas of psychological research that Cooper identifies as relevant to historical thinking—creative thinking, changing perspectives and psychodynamics—are equally essential to the development of spiritual and moral understanding:

> By making sense of the actions of others, children will be able to develop their own moral values, through the development of historical imagination

children may come to understand that belief systems other than their own have existed and do exist, and through the analysis of decisions taken according to such systems and the resulting outcomes, we enable children to reflect on their own implicit belief systems and the likely consequences of their moral action.

(Baldwin 1996:212)

According to Baldwin the curriculum is 'a selection from culture' and thus has an underlying moral stance that needs to be revealed. He is referring to the history curriculum, but it could refer to any part of the overall curriculum. To some extent moral education can be fulfilled within the school implicitly by the choices made about the content of the curriculum. This is particularly relevant for subjects such as history and religious education, although English literature, science, drama and art can also have contents that involve moral discussion. Baldwin suggests that:

By exploring the operation of different moral codes it is hoped that children's own moral choices will be given greater substance, and by carefully teasing out the differences between moral analysis and judgement they may be better equipped to understand the moral positions of others in conflict with their own.

(ibid.:214)

Baldwin suggests that the way in which the teacher approaches conversations with pupils is important, and that the relationship between teacher and pupil should be one of equality. This reflects the prominence that the Children and Worldviews Project gives to the quality of the relationship between interviewer and child. For them, the role of the interviewer is to facilitate conversation between children, while for Baldwin the conversation is between the child and the historical text. Both approaches use conversation as a means of moral development.

Michael Oakeshott's approach

In *The Rationalism of Politics* (1962) Oakeshott suggests that there are two forms of moral life, both of which depend on education, albeit different sorts of education. The first form of moral life does not rely on the time, the opportunity or the inclination to reflect on the possibilities for action, but acts out of habit. It is neither rigid nor unstable, and its history is one of continuous change, the sort of change to which a living language is subject. It is learned by children just as they learn their native language, by being exposed to it every day, by imitation and thus by habit: 'by living with people who habitually behave in a certain manner we acquire habits of conduct in the same way we acquire our native language' (Oakeshott 1962:62).

Here I shall consider what happens when the moral language at home and that at school are different, as can often be the case. The school automatically assumes that its one is the right one, so there is no discussion about it and the children are confronted by the conflict set up by the differences between the two habits. Children first acquire the habits and affections of their home life, and when they go to school for the first time they can be presented with a different 'language' (in the moral sense) by which to live and different habits to acquire. The child who will be most successful in that situation is the child who has little new to learn, the child whose home life has the same habits and affections as school life. In other words, the white, middle-class child. This means that there will be no conflict for such children, no new habits to learn, and they can immediately apply themselves to learning all the other things that they have been sent to school to learn. For the child whose moral language is different, by virtue of class, culture or any other reason, the situation is very different. Before any learning in curriculum subjects and skills can occur, she or he must observe, sort out the differences and acquire or at least ape the habits of the school community. This is a huge burden for a young child just starting school and it is not openly acknowledged or planned for. In fact, with the recent initiatives to move academic learning further and further down the school, there is even less time for the child to make these adjustments.

For some children the task is too great. The new habits are too difficult or too alien for them to acquire and they never adapt. In my work as a home tutor for education welfare I saw these children when they were finally excluded from school as failures. Simon was one of those children. He was twelve years old when he was assigned to me, and for the most part I taught him in his own home so I got to know the family well. Simon's mother was strong and clever, though comparatively uneducated. His father was illiterate and at one point he asked me to teach him to read. There were six children: three boys and three girls. One girl and one boy had learning difficulties. Simon was not one of them; he and his elder brother were bright and personable, though neither was successful in school and Simon's school career was disastrous. He did not want to learn, he misbehaved and he disrupted other children's learning. Eventually he was excluded from the school at the age of twelve and later on there was some speculation as to whether he had started the fire that destroyed the sports hall, though it was never proved. When I came to teach him he had no self-confidence at all about any of the skills that were relevant to the school situation. He could draw very well and he showed me one of his pictures. When I praised it he tore it up, saying that nothing he did could be good because he was thick. I worked with Simon for four years, until he was old enough to leave school, but we did not achieve much.

So why did Simon behave the way he did? Once the process had started, it is comparatively easy to see why he became more and more alienated from school. When children constantly behave badly and disrupt the learning of the other members of their class, the only response the teachers can make is to criticise them. The children's subsequent lack of effort to please a constantly critical audience means they achieve very little compared with their peers, therefore earning more criticism. The understandable result is anger and a desire to revenge themselves on a system that is alien to them and judges them. So perhaps they set the school on fire. But what went wrong at the beginning? What started the whole process? Obviously this does not happen with all children—many children adapt perfectly well to school life, and succeed. Let us look back at Simon's home life to give us some clues. How were the moral 'habits and conduct' different in his home from those in school?

When children like Simon first go to school the moral habits of their home lives are all they have known. They are not necessarily aware that their home lives might be judged as inadequate in any way. When they get to school, and their behaviour is criticised, it is also a criticism of their home life, to which they may well feel a strong loyalty so the acquisition of the necessary new habits is a process that should be conducted with great sensitivity by the teachers involved. I do not think this is done in the majority of schools today and I am not sure whether it was attempted in Simon's case.

Simon's home life could be classified as working class and the family exhibited the attitudes towards education that were identified by Hyman (1967) and others so long ago. There were very few books, although his mother did read popular romantic fiction. His father had a steady job, though this was unusual in the extended family. However he did not, could not, expect any promotion because he could not read or write. There was a hand-to-mouth attitude, whereby money was spent as soon as it appeared and there was disregard to the value of what was bought. At Christmas a large amount of money was spent on cheap toys for the children, toys that were broken within days and then thrown away. They lived in a council house and Simon's father was often ill, so they frequently lived on child and sickness benefit and any bits of work the mother could do when she was not looking after the children. There was no sense of planning for the future and state provision was relied on when no one was working.

Schooling is about planning for the future. It depends on an assumption that self-improvement is possible and worth pursuing, but Simon's background was not conducive to fostering this assumption. Simon's father had seen the value of a 'steady job' eroding and his practical skills were no longer appreciated, and he had communicated his disillusionment to his family. His children had seen that that attitude had got him nowhere, and they knew that the way to make real money in today's society was to be a footballer or a pop star, and not to get your GCSEs. They also knew that society did not respect or appreciate them, so their answer was to exploit society. Thus Simon went to school, the third child in this large family, already aware that he was not respected, aware that education would not help him much, not feeling that he had much to contribute to society, not feeling that a job was even really necessary in the future. How could he relate to a school community that was all about deferred gratification, a long process that culminated in a good job, a community in which the members were supposed to value and respect each other. This was not his experience, these were not his habits or his learned conduct.

Later in this book we shall suggest how we might make the task of adjustment easier for these children, how we might show the necessary respect for their differences.

Oakeshott's second form of moral life is one with which we might be more familiar, or at least would recognise as overtly 'moral'. This form is characterised by 'the reflective application of a moral criterion' (Oakeshott 1962:66). He claims that 'it appears in two common varieties: as the self-conscious pursuit of moral ideals, and as the reflective observance of moral rules' (ibid.). We would suggest that it is these two 'common varieties', particularly the second one, that are the aim of schools when they morally educate, regardless of whether they have reflected sufficiently to be aware of that fact. The 'rules' to be followed are first determined, and then applied when appropriate. It is important that the actor is a separate, autonomous self and capable of reflecting and deciding what should be done in respect of the rules. According to Oakeshott, in order to do this 'we require an intellectual training in the detection and appreciation of the moral ideals themselves ... training in the art of the intellectual management of these ideals ... [and] training in the application of ideals to concrete situations' (ibid.:72).

He goes on to describe moral societies based on these two ideals, with one or the other dominating. He is very concerned about the effect of living with the ideal always pursued, but finds the alternative, the 'habit' of morality leavened with a little idealism, to be workable, flexible and tolerant.

> Moral ideals are not, in the first place, the products of reflective thought, the verbal expressions of unrealised ideas, which are then translated into human behaviour; they are the products of human behaviour, of human practical activity, to which reflective thought gives subsequent, partial and abstract expression in words.
>
> (ibid.:72–3)

Oakeshott likens this way of living morally to the production of a poem: the writing of the poem or the living of the moral life produces the work of art—the poem or the life. It is not the other way round, that the poem or the life is the translation of an idea or an ideal into concrete expression. This is reminiscent of Foucault's idea that the self is a 'work of art' because it is constructed partly by the 'artist' and partly by the contingency of experience. Oakeshott considers that society is dominated by moral idealism; that we have built a Tower of Babel in an effort to reach heaven, but have succeeded only in bringing about chaos. Of course he was speaking in 1962, though nothing much seems to have changed since then. Even the challenges of postmodernity have not really changed the way in which we live. If anything it might be said that we have gone even further down the road that Oakeshott envisaged.

We can ask the question 'where is moral education in our schools?', but we have no subject called moral education so how can we track it down? We know that it exists, if only because Ofsted inspectors have to inspect the provision made by schools for both moral education (development?) and spiritual, social and cultural education. So we can ask where the inspectors look, but we can find it ourselves in the everyday workings of the school. We can find it in both of the guises that Oakeshott identifies. It is present as the rules and precepts that the children must learn and follow. It is interesting that these rules also appear in two guises: the negatively prohibitive 'no cheating in examinations' and 'bullying will not be tolerated'; and the positively encouraging 'be kind to each other' and 'look after those weaker than yourselves'.

We can also find it in the 'tradition' of the school, or in other words the school ethos. This is the moral education that Oakeshott thinks children acquire 'by living with people who habitually behave in a certain manner' and thus 'acquire habits of conduct in the same way we acquire our native language' (ibid.:62). Children are morally educated by the habits that they see others exhibiting. They see teachers treating each other, and children, with respect; they see children treating the school buildings and grounds properly; they see older children looking after younger children and the disabled; they see cultural differences valued. Or not.

We cannot ensure that everyone behaves in the way required for moral education (how do we know what that way should be?). All we can do is allow the opportunity for discussion and narration so that children can work it out for themselves. In this way they can become familiar with the opinions, feelings and concerns of others and recognise the complexity of moral discourse, the moral discourse of their own community, the way in which moral discourse differs between communities, their own personal moral discourse and the possibility of solving moral problems by communication. Also, conversation allows the differences in moral 'language' to be revealed and communicated. This does not necessarily mean that children will conform immediately to the prevailing 'habits and affection' of the school, but it will allow them to become aware of the nature of the differences. In the absence of conversation with a teacher and other children, who 'must listen carefully, respectfully and responsively' (Tappan 1991), children will simply become alienated from a moral culture that cannot be reconciled with that to which they are accustomed.

Citizenship

Differing views of what citizenship should mean is provided by two moral visions identified by Kohlberg (1984) and Gilligan (1982): justice (equity), with its underlying conception of an autonomous self; and care (attachment), which requires a self-constructed relationship. The first depicts citizenship as an awareness of laws (rules) and how and why we must obey them; and the second provides an alternative conception that involves an awareness of relationship and how this holds the community together and gives us reasons for making it work. Arendt (1958:23) challenges the first view when she notes:

> the overriding value psychologists have placed on separation, individuation and autonomy. To see self-sufficiency as the hallmark of maturity conveys a view of adulthood that is at odds with the human condition, a view that

cannot sustain the kinds of long-term commitments and involvements with other people that are necessary for raising and educating a child or for citizenship in a democratic society.

It seems likely that the proposed citizenship curriculum for the UK will conform to the latter conception. The report of the advisory group chaired by Professor Bernard Crick (QCA 1998:13) describes citizenship education as having 'three heads on one body: social and moral responsibility, community involvement and political literacy', but the subsequent description of the essential elements to be reached by the end of compulsory schooling leads us to believe that the conception of the self as autonomous rather than relational and the justice orientation of morality lie behind this curriculum.

It is likely that the citizenship curriculum will follow the recommendations of this report very closely. If this proves to be the case, then the situation will be as Benhabib (1992:154–5) suggests when she says that

> The transition to modernity does not only privatise the self's relation to the cosmos and to ultimate questions of religion and being. First with Western modernity the conception of privacy is so enlarged that an intimate domestic–familial sphere is subsumed under it. Relations of 'kinship, friendship, love and sex', indeed, as Kohlberg takes them to be, come to be viewed as spheres of 'personal decision making'.
>
> An entire domain of human activity, namely, nurture, reproduction, love and care, which becomes the woman's lot in the course of the development of modern, bourgeois society, is excluded from moral and political considerations, and relegated to the realm of nature.

I suggest that the skills mentioned in the above extract—the skills of relationship—are a prerequisite for the 'action' of citizenship. Not the knowledge of citizenship, but the doing of it. For us in the West, citizenship means the action of democracy. It means taking part in the decision making that allows a community to work, to operate in a global arena. In order to take part in community building and maintenance, and relations with other communities, children must first have self-knowledge, and then they must be able to put themselves in another's place, that is, be able to empathise, to understand what the consequences of a particular decision might be for another individual. Without this, and without a framework of values, it is impossible to take part. Unless all citizens take part in a democracy, that democracy is not a democracy at all, but an oligarchy, with decisions being made by the few who are informed and imbued with the necessary skills and the desire for power. The empowerment of the population will only occur when children are educated in autonomy, when they are empowered by the facilitation, practise and accomplishment of these skills.

Furthermore, these are not just the instrumental skills of democratic participation, they are also the basic skills of being human. In the West we purport to believe that democracy is not only the most efficient way of running a community, but also the fairest, the most moral way. We also believe that it gives citizens the best quality of life. Thus subsumed within education for democratic participation are spiritual and moral education: moral education allows children to understand what is good and to work towards it; and spiritual education allows children to pay attention to their 'inner' life. However democratic participation cannot be achieved by telling people what they should know and what they should do. It is a much more risky business than that. In order for democracy to work people must be educated and then trusted to act morally, in the best interests of themselves and others. This has always been the uncomfortable part of democracy, and thus is also the uncomfortable part of citizenship education. No one can be sure of the outcome of allowing the people to decide. The process, by definition, cannot be controlled from above. Thus in espousing citizenship education we are flying in the face of the recent trends in curriculum development, which have further prescribed both the content of the curriculum and the teaching methods. In this particular area of education autonomy is the learning objective.

Anthony Giddens (1999) draws a parallel between the characteristics of intimate relationship, which in its ideal form he calls emotional democracy, and public democracy. In an intimate relationship both partners should have equality of opportunity, which is achieved by good communication or dialogue. There should be openness and trust and reciprocated respect. The relationship should be free from arbitrary power, coercion or violence. Giddens claims that, as well as characterising the ideal couple, these are the very qualities that constitute an ideal public democracy.

It therefore stands to reason that if we encourage and develop the qualities of relationship, as identified by Giddens, in young children in school, and make sure that they understand and reflect on those qualities, we are laying the foundation for an understanding of public democracy, and an ability to participate in the processes of that democracy. Although Giddens was speaking particularly about intimate relationship, he extended the application of his analysis to the parent–child relationship, and I would extend it further. In fact those qualities describe an ideal in any relationship on the continuum between extremely intimate coupledom and relations between members of a democratic community.

It appears that, in the UK, spiritual and moral education, health education and PSE are all to come under the umbrella of citizenship. If this proves to be the case, then a radical (historical?) solution would be to open up a space in the curriculum and allow schools to fill that space in a number of possible ways. The goal would be to address all the above areas, but not in a prescribed manner. Schools would be able to respond to:

• The expertise of their staff.
• The needs and desires of their pupils.
• The reality of their community, both within and outside the school.
• The needs and desires of the staff.

The pedagogy would demand the autonomy of the pupils and the trust of the staff in the ability of the pupils to respond to that delegation of responsibility. No-one can grow into citizenship unless that trust and that autonomy is there. We can teach citizenship all we like, but learning will not take place unless there is ownership of the process by the learner. Citizenship involves responsibility and the power to make changes, and the pupils must have these in order to understand how they are to be managed.

The pupils could find a project to work on and manage during this curriculum space. The nature of the project would be responsive to the above list. It might be:

• Setting up a small company to produce and market a product.
• Identifying a community need and responding to it.
• Constructing something as a team.
• Fundraising for charity.
• Setting up a research project to gather information to inform government.
• Putting on a dramatic production.

All of these would involve teamwork, financial acumen, management, interpersonal skills, need analysis and so on. Thus other areas of the curriculum would be drawn into citizenship—maths, English, science, design and technology, art, music and so on—and citizenship would become an active and experiential project.

In the report by Crick (1998) discussed at the start of this section, race or racial identity is not mentioned. Hidden in this report is the idea of Britishness and its celebration. At the beginning and end of the report the Lord Chancellor is quoted saying 'We should not, must not, dare not, be complacent about the health and future of British democracy. Unless we become a nation of engaged citizens, our democracy is not secure' (ibid.:8). There is nothing in the suggestions for the curriculum about teaching alternatives to democracy. The report ends with a further quote from the Lord Chancellor:

> A healthy society is made up of people who care about the future. . . . People who want to be practising citizens. Before this can happen they need to have a sense of belonging—of identity—with the community around them. . . . Our goal is to create a nation of able, informed and empowered citizens.
>
> (ibid.:8)

Audrey Osler (1999:) has this to say about the Crick report:

> There are a number of other phrases and recommendations which give the report what is, in my judgement, a somewhat colonial flavour. In discussion of the need to consider questions of national identity in a pluralist context the report refers to 'due regard being given to the homelands of our minority communities and to the main countries of British emigration.' As well as

being somewhat patronising in using the term 'our minority communities', this statement also makes the assumption that members of minority communities, including those who are not of a migrant generation, will necessarily see the countries of their family's migration as their 'homelands' rather than Britain. Furthermore, it precludes the notion of multiple identity, and that as a consequence of a multiple or hybrid identity an individual may have more than one 'homeland'.

Although the Crick report is yet another well-meaning attempt to include moral education explicitly in the curriculum, the omissions noted above and its assumptions about identity mean that any curriculum based on it must be challenged.

6   Narrative constructions towards community

Jane and Clive Erricker

Introduction

In pursuit of our new understanding of religious, spiritual and moral education a jigsaw of constructions has informed our thinking. In this chapter we shall consider the separate pieces before going on to join them together to form the whole picture. They are:

- Constructing a self.
- Constructing childhood and adulthood.
- Constructing a pedagogy.

The elements contained in each of these discussions inform our thinking throughout this book, but particularly in Section III, where we put our ideas into action by addressing classroom practice.

Constructing a self

> Identity! That was the word. That was the key to the whole human problem. Unless a man understood, however dimly, what he was and how he was linked with his fellows and with the cosmos, he could not survive. Put him in a padded cell, separate him from the sight, sound and touch of the world, and you would in a short time reduce him to madness and physical disorder.
>
> (West 1965:75)

In previous chapters we criticised approaches to religious, spiritual and moral education and began to indicate a different approach to, and reconfiguration of, these subjects in school. In this chapter we would like to suggest that spiritual and moral education requires an approach that has as its foundation a different understanding of the nature of knowledge and of the self who is doing the knowing. These two are very closely related, indeed it is very difficult to discuss one without reference to the other.

Our different understanding of knowledge can be described as 'narrative', that is, instead of knowledge being something 'out there' towards which we can work at understanding, it is conceived of as constructed by us as a result of the stories we tell ourselves about our experiences. So it is subjective rather than objective. Lyotard (1984) makes a distinction between these two types of knowledge when he describes 'scientific' knowledge as having been privileged in modern culture, and narrative knowledge as more prevalent in 'primitive' or 'traditional' cultures. He suggests that knowledge (savoir) cannot be reduced to science or even to learning (connaissance) but also 'coincides with an extensive array of competence-building measures and is the only form embodied in a subject constituted by the various areas of competence composing it' (ibid.:18–19). He includes 'notions of "know-how", "knowing how to live", "how to listen"' (ibid.:18), and suggests that value judgements are made on the basis of custom:

> What is a 'good' prescriptive or evaluative utterance, a 'good' performance in denotive or technical matters? They are all judged to be 'good' because they conform to the relevant criteria (of justice, beauty, truth and efficiency respectively) accepted in the social circle of the 'knower's' interlocutors. . . . The consensus that permits such knowledge to be circumscribed and makes it possible to distinguish one who knows from one who doesn't (the foreigner, the child) is what constitutes the culture of a people.
>
> (ibid.:19)

Lyotard is saying that value judgements are made on the basis of custom, and this is an idea extended by Oakeshott (1962:62), when he says 'by living with people who habitually behave in a certain manner we acquire habits of conduct in the same way we acquire our native language', and

> Moral ideals are not, in the first place, the products of reflective thought, the verbal expressions of unrealised ideas, which are then translated into human behaviour; they are the products of human behaviour, of human practical activity, to which reflective thought gives subsequent, partial and abstract expression in words.
>
> (ibid.:72–3)

Now 'custom' can be identified as the way we usually behave, and that is communicated within a society by the stories we tell, stories about ourselves and about others, both historical and contemporary. Thus our culture, our identity, what we 'know' and our sense of what is right and what is wrong is constructed by the stories we tell each other. This story telling is put into a political context by Carroll (1987:72), who, in a commentary on Lyotard, states that

> Lyotard's postmodern disbelief in metanarrative is rooted in a confidence in the potential critical force of small narratives, at least insomuch as their conflictual multiplicity and heterogeneity resist totalization—and he sees,

moreover, narrative heterogeneity to be indicative of the complexity and diversity of the social fabric itself.

It thus legitimates the multiplicity of 'right and wrong' perceptions that result from a morality based on our stories. According to Carroll, Lyotard suggests a notion of narrative pragmatics where

> Pragmatics is a word that designates the set of very complicated relations that exist between the person who narrates and what he is narrating, between the person who narrates and the one who listens to him, between the latter and the story told by the former. The critical advantage of narrative pragmatics for Lyotard is that in order to talk about narrative it does not implicitly or explicitly assume a metanarralogical position, one that gives the rules according to which narrative should be judged, one that proposes laws which determine the truth of narrative, the nature of the real to which it is supposed to conform, and the ideal form narrative must be modelled after. On the contrary, a critical pragmatics admits that one can only analyse, respond to, and counter narratives with other narratives.
>
> (Carroll 1987:76–7)

This suggests that if we accept the idea of narrative knowledge, the only way in which we can 'teach' it is to allow the reciprocal encounter of personal narrative. As Code (1991:309) suggests, we would like to 'remap the epistemic domain into numerous, fluid conversations', bearing in mind the moral, political and practical consequences of that position, demonstrated by Lyotard.

Taking these ideas into the classroom, if knowledge is fluid, contingent and constructed by the narration of stories, then what the children know becomes less important than how they operate. Skills become more important than knowledge and this is the position we would take with regard to spiritual and moral education. As well as taking into consideration possible changes in epistemological position, moral education should be informed by psychological research into moral development and the theory that comes from that research. We need to understand how we think children develop in a psychological sense before we can suggest how we might help them along the way. This is the way in which education is informed by psychology. If we are not informed by psychology—that is, by research into how learning takes place—when we educate, then we run the risk of either trying to force children to do something before they are ready (an idea of course that has at its roots a concept of psychological 'readiness' that may be open to debate) or—to look at it another way which avoids some of those assumptions—trying to make children learn using a methodology, a progression, that is alien to them and that they will resist, rather than a methodology or progression that is defined entirely by them themselves, that will feel natural to them and that they will partake of willingly and efficiently.

If we use work on moral development to inform moral education, then there are certain conceptions that underpin various visions of how moral development occurs. One of these is the notion of a morally developed person. If we want children to develop morally, what do we see as the end point of this development? How can we help a child 'develop' if we do not know what she or he is developing towards? In asking this question, of course, we are asking one of the oldest questions in the world. Plato, Socrates, Kant, Hume, all these and countless others asked variations on the questions 'what is a good person?' and 'how should that person live?' Even deeper underneath is the question of the nature of that person, that self, who is to be these things, who is to develop and be 'good'. Enlightenment notions of the self who is to be good depict this self as autonomous, detached, objective, separate. As Hekman (1995:2) observes:

> The paradigm of this tradition is Kant's self-legislating moral subject. For this subject, rationality and morality are mutually dependent: this explains why Kant excludes those incapable of full rationality, such as women and idiots, from the moral sphere. Essential to this moral tradition is the ability of the subject to abstract from the particularity of his (as the writers in this tradition invariably designate the subject) circumstances and to formulate the universal principles that define the moral sphere.

Women and idiots are excluded because their thinking cannot be rational as they are too attached. Presumably young children too are excluded as not capable of fully rational thought. Piaget would place many of them at the stage of concrete thinking rather than the abstract in his theory of cognitive development. So to be a 'moral subject' one first of all has to be fully 'rational', that is, capable of thinking in the abstract, which means someone, a self, who can extract their thinking from the implied confusion of the concrete and the attached.

This philosophical view is supported by the Freudian explanation of how this self comes to be, in the realisation of separation from the mother as the one who meets basic physiological needs at a very early age. This view is challenged and extended by Nancy Chodorow, who is persuaded by the arguments of Michael and Alice Balint and of Bowlby when they developed the theory that 'infants have a primary need for human contact for itself' (Chodorow 1978:64). She goes on to say that

> a person's self, or identity, has a twofold origin and twofold orientation, both of which derive from its early relational experiences. One origin is an inner physical experience of body integrity and a more internal 'core of the self'. This core derives from the infant's inner sensations and emotions, and remains the central, the crystallisation point of the 'feeling of self' around which a 'sense of identity' will become established. . . . The second origin of the self is through demarcation from the object world. . . . The development of the self is relational.
>
> (ibid.)

Winnicott suggests that 'a good relationship between infant and caretaker allows the infant to develop a sense of separate self—a self whose existence does not depend on the presence of another—at the same time as it develops a sense of basic relatedness' (quoted in ibid.:68).

The above refers to a child's development in the first year or eighteen months, but Chodorow extends the time frame when she says that, 'By the end of the first few years, a sense of identity and wholeness, a sense of self in relationship, has emerged' (Chodorow 1978:73).

Carol Gilligan (1982) develops her notion of the self, based on a critique of Lawrence Kohlberg's view of moral development (which will be discussed in more detail later), and gives us a sense that the process of self-construction is ongoing. Her 'self' is attached, relational and subjective, the notion of separation playing a lesser part in the theory: 'we know ourselves as separate only insofar as we live in connection with others, and that we experience relationships only insofar as we differentiate other from self' (Gilligan 1982:63). Judith Jordan also argues for a new paradigm: 'Rather than a study of development as a movement away from and out of relationship, this approach posits growth through and toward relationship' (Jordan 1991, quoted in Hekman 1995:74).

This point is illustrated and extended by a story concerning Carol Gilligan herself and her recollections of Lawrence Kohlberg, with whom she worked and later disagreed as she developed her own theories of moral development. At a conference on moral education (Association of Moral Education conference 1997) Gilligan gave the keynote address, the Kohlberg Memorial Lecture. She spoke of the friendship between Larry and Carol, and how she did not recognise in that relationship the Kohlberg and Gilligan who were quoted in the academic literature, and whose disagreements were highlighted. Here we have two selves apparently in one person. There is the self constructed by Carol herself, in relationship with Larry, and there is the Gilligan, constructed by the academic community, who 'quarrelled' with Kohlberg. The Carol constructed by Carol herself in relationship with Larry is certainly not the Gilligan constructed by the others. But the Carol constructed by Carol in relationship to someone else is also different. So we have not just one constructed self, but many constructed selves. This idea of multiple constructed selves will be important in our later discussion on suggested methods of education in the classroom.

Susan Hekman (1995) develops the idea of a relational self and articulates her notion of the 'discursive self'. She analyses the movement in contemporary moral theory from the modernist position defined by Descartes, an autonomous ego with essential qualities divorced from contingent circumstances, to a constructed, embodied self defined by Marx as historically situated and by Freud as sexed (ibid.:72). However she notes that more radical steps were taken towards a constructed, anti-Cartesian self by object-relations theorists, who 'seek to describe a self that has no separate, essential core but, rather, becomes a "self" through relations with others' (ibid.:73). She quotes Chodorow's statement that 'Differentiation is not distinctness and separateness, but a particular way of being connected to others' (Chodorow 1978:257). Hekman goes on to explain the paradigm shift in psychoanalytic theory away from Freud's drive theories as an explanation of the self, towards a relational self. In Mitchell's words, 'I become the person I am in interaction with specific others. The way I feel it necessary to be with them is the person I take myself to be' (Mitchell 1988:276). In other words I understand myself as a self because of the way I behave with and to others and the way in which others behave to me.

Now there is a huge difference between those who believe themselves to stand alone, their selfhood all their own, distinct, protected and controlled by themselves, and those whose selfhood depends on their relationship with others. The latter need relationships, depend upon them for their selfhood. Their selfhood is not entirely in their own control, their position is more insecure. It is also possible that their selfhood is contingent on circumstances and is likely to be changed. It sounds more risky to be that sort of person.

Gilligan and Hekman gender this vision of the self by claiming it for women. According to Hekman (1995:74), 'feminist psychoanalysts have recognised the significance of the relational theory of the self for a feminist understanding of psychological development'. There is certainly a 'common sense' perception of men as more detached and autonomous, more self-reliant in their personal assessment, and women as more dependent on relationships for their self-esteem. However it is difficult to determine the contribution of society's constructed expectations in this judgement.

Hekman identifies the relational self as the 'product of discourses' in the following statement:

> The epistemology implicit in her [Gilligan's] work replaces the disembodied knower with the relational self. The knowledge constituted by this relational self is a very different kind of knowledge. The relational self produces knowledge that is connected, a product of discourses that constitute forms of life; it is plural rather than singular.
>
> (ibid.:30)

She goes on to articulate a concept of the subject/self which she calls the 'discursive subject'. This is 'neither relational, feminist, postmodern, nor a product of theories of race and ethnicity, yet it borrows from each of these discourses' (ibid.:109). Its 'identity is (not) disembodied, given, transcendent. It is (not) what the subject "discovers" as he "finds" himself. For the discursive subject, by contrast, identity is constituted, multiple, and fluctuating. The subject is a work of art, fashioned from the discursive tools at the disposal of the situated subject' (1995:109).

We take this to mean that the nature of a discursive identity depends on the nature of the discourse. In other words, who you are depends on what happens to you, to whom you talk and how you talk, and through this you construct your self. We argue that the discourse (narrative) is essential to the process, that the talking out loud, the communication with another, is essential to the process of construction. The use of language constructs the self. The dialogic process constructs the self and because of this the self is necessarily fluid, changing, contingent, responsive. Of course the 'true' nature of communication can always be challenged. How on earth can I know what you are talking about? I do not even know who you are. You do not even know who you are. But we can get by because my ideas of who I am change in response to you and the dialogue we engage in, and your ideas change in response to me. Thus our communication consists of an offering by each of us to the other, an offering that is interpreted and incorporated and changes my idea of who I am, and likewise with you. I can carry out the process with myself, refining and adjusting my notions of myself in silent dialogue, but the process is richer in dialogue with another.

This idea of the self as fluid and contingent is supported and illustrated by the changing nature of the stories we tell. One of Jane's experiences with a particular student can act as a particular example:

> A student of mine, Katy, had an unpleasant experience. She was shopping in town, and a woman came up to her and explained, in some distress, that she had had her car clamped and she had to get to a hospital to see her nephew, who was very ill. This woman was black, and said that because she was black no one would help her. Would Katy give her some money so that she could get the clamp removed? The woman asked for three hundred pounds and Katy got the money out of the bank and gave it to her, arranging to meet her later to get it back. A couple of hours later Katy began to realise that she had been deceived and came to me for help. I listened to her story and then we went to see various people to deal with the problem, ending up at the police station. I heard Katy's story five or six times and each time it was different, not hugely, but significantly. More importantly it seemed to come from a different person, a different self, each time. As Katy told the story each time, her view of herself changed in that dialogue, depending on the response of the person she was talking to. Put simplistically and as an example, my very sympathetic response produced a victim, while the policeman's critical response produced a fool. Her final 'self' after the experience had ended would have been neither of these but something different dependant on subsequent experiences.

The point is that the self constantly changes, and changes in dialogue and because of dialogue, and that this process is unavoidable and necessary. The self is a 'work of art' because it is constructed partly by the 'artist' and partly by the contingency of experience.

This notion of a dialogic self, reliant on the participation of another for its construction, collapses the self/other dichotomy, which has proved to be such a powerful tool in the white, Western, male hegemony of theory and identity. Women do not have to be identified as in binary opposition to men, and the same applies to black and white, Western and non-Western, and, importantly for our purposes, adult and child, or one-who-knows and one-who-does-not-know. Instead, without the opposition and the concomitant privileging of the first term, identity and self become Derridean undecidables.

What does this vision of the self as discursive mean for moral education? In order to answer that we must first deal with notions of moral development, upon which moral education has been seen to depend in recent decades, and which originate from the work of Piaget and Kohlberg.

Piaget explains his theory of the development of moral judgement in the child in *The Moral Judgement of the Child* (1932), where he examines children's behaviour at different ages while playing games. According to Piaget, 'All morality consists in a system of rules, and the essence of all morality is to be sought for in the respect which the individual acquires for those rules' (ibid.:1). He was interested in establishing how children come to respect these rules and he approached the problem in two steps. He looked first at the extent to which children were aware of the rules as something that should influence their play, and then at the extent to which the rules actually did influence their play. His conclusions about the development of children's moral judgement mirror his theories about their cognitive development, as they move from egocentricity and concrete thinking towards abstraction. He found that children progress, in a sequence of defined stages, from heteronomy—that is, a belief that rules are external and sacred—to autonomy, an understanding that rules are the result of consensus among the players.

Piaget extends his notions of children's attitudes towards the rules of games to their moral judgement more generally, and explains the ongoing process of development as follows: 'reason works over moral rules, as she works over everything, generalising them, making them coherent with each other, and above all extending them progressively to all individuals until universality is reached' (ibid.:380).

Lawrence Kohlberg articulated his theory of moral development, which both expanded and complemented Piaget's work, in many books and papers in the 1970s and the 1980s. Like Piaget, he was more concerned with the reasons that people give for their moral stances than with people's moral behaviour. This is a necessary distinction if Hartshorne and May's conclusion is correct that 'There is no necessary relationship between what people say about morality and the way they act. People who express great disapproval of stealing and cheating may actually steal and cheat as much as everyone else' (quoted in Duska and Whelan 1977).

Kohlberg's theory of moral development was developed from empirical, longitudinal data gathered from a study of boys and young men. Moral dilemmas were presented to the subjects and subsequent interviews were aimed at determining the subjects' reasons for suggesting particular courses of action. From the data he identified six stages of moral judgement, which he organised into three levels with two stages at each level. He suggests that stage development is invariant, that subjects cannot understand moral reasoning that is more than a stage above their own, that subjects are cognitively attracted to reasoning at the level above their own, and that movement through the stages occurs when cognitive disequilibrium occurs. The stages demonstrate a progression from responsiveness to rules (but only because of possible punishment for infringement), to an instrumental view that considers as paramount the satisfaction of one's own needs, to a desire to fulfil the expectations of one's own societal group, to an effort to define universal moral principles. There is a move from heteronomy to autonomy, and a need for the subject to work cognitively in the abstract in order that he or she might appreciate universal moral principles, but the stages are developed in much greater detail than Piaget's work demonstrates.

These accounts and explanations of moral development have been challenged on the grounds of the concept of the self underlying them, gender bias and the underlying modernist notions of linear progression over time. Gilligan (1982) replaces these theories with a relational self, a care orientation rather than a justice orientation, which exists alongside Kohlberg's justice-focused judgements of a person's moral capabilities, and a concept of development that is a realisation of full potential rather than achievement of an already determined, fully morally developed personality.

To explain this in greater detail we turn to Seyla Benhabib's analysis in *Situating the Self* (1992). In a chapter entitled 'The Generalized and the Concrete Other' she describes and analyses the critique of Kohlberg's theories put forward by Carol Gilligan, who re-examines some of Kohlberg's data and identifies several discrepancies, one of which is the persistently low score that women achieve in Kohlberg's hierarchy of moral judgement compared with their male peers. Benhabib explains this as follows:

> distinguishing between the ethical orientation of justice and rights and the ethical orientation of care and responsibility allows her to account for women's moral development and the cognitive skills they show in a new way. Women's moral judgement is more contextual, more immersed in the details of relationships and narratives. It shows a greater propensity to take the standpoint of the 'particular other', and women appear more adept at revealing feelings of empathy and sympathy required by this.
>
> (Benhabib 1992:149)

She also claims that

> The contextuality, narrativity and specificity of women's moral judgement is not a sign of weakness nor deficiency, but a manifestation of a vision of moral maturity that views the self as a being immersed in a network of relationships with others. According to this vision, the respect for each other's needs and the mutuality of effort to satisfy them sustain moral growth and development.
>
> (ibid.:149)

Benhabib pays tribute to Carol Gilligan's work when she says that 'It is Carol Gilligan's lasting contribution to moral theory and moral psychology that she has made us aware of the implicit models of selfhood, autonomy,

impartiality and justice sustained and privileged by ... dichotomous reasoning'
(ibid.:170).

To summarise our position so far, in this section we have used the work of
various authors to argue for an idea of the self that is constructed in narrative, in
dialogue and in relationship, rather than a self that is autonomous, self-sufficient
and predetermined, and a morality that has as its foundation the notion of care,
contextuality and empathy rather than abstract rules and objective justice. We
are working towards a moral education where these ideas are constructed and
communicated as and in narrative. On this basis it is necessary to reconsider both
our understanding of the relationship between childhood and adulthood, and the
teacher–pupil relationship that underpins pedagogy. This will be done in the next
two sections.

Constructing childhood and adulthood

Our conceptual construction of childhood is a vital factor in the way in which
we conceive of the parameters of learning and development in schooling. It also
intrinsically relates to constructions of selfhood. In this section we shall examine
constructions of childhood and how they relate to constructions of adulthood.
Childhood, we suggest is a conceptual construction imposed by adults, as well as
a way of determining when we reach an age of full legal responsibility and
obligation. In other words it confers protection and repression at one and the
same time. Those passing through the later stages of this period, becoming aware
of their ability and desire to construct their own culture independent of this
distinction, often voice this in a form of revolt that, as adults, we accommodate
as 'natural' rather than indicative of the need to reconstruct our cultural
categories. To do the latter would be to redesign and reconstruct our own
conception of ourselves as adults. We would have to take 'children' seriously.
Those whom 'children' take seriously, within their own culture, we regard as
icons of popular 'youth' culture. Thus we ensure that they are not to be taken
seriously, despite the fact that they often find and express the views of dissident
adult voices, as the following illustrates. In 1995 the band Manic Street Preachers
produced a CD entitled *The Holy Bible*, on the back cover of which is a quotation
from Mirbeau:

> You're obliged to pretend respect for people and institutions you think
> absurd. You live attached in a cowardly fashion to moral and social
> conventions you despise, condemn and know lack all foundation. It is that
> permanent contradiction between your ideas and desires and all the dead
> formalities and vain pretensions of your civilisation that makes you sad,
> troubled and unbalanced ... at every moment they suppress, restrain and
> check the free play of your powers.
>
> (Octave Mirbeau, *The Torture Garden*, 1898)

In engaging with young people, the extent to which they listen is very likely to
be related to the respect we confer on them. The beginnings of such respect are

likely to be engendered by allowing them to represent themselves according to their own self-designation. As an illustration of this we offer the following account of Clive's experience.

> In 1998 I gave a talk to 150 fifteen year olds. This was after the first phase of our research into children's worldviews. I took quotes from young people between the ages of seven and ten to show them on OHTs. But, first I asked a question: 'How many adults here? Please put up your hand.' After they had lowered their hands, I asked, 'How many children here? Please put up your hand.' This left a large proportion of the audience who had not raised their hands. I asked, 'You who have not put up your hands, how do you describe yourselves?' The answer was 'Young adults'. The importance of this procedure relates to what followed, I wished them to take seriously the narratives of people younger than themselves. To confer this respect it was important that respect was first conferred on them by one older than them. The important principle to be invoked was that of self-definition, before respect would be conferred.

The construction of childhood often works against such a principle of engagement, as evidenced by an examination of the following studies.

The history of the visual representation of childhood in the modern era has been well documented by Anne Higonnet in *Pictures of Innocence: The History and Crisis of Ideal Childhood* (1998). In the introduction she asserts that

> Pictures of children are at once the most common, the most sacred, and the most controversial images of our time. They guard the cherished ideal of childhood innocence, yet they contain within them the potential to undo that ideal. No subject seems cuter or more sentimental, and we take none more for granted, yet pictures of children have proved dangerously difficult to understand and control. This book is about how pictures have represented children, and about how an ideal of childhood innocence has entered a crisis out of which a new definition of childhood is emerging.
>
> (Higonnet 1998:7)

Higonnet's book is a collection of analyses of paintings and photographs produced during the last three or four centuries. In this book she draws attention to the difference between 'romantic' and 'knowing' images of children. The key to the difference is that knowing images 'endow children with psychological and physical individuality at the same time as they recognise them as being childlike' (ibid.:12), whereas romantic images, introduced in the eighteenth century, were 'a visual invention of childhood innocence' promoted by the great portrait painters of the day, notably Sir Joshua Reynolds and Sir John Everett Millais (ibid.:9). Previously, Higonnet notes, children had been understood as 'faulty small adults in need of correction and discipline' (ibid.:8) within the influence of Christian culture.

Higonnet points out that in these images we are presented with cultural inventions requiring representation, and in the case of the modern (romantic) conception of childhood, the 'fictions about the lived experience were more consistent, more convincing and more beautiful than any lived experience could ever be' (ibid.:8). Significantly, this representation was the first to be promoted by the advances in and new technologies of portrait painting and the printing of images for a mass market. Reynolds' *Age of Innocence* thus offers the cultural construction of childhood innocence as 'natural', in contrast with earlier depictions of childhood such as Van Dyck's *George Villiers, Second Duke of Buckingham and Lord Francis Villiers* (1635), in which the children look like and are dressed as small adults from an aristocratic family who are presented to project their future adult status. The issue of social status and class is, of course, bound up in such representations, along with the question of the audience for whom the image was constructed. Here we can infer echoes of educational provision related to the particulars of childhood status within the social structure. This topic will be returned to later.

Millais' painting *Cherry Ripe* is the most obvious example of the beginnings of the romantic image of childhood entering the popular imagination through the production of best-selling prints and then advertisements and the mass market of industrially produced illustration. If we compare the romantic and the previous Van Dyck images of childhood with an early 'knowing' image, that of Lewis Carroll's photograph 'Alice Liddell as the Beggar Maid' (1859), some interesting issues arise. First, the introduction of sensual sexuality in the pose for the viewer. She is there for him and is already corrupted. Second, she belongs to the lower classes and is in a sense an 'outcast' in terms of social class, Christian mythology, moral virtue and the productive economy. That this construction is for the particular delight and satisfaction of the idiosyncrasies of Charles Dodgson does not detract from its larger signification.

Higonnet also draws our attention to the depiction of cherubs and cupids in Western art. They contrast, with the former representing the Christian teaching of the transcendent and the latter the temptation and lust inherent in the human condition (Higonnet 1998:18). The tension is between Christian conceptions of virtue and innocence and Dionysian conceptions of desire. The latter are given full rein in works such as the *Rape of Europa* by Titian (1560) prior to the eighteenth century. The former appear in such Renaissance Madonna and Child paintings as Raphael's *Sistine Madonna*, where the assembled characters look up melancholically contemplating the mission and destiny of the naked infant above them, nestled in the arms of his mother. Leo Steinberg (1996) has argued, and Higonnet agrees, that the composition of the picture affirms rather than denies the sexuality of Christ in the way his right thigh extends across the genital area so making an equilateral triangle with its apex at the crown of the madonna's head, in order to affirm the doctrine of the Incarnation. However, it is precisely this device which marks out the difference between the Dionysian and the Christian transcendentalist conceptions.

Here is a means of asserting immanence, however unpalatable to Protestants, without denying transcendence We are drawn to the child's vulnerability in relation to the sufferings he will undergo for the sake of humanity. He is a knowing child, not in any sexual or corrupted sense but in his awareness of the transcendent. His innocence, as one who will never sin, is thus assured. Even if his genitals were apparent they would appear in this setting as a worthless appendage. When we are introduced later to the Romantic conceptions of childhood, we are presented with children whose innocence is quite different from that of the Christ-child. They do not 'know' in either sense and their innocence is equivalent to an idyllic or blissful ignorance. The state in which they are depicted is the state in which we must keep and protect them as 'children', as if it were ever possible! Thus we come to conceive of them as being in this state by virtue of having presented them to ourselves, as adults, in this way.

Our Western construction of childhood, historically speaking, is concerned with the affirmation or negation of these two contrasting depictions of innocence and desire, but also it is confused by the romantic vision of the child as living in a contrary world to that of the adult before the Fall. Thus the contradictions in our attitudes towards childhood are established. We wish children to grow and learn, but not to become what we are or know what we know as adults. We wish children to remain in innocence, but an innocence protected by ignorance. We may wish children to be acquainted with and nurtured in the Christian vision of redemption, but without experiencing why it is necessary. We use the Christian myth as a protective device for attempting to ensure these aims are fulfilled, and we oppose any reflection either on its existential meaning or on the questioning of the same. We confuse experience with corruption, insofar as it opposes the innocence being protected, which consists of concealment from the vagaries and sufferings of the human world and its sexual delights and desires. Thus we have the retardation of the development of children for all the right (conscious) motives and wrong reasons. Could it be that secretly we see childhood as the projection of a world we want but can never have? Romanticism then becomes blended with a sentimentalised form of Christian understanding that starves children rather than nourishes them, in the context of the experiences they have but cannot voice.

To preserve both our idealised and our perverted hope for their future and to protect them from our inadequacy in dealing with (and disillusionment with) the realities of our own human experience, we offer them an education that refuses to acquaint them with our realities (or at least the aspects of them that we regard as 'negative') in the hope that they will not experience them. We do this at the same time as those experiences start to impinge on them. Thus regardless of any advantage in other educational matters (in terms of knowledge and skills), we ensure they are disadvantaged.

Alongside Higonnet's study we can place James and Prout's *Constructing and Reconstructing Childhood* (1990). In drawing attention to an emergent paradigm developed in this collection of studies, Allison James and Alan Prout speak of it challenging our present construction of childhood (ibid.:1–6). One of the contributors in a chapter entitled 'Constructions and Reconstructions of British Childhood', focuses on 'the change from an ideal childhood (as represented in Higonnet) fragmented in the main by geography and by class experience to one that was much more uniform and coherent' (Hendrick 1990:35). Tellingly, Hendrick explains the short-lived dominance of the construction of the 'Romantic child' with the phrase 'Poets are no match for political economy' (ibid.:39). Thus the original invention of Rousseau, which suffered as social change in the form of the reaction to the French Revolution and the impact of the industrial revolution, emphasising the suppression of civil liberties and the demand for free labour respectively, was replaced by one that emerged as 'adult–child relations [were pushed] in the opposite direction' (ibid.:39). Hendrick quotes the 'counter-revolutionary' writer Hannah More as representative of this contrasting model, which regarded it 'a fundamental error to consider children as innocent beings . . . rather than as beings who bring into the world a corrupt nature and evil dispositions, which it should be the great end of education to rectify' (ibid.:39; Robertson 1976:421). This view was supported by Evangelicals and the upper classes, Hendrick explains, because 'she articulated their desire for a settled society, characterised by order, obedience and authority' (Hendrick 1990:39); needless to say *their* authority. The significant epistemological difference in these constructions was embedded in the question of whether childhood had its own nature, different from adulthood, or whether it was an immature form of the latter. Once the quality of 'innocence' is removed from the former view (which ironically implies some contrasting condition in adulthood), it is possible to be far more pragmatic about what the education of children is for. The wedding of Protestant Evangelicalism and the needs to be serviced due to industrialisation creates the link between instruction and skilling, as a preparation for work and the attainment of adulthood.

To make this equation in the way we have done above is only fully possible in hindsight because it does not represent the sort of statement that could be made at the time when children were exploited for factory labour and there was not as yet a public school system for the education of the poor. However the seeds were sown. Hendrick charts a progressive shift from the first Factory Act of 1802 towards a concept of *universal* childhood that takes in the constructions of delinquency and the child as being in need of 'protection, guidance, discipline and love of a family' (ibid.:43–4), and the emergence of schooling as a paternalistic concern for the innocent and exploited child as well as attempting to ensure social order. Hendrick quotes a government report that affirmed the 'need to produce educated men who "can be reasoned with" ' (ibid.:45). Tellingly he observes that the vision of a *'national* childhood' (ibid.:46), which demanded obligatory daily school attendance, was driven by a class-based political end, namely the reformation of working-class morals (ibid.:46).

At the end of his deconstructive history of childhood constructions Hendrick points to the way in which the importance of the family and family upbringing emerges, especially in the twentieth century, and how this construct represents a 'bourgeois "domestic ideal" with its emphasis on order, respect, love and clearly defined age and gender distinctions' (ibid.:55–6). In other words, this is a protective and instructive 'natural' environment that is self-evidently universalisable in application. Therefore it would be both morally indefensible and rationally implausible to argue against it. Of course there is no such thing as *the* family, but it serves a particular hegemonic purpose in relation to class and children: that of preserving social order and ensuring the efficiency of economic enterprise. What were not addressed throughout this history were the 'personhood of children' and the proposition contained in the *Cleveland Report on Sexual Abuse* that 'the child is a person—not an object of concern' (Hendrick 1990:56).

The important issue that Hendrick's analysis makes clear is expressed by Freeman and quoted in Hendrick by way of conclusion: 'Reformers have usually treated children "as things, as problems, but rarely as human beings with personality and integrity"' (ibid.:56; Freeman 1983:24). We can refer to this succinctly as the objectification of children as 'other' for particular social purposes that do not involve the empowerment of children. By this we mean that the varying contested constructions of childhood all came to serve the ends of adult empowerment. They did so for various purposes connected to Protestant doctrine, the mistrust of the lower classes and desire to preserve an established class order, and the greed of industrial entrepreneurs and manufacturers. Zipes (1997), in a study with a different focus, illustrates how these purposes were also influential in relation to the moralism and commodification that affected fairy tales, as instructive literature for children's consumption.

In relation to education during this period, the influence of these dominating factors were reflected in the struggle to establish a system of state schooling. This is charted by H. C. Barnard in *A History of English Education from 1760* (1961). Barnard exposes the theoretical justification for cruelty to children 'afforded by the current [late eighteenth century] political theory of *laissez faire*' derived from Adam Smith's *Wealth of Nations*, published in 1776 (Barnard 1961:xvi); the justification established for Sunday Schools providing religious instruction, a learning by rote, in the same period (ibid.:9); and the acceptance of the 'monetorial system' introduced by Lancaster and Bell in the early nineteenth century as a basis for 'the mass production of education' (ibid.:54). This was perspicaciously described at the time as 'the division of labour applied to intellectual purposes. . . . The principle in manufactories and schools is the same. . . . In short it [schooling] substituted machinery for personality and forced facts into the pupil's memory in a purely mechanical way. . . . The children did learn something; they were taught to be quiet and orderly; and above all the system was cheap' (Bernard, quoted in ibid.:54).

Barnard goes on to comment on the way in which these features continue to shape our historical and contemporary educational tradition despite the more radical reformers such as Rousseau, Pestalozzi, Fellenberg and Robert Owen. However, he maintains that 'The effort to overcome [these obstacles to effective educational provision] has never relaxed; and that continued and increasing effort is an important feature of all the subsequent educational history of this country' (ibid.:62).

There is no doubt that the drive for the efficient and domiciled utilisation of the masses for economic purposes was the argument that established a state system of schooling, rather than a concern for the development of their human capacities as individuals. The rhetoric of current educational provision and its regulation in schools is in direct descent from this view. Little account has been taken of the radical tradition that education should be instigated for the value or empowerment offered to those whom it purports to serve—children. Thus we can observe the way in which the constructions of childhood operate in the political and economic domain, and how education serves the dominant ideology that determines the constructions to be put in place. We may no longer be cruel to children, but our system is hardly sensitive to their needs.

Furthering our investigation, and making use of a source of yet another kind referred to earlier in this study, we can identify how marginalisation takes place in other contexts. In *Unveiling India* (1987), the first chapter of which is entitled 'Outside the Frame', Anees Jung speaks of her experience as a child in India, and in particular refers to family photographs as follows:

> I was three years old when I was first photographed. It was a garden party for children . . . I am in the arms of a radiant father. None of the little girls is on the ground. Each is held aloft by a father or an *ayah*, but not a mother. There are no mothers in the photograph.
>
> (Jung 1987:13)

Jung's main point, and the research in the rest of her book is driven by this, is that women in this social context are excluded from public life: 'My mother, like all mothers of children photographed in the garden party, remained behind the *chilman*—their part of the house which was never allowed to enter the picture frames that ceremonially documented the high points in family history' (ibid.:14).

Our purpose in referring to Jung is not to accentuate the issue she pursues regarding the place and voice of women in Indian society and the inequality that is involved, important though this is. Rather we wish to draw a parallel between this and how childhood experiences are outside the frame of educational enterprise in our society. Imagine the classroom as a photograph, with the lesson proceeding between teacher and children. The frame extends across say forty minutes, or the time of the lesson. Thus we translate Jung's visual metaphor into a temporal one. Who is in the frame? Not in terms of who is present but in terms of who is heard and what is talked about. Who is in the frame now and whose voices are heard and reflected upon and engaged with? What is the nature of the photograph produced at the end? What will the children remember and talk about afterwards in relation to that experience? Will they remember it at all? Will it enter the 'family album' of events to be recounted as significant in their life? And to whom will it be recounted and for what purpose? Will it be handed down as part of an ongoing album of significant events? If so, on what basis and for what purpose? Enlarge this one photo into an album of educational experience. What do we have now? Would this represent a sequence of photographs (experiences) of being in school, or would the experiences be derived from elsewhere (or nowhere, no album at all)? What, if any, is the relationship between formal education and the autobiographies of individuals? If there is no relationship there is no spiritual development in schools, so what is the purpose of religious and moral education in the lives of individual children? Learning about or learning from the beliefs and practices of different religions is not enough if it does not ensure that they, the children, are in the frame, at the centre of the photograph, in the same way as Anees Jung's father (but not her mother). Is it right to give them rules to live by but not involve them in determining what the rules might be and what ends they might serve? If children and young people are not at the centre of the frame of education everything else will be either forgotten, perceived as irrelevant or even resented.

We might reconstruct our understanding of religion, morality and their relationship to spirituality with this in mind, and recognise that there is a fluidity of terms for young people across the issues of faith, religion, values and identity in their lives that we have to excavate rather than prescribe in relation to their perceived purposes and understandings. This examination of the issues of identity, representation and participation is germane to the concerns of pedagogy: what we teach and how we learn. Unless we take the issues of self-identification, representation and relationship seriously in relation to learning we cannot expect positive outcomes. In the next section we shall examine the implications raised so far for the purposes of pedagogical theory and practice.

Constructing a pedagogy

Relating the above enquiries into constructions of relational identity to our pedagogical purposes indicates why children and young people often respond negatively to religious and moral education. It is not because the issues involved do not have intrinsic interest for them, but because the issues are not the open focus of enquiry. There is an agenda, devised through curriculum circumscription and desirable outcomes, that precludes this possibility. This agenda seeks to produce certain types of citizen, valuing certain religious constructions of human purpose, even if not subscribing to them, and agreeing a consensus of normative morality. The problem is not whether these are good aims, but that they are imposed aims. Pupils and students know that they are expected to buy into them. This limits the possibilities of response and involvement in the process of development.

A review of recent pedagogical approaches to religious education

By providing a short critical review of recent pedagogical debates we can determine how a shift to what has been argued for so far would result in a revision of our practice. Clearly, in the light of the above discussion, the idea of a pedagogy that is neutral and objective or inculcates nurture into certain values derived from Christian teachings, appears naive in the first case and could be criticised as damaging in the second. Nevertheless, until recently, the debate has been across these positions as far as religious and moral education have been concerned. Jackson (1997:36) distinguishes between 'neutral' and 'impartial' in relation to the faith or non-faith stance of the teacher and the effective delivery of RE, and this can be seen as signalling the problem of appealing to neutrality and objectivity in the teacher's role while still allowing the teacher a privileged position in the discourse of the classroom in relation to the judgements we might expect students to make. Conversely the impartial teacher acts as a role model for not making judgements. This possibility of taking an impartial stance suggests that Jackson's approach distances itself from student interaction, and the possibilities involved in that for their development, in favour of a more content-oriented model, that is, focusing on what is brought in to the classroom, even though there is a hermeneutical complexity in the approach Jackson advocates.

Grimmitt provides us with a different and more radical example of a shift in this debate. Grimmitt moved from a relatively naive position of liberal neutrality in his earlier work—'If RE teachers could adopt the attitude of a shopkeeper with wares in his window which he is anxious for customers to examine, appreciate and even "try on" but not feel under any obligation to buy, then many of the educational problems connected with RE would disappear' (Grimmitt 1978:26)—to being the initiator of the parlance of 'learning from'. 'When I speak of pupils *learning from* religion I am referring to what pupils learn from their studies in religion about themselves' (Grimmitt 1987:225). Later he moved still further, arguing that students should be equipped with 'skills of ideological criticism to promote an increased critical consciousness of their own cultural/religious perspective and that of others'; an 'awareness of the processes by which ideologies influences attitudes, values and beliefs, and in doing so, shape the human person' (Grimmitt 1994:138).

Grimmitt's latter position deserves further analysis, not least because he is concerned hermeneutically to challenge ideological perspectives. The tension between educational aims and religious absolutism is, for Grimmitt, the paramount issue to be addressed. Religious education has sought to deal with this in two ways. The first he labels cultural absolutism: the host culture, as in 'British culture', determines the values upon which education is based, and education is the transmitter of those values. The second he labels 'cultural relativism': the descriptive imparting of the cultures of different ethnic groups in a non-evaluative way. Both of these approaches he regards as misconceived and inadequate. The first, like religious ideologies themselves, is intransigent about preserving the relationship between ideology and identity. It affirms 'ideological enclosure' (ibid.:140). The latter, by advancing a neutrality of view, does nothing politically to challenge absolutist views. Grimmitt quotes Frazer in this respect. 'Neutrality is a way of giving in to power and money pressures, of making straight the way of the powerful' (Frazer 1975:27).

As a result, Grimmitt considers that RE can only make a positive contribution to the development of a pluralist society by helping pupils to engage in 'ideological exploration', which for him means an 'inter-faith education', in order to bring about a 'change in human consciousness' (Grimmitt 1994:139). This would result in 'the progressive development of intercultural communication and understanding' (ibid.:139). This leads him to reflect on the core universal spiritual values upon which this needs to be based. He lists seven values, of which the last is given precedence as the foundation of the others: 'the value of human spirituality and the desirability of spiritual development'. This is justified, for Grimmitt, because 'the "givens" of the human condition possess a "spiritual nature" or "spiritual essence" of their own' (ibid.:144).

We can applaud the boldness of Grimmitt's stance, and his attempt to construct a pedagogical position that challenges ideology with a clear purpose for pluralism that is progressive in design. He attempts to move towards a position that is consistent with antiracist education and to bridge the values chasm between the two subjects. Our misgivings centre on Grimmitt not going far enough to overcome the ideological problem. His desire to make ideological criticism the focus of pedagogy is suitably reflexive in principle, but it is likely to take the form of a criticism of ideologies rather than a reflexive consideration of one's own (the teacher's and student's) in practice. The scope of the subject is still limited to interfaith education. We recognise that Grimmitt wishes this to be open to interpretation beyond religious faith, but he still uses terminology that belongs to religious discourse and does not provide sufficient justification of its non-religious possibilities. The identification of universal, core spiritual values is a way of trying to create a new foundation for the subject, but his main value, quoted above, is open to translation within any number of competing and opposing ideological frames of reference. We can outline the problem step by step.

The teacher is to be neither neutral nor impartial on the question of what values he or she stands for. Those values reflect 'bringing about a planned policy of change whereby ethnic minority groups ... are brought within a fully participatory form of power sharing, affording them equal access to basic human rights' (ibid.:137). These rights are intrinsic to the development of an individual's 'spiritual essence'. Therefore in any particular case we must respect these rights. So far so good. However let us take the case of sexual orientation. Do we oppose the repression of homosexual practice on this basis? Grimmitt does not offer differences in sexual preference as an example, but it must surely be included in his agenda. If we do, even simply as a way of siding with a form of heterodoxy, as opposed to the more significant criticisms of it as deviance, perversion or evil, then we are effectively opposing the foundations of religious ideology itself. In other words Grimmitt appears to be seeking both to preserve the rights of religious and nationalist ideologies to representation and to undermine them by his critical 'ideological exploration'. Presumably, in this way he hopes that reason, morality, persuasion and changes in consciousness will ensure that justice is achieved without conflict as a result of education. This contrasts with Brian Wren's observation:

If justice can only be guaranteed by equality of power, and if power is never surrendered by moral persuasion alone, it follows that justice in society can only be established through conflict. Reason, morality and persuasion can ease the conflict, but they can never wish it away.

(Wren 1977:65; quoted in Grimmitt 1994:136)

We also need to be reminded that, as Mantin (forthcoming) points out, equality and justice are terms used by particular dominant bodies to serve their own purposes. They are terms enclosed by specific frameworks of meaning, designed to erase the realities of cultural difference. They are employed to work towards consensus and inclusivity rather than in recognition of difference and exclusivity. They are cosy words that massage the liberal conscience.

Grimmitt's argument seems to be sound in its aims but not in its implementation. By seeking to preserve religious education as a discrete subject, and yet oppose the ideologies upon which its content is based, he must either affirm the pedagogy he espouses, in which case the subject as it stands is undermined, or affirm the central importance of the ideologies within human spiritual and cultural development, in which case his pedagogical purpose is undermined. Perhaps, rather like David Hay, the idea of an essence to human spirituality, yet to be discerned but ultimately uniting, despite its present flawed and imperfect expressions, leads Grimmitt to persist with the idea of RE as a subject that can act as a vehicle for this. Perhaps the threat of secularism is still deemed too great to discard it.

If we are to find a new pedagogical purpose we have to do so within a new circumscription of the subject itself. That means rejecting the title 'religious education'. It also means rejecting the rights of religious ideologies in educational and political terms. They have a right to representation but not a right to influence the approach to children's spirituality or the values that underpin pedagogical purpose. If young people are to be prepared for making their way in an increasingly plural society—in which social values and identities are more fluid, and in which orientation and purpose entertain sexual, economic, political, moral and spiritual complexities in the construction of lifestyles—the most important task is to equip them with the possibilities and qualities of empowerment, discernment and sensitivity. In this case, at the centre of education must be an attempt to focus on what will enable such possibilities and qualities. To do this we must reconceive our central purpose. We must construct a new 'root metaphor' that signals a pedagogical purpose that goes beyond (whilst appropriately acknowledging) the concerns debated in religious and moral education.

Towards a narrative pedagogy

'Root metaphor' is a term used by Liam Hudson in *The Cult of the Fact* (1976). We use it here in his sense of the core or basic activity that characterises a subject. Speaking of psychology, he suggests that the transition of the character of psychology as it moved from the first through the second half of the twentieth century was due to the different activity it carried out, the conceptions behind that activity, and its understanding of its purposes and outcomes. 'Where, schematically speaking, psychology has in the past been conceived as contact between two sets of objects—or logical systems—via a measurement technology, it would in future be seen as mutual infiltration between at least two systems of meaning' (ibid.:163).

For Hudson the systems of meaning lie in the minds of the 'person dressed as psychologist' and the 'plain man to be explained'. Out of this comes interpretative activity. This activity is what he calls hermeneutics. Hermeneutics thus becomes the root metaphor. 'And we, all of us, are interpreters, "*hermeneuts*"— creatures who pan for sense in the muddy waters of human transaction, and who, if we are interested in people, collect this sense into the bundles of remembered event, belief and fantasy that constitute the human biography' (ibid.:163).

However, Hudson's notion of 'human biography' has an essentialist ring to it, in much the same sense as Grimmitt's 'spiritual essence'. We need to remember that each individual autobiography is unique in character as well as relating to a larger interpreted picture. Paul Ricoeur indicates how this interpretive process is metaphorical in character and imaginative in design and has, as its object, the construction of a narrative plot conferring signification on events. This in turn creates a logic of prediction. In other words the narrative can accommodate past, present and future in a schematised whole.

> The productive imagination at work in the metaphorical process is thus our competence for producing new logical species by predictive assimilation, in spite of the resistance of our current categorizations of language. The plot of a narrative is comparable to this predictive assimilation. It 'grasps together' and integrates into one whole and complete story multiple and scattered events, thereby schematizing the intelligible signification attached to the narrative as a whole.
>
> (Ricoeur 1984:x)

As a further explication of this idea Ricoeur states previously:

> With narrative, the semantic innovation lies in the inventing of another work of synthesis—a plot. By means of the plot, goals, causes, and chance are brought together within the temporal unity of a whole and complete action. It is this synthesis of the heterogeneous that brings narrative close to metaphor. In both cases the new thing—the as yet unsaid, the unwritten— springs up in language. Here a living metaphor, that is a new pertinence in the predication, there a feigned plot, that is a new congruence in the organization of the events.
>
> (ibid.:ix)

Ricoeur is quick to point out, however, that this is not to propose what we would normally call a truth claim. The possibilities of the temporal imagination impose on us a liminal experience of being suspended between fact and fiction, which forces us to resort to 'poetic composition to re-figure this temporal experience' (ibid.:xi). He enlarges on this by saying, 'I see in the plots we invent the privileged means by which we re-configure our confused, unformed, and at the limit temporal experience' (ibid.). 'In this way, metaphorical redescription and mimesis are closely bound up with one another, to the point that we can exchange the two vocabularies and speak of the mimetic value of poetic discourse and the redescriptive power of narrative fiction' (ibid.).

Ricoeur's theoretical statement offers a way forward in terms of pedagogical practice, but not one in which the teacher is the impartial observer or orchestrator and facilitator of events. He or she is the one who 'pans for sense in the muddy waters of human transaction'. The classroom is the site of these transactions or multiple stories. As a means towards the practical implications of putting such a pedagogy into action we can turn to the writings of Walter Benjamin. Benjamin's use of the term 'storytelling' opens up a line of enquiry with radical pedagogic implications. Benjamin's concern is to identify the way in which we have lost sight of the importance of the role of the storyteller. He does so by contrasting what is imparted in this role with our modern emphasis on the communication of information.

One way of understanding the import of Benjamin's observations is to identify the loss of interpersonal understanding and the effect this has on the construct of meaning-making or the ability—as Susan Sontag comments in her appraisal of Benjamin and his work—to construct autobiography as what 'has to do with time, with sequence and what makes up the continuous flow of life' (Sontag 1979:12).

This is not to suggest an even progression of life's events towards seamless meaning and pattern since Benjamin emphasises discontinuities, especially in the 'Berlin Chronicle' (Benjamin 1979), but to recognise the need to construct an understanding of the way in which life's vicissitudes and disjunctures can at least be placed alongside each other and arranged. Pedagogically this has little to do with the recall of information and arranging such information into predetermined categories that might be constituted according to the structures of curriculum knowledge, even if the object is then to reflect upon and utilise such knowledge. In effect Benjamin's concerns act as a means of subverting the importance of such an institutionalised structure on the basis that it is ordered according to informational criteria. Benjamin identifies the role of the storyteller as paramount:

> The storyteller joins the ranks of the teachers and sages. He has counsel—not for a few situations . . . but for many. . . . For it is granted to him to reach back to a whole lifetime (a life, incidentally, that comprises not only his own experience but no little of the experience of others). His gift is the ability to relate his life.
>
> (Benjamin 1970:108)

The problem now arises of how we can recognise Benjamin's imperatives within an institutional framework. We can compound this problem before resolving it. Benjamin refers to notions of 'ideas and experiences as ruins' and advances the notion that 'to understand something is to understand its topography, to know how to chart it. And to know how to get lost ... space, in its temporal, geographical and experiential senses, is teeming with possibilities, positions, intersections, passages, detours, U-turns, dead ends and one way streets' (Sontag 1979:13).

Benjamin likes finding things where no-one is looking, that is by making connections across usual classifications and in 'hidden' and apparently irrelevant or everyday places and circumstance, rather than relating to 'important' events and predetermined lines of enquiry and classification. Benjamin refers to his acquisition of learning as being derived from 'strolling about the world' and finding things where 'no-one was looking' (Benjamin 1979:17), and as a collector he created odd arrangements in his library that reflected the strategy of his work, specialising in children's books and books written by the mad. From this we can derive a specific metaphorical understanding. Benjamin was attempting a reconstruction of order according to his temperament that defied orthodoxy in learning—a rehabitation of the world according to the determinants required by his experience. It was a recharting of the geography of human location, the literal classification of which, in his library, was a reflection of his psychological process of meaning-construction. Importantly Benjamin links the above to the idea that 'in every era the attempt must be made anew to wrest tradition away from a conformism that is about to overpower it' (Benjamin 1970:257). This can be achieved by recognising the importance of the 'gift for listening' (ibid.:91).

'For storytelling is always the art of repeating stories, and this art is lost when the stories are no longer retained. This, then, is the nature of the web in which the gift of storytelling is cradled. This is how today it is becoming unravelled at all its ends ... the gift for listening is lost and the community of listeners disappears' (ibid.:91).

Relating this to children we arrive at the idea of enabling children to become storytellers within such a community, which in turn implies we must become storytellers ourselves. The process is developed by facilitating the exchange of experiences, acknowledging that this involves an honesty and trust that facilitates the creation of community. Seeing this as the basis of spiritual development demands revision of our notions of curriculum and schooling. It also revises our understanding of the function of teaching. In his essay 'The Task of the Translator', Benjamin says: 'For to some degree all great texts contain their potential translation between the lines ... the interlinear version of the Scripture is the ideal of all translation' (ibid.:82). Here Benjamin is arguing for freedom to convey the sense of the original within a 'linguistic flux. ... The basic error of the translator is that he preserves the state in which his own language happens to be instead of allowing his language to be powerfully affected by the foreign tongue' (ibid.:80–1).

Our contention is that what Benjamin says about translation is also required in translating within a language, as story and sense move from one person to another and become situated within a new experiential context. Through this idea of intertextuality, interlineality and the exchange of experiences meaning comes alive and reasserts itself. The teacher is the facilitator of this in the classroom. This is his or her craft, so that telling and listening occurs and community is established.

This is what we might call the construction of both autobiography and community. What Lyotard (1984:18–23) refers to as the pragmatics of narrative knowledge. What is transmitted through these narratives is 'the set of pragmatic rules that constitutes the social bond' (ibid.:21). If we apply this to the community of the school we may call this process a narrative pedagogy.

A narrative pedagogy is characterised by significant differences from a pedagogy in which the content of the curriculum is the determining factor for the promotion of learning. The aim is to go beyond what is already known. Knowing constitutes what the community of learners brings to the subject of study and how the subject of study, as well as the learner's knowing, become changed as a result of the event. Gregory Ulmer, commenting on Derrida's pedagogical ideas, puts it in this way: 'The practical consequences are simply stated—every pedagogical exposition, just like every reading, adds something to what it transmits. . . . Adding, here, is nothing other than giving to read' (Ulmer 1985:162). Thus it becomes a pedagogy committed to change rather than reproduction in the *mise en scène* of the classroom. For Pautrat, working with a similar understanding of the dynamics of knowing developing in the classroom situation, this pedagogy is paradoxical because it attempts to teach the 'unteachable relation to truth' (Pautrat in Ulmer:173–4).

The paradox resides in there being no knowledge outside the 'scene of instruction'. It is generated within it by the participants, and therefore has an affective and dynamic quality involving all the actors in that scene in its construction. Inevitably knowledge, as something static and known (ideological truth), cannot be the controlling influence in this process, since the process itself would be prevented. In Derrida's understanding, following Artaud, the classroom becomes a theatre where knowledge (in the ideological sense) cannot be re-presented, there can only be the unfolding that occurs, as in a play in which all involved are performers. Knowledge as a result ceases to be a mimetic activity, a citation of what is to be learned (Ulmer 1985:174–7).

The radical shift in this understanding of pedagogy is the removal of the preferential status given both to the text introduced and to the teacher as the introducer of that text, as the locations of knowledge. Pedagogy as an activity, following the trajectory of the commentators introduced above, takes a significantly different purpose to that which we presently assign it. It does not presume the inculcation of a knowledge that is introduced into pedagogical activity from outside, based on the intrinsic worth of that knowledge. It does not presume aims to be met beyond the dynamic process that occurs within the learning community. It does presume that the learners are there to develop their own potential in relation to the circumstances of their own lives. It also presumes that the community itself will be the site of this development, and for that to be so it must be mutually enriching and empowering for its participants. It follows that the role of the teacher is to facilitate this development and be a participator in it. This brings us back to Lyotard's understanding of savoir and Hayden White's understanding of poetics. As a form of values education, it becomes the development of individuals in the community by these means and toward these ends. Effectively this is what occurs in faith communities, thus what we are advocating is that the school community should be enacting what faith communities (potentially) enact rather than being a place where we import the study of faith communities as the object of study. This does not preclude the school community being a place where we also seek to understand communities beyond our own, but we can hardly make much sense of that unless we are primarily seeking to act as a community ourselves, with all that that entails.

Conclusion

This brings us back to the three elements of this chapter. Our primary educational aim is to attend to the construction of self in community. In order to address this we have to consider the constructions of childhood and adulthood we bring to the classroom and the type of relationship we are attempting to foster. This leads us to consider the pedagogical theory and practice we wish to implement. This will in turn depend on how we attend to and understand the purposes of spiritual and moral education. It is, perhaps, paradoxical that religious education, because of the exclusivity implied in its title, appears anachronistic within this design. And yet it is largely religious education, with its unresolved tensions, that leads us to this point. Through its development, debates and concerns, its oppositional challenge to the secular and materialism, its particular and unresolved relationship with spiritual and moral education, and its recognition of diversity and cultural difference, it has been a vehicle for important issues often not collectively debated elsewhere in education. But the resolution of these issues, or at least debating them with some success, is hampered by religious education remaining just that and only that. To transform religious education into something broader is not to do away with much of what it presently addresses, but to place it in a new and more appropriate educational perspective. This perspective is concerned with human narratives rather than doxic truths or the teaching of 'world religions'. It is inclusive in intention rather than exclusive, and performative rather than reactive.

Section III

Pedagogy: putting theory into practice

7 Principles of pedagogical practice

Clive and Jane Erricker

Introduction

This chapter and those that follow show how we can address spiritual, moral, social, cultural, emotional and religious education, not separately, but as interwoven and interdependent factors in a narrative approach. We offer different processes and strategies for doing this.

We have designed this section to follow a particular pattern. It works from the overarching issue of how we construct the idea of our own personal biography, the story of who we are, in a relational way. The activities described in later chapters are all techniques to help that process.

Construction site

> Pedantic brooding over the production of objects—visual aids, toys, or books—that are supposed to be suitable for children is folly. Since the Enlightenment this has been one of the mustiest speculations of the pedagogues. Their infatuation with psychology keeps them from perceiving that the world is full of the most unrivalled objects for childish attention and use. And the most specific. For children are particularly fond of haunting any site where things are being visibly worked upon. They are irresistibly drawn by the detritus generated by building, gardening, housework, tailoring, or carpentry. In waste products they recognise the face that the world of things turns directly and solely to them. In using these things they do not so much imitate the world of adults as bring together, in the artefact produced in play, materials of widely differing kinds in a new, intuitive relationship. Children thus produce their own small world of things within the greater one. The norms of this own small world must be kept in mind if one wishes to create things specially for children, rather than let one's adult activity, through its requisites and instruments, find its own way to them.
>
> (Benjamin 1979:52–3)

What Walter Benjamin says of children actually applies to us all. Pedagogically his point is that what matters is to find out what is of interest—what *matters* to those involved in learning. This is the construction site where learning, development, growth—call it what we will—takes place. It is certainly not about the production of specific tools or objects, but using what is already there, their experiences and their psychological places of interest.

Up to this point this book has been written in the familiar, rational, academic style that characterises the theoretical discourse of all disciplines, including education. However we have argued that this idea of theorising should not be the basis of practice, because the power relations so constructed result in the disempowerment of the learner and the teacher. This is due to the construction of knowledge assumed within it, upon which the curriculum is based. This in turn ensures a hierarchical relationship of knowledge holders, from the theorist to the teacher practitioner and lastly to the child. In effect the child has to be understood as the one who does not know, the one to whom knowledge has to be imparted, the one to whom it has to be *given* as a commodity. We know that teachers have often struggled against this, and that the rhetoric of official documentation and the defence of that documentation protests that this is not the case. However, systemically, the struggle in terms of allowing the time to pursue a different educational process that privileges the learner and his or her capacities is always an uphill one, and is ultimately defeated in its possibilities by the model of education that we employ.

Arguing that the good teacher does this and the bad teacher does not is a way of preventing the radical thinking and change of practice that needs to be employed. In the following section we have attempted to model a different pedagogical approach, both in our suggestions for classroom practice and in the way the section has been written. The style of writing requires that, in places, the reader is given stimuli in order that he or she can use his or her own experience to construct the meaning and significance of that stimulus within his or her own narrative framework. This is what we understand 'knowledge' to be: a process of construction that is then voiced in a community of learners. In turn that 'knowledge' is affected by the 'knowledges' within the community itself. This will be illustrated as you the reader and actor carry out the process.

We might call this process 'interlinear', but this word suggests a contiguity that is not easily communicated in a book, which is necessarily linear—temporally, spatially and cognitively. There is no single author but an editor who situates experiences—texts: the written word, the spoken word, visual images, sensory stimulation—in relation to each other in the process of narrative construction. This construction includes the notion of selfhood.

Decisions on values are an integral part of this process. We decide what we should take on board and what we should reject. We ourselves have gone through this process in our own narrative construction and in the process of deciding which quotes to put in this book. The following texts are 'points of view' to stimulate the process of 'narrative engagement', they are not presented as texts to be learnt, followed or accepted. Representation, a key issue discussed earlier in this book, we do not employ as relating to a subject such as RE. We employ it as relating to issues to be addressed. Representation cannot start with representing a body of people identified as a religion, tradition or group. It must start with the voice of someone (who may belong to one of the above collectivities). The point is that representation should not be legitimated on a collective basis. If we were to insist on this, or collude with this, we would have already taken a political decision involving editorship, and censorship, which, if not undemocratic, would be no more than a representational democracy, serving to ensure order, orthodoxy and, educationally speaking, marginalising the individual in the classroom. The message is that we are studying *them*, not raising and responding to issues important to *us*. This does not prevent us from bringing to the classroom what is important for others, indeed we must, but we must do so this way round. Otherwise next to nothing in the way of education, as we have characterised it, will happen—or at least only inadvertently.

Connected to the above points is the idea of the teacher as actor and participant. He or she is part of the process and cannot simply be a facilitator from outside, a referee or an umpire. That does not mean the teacher does not exercise leadership, adjudication and so on where required, but the teacher is not neutral (which is not to say the teacher is not fair). If we ask our students to express themselves, we as teachers must be willing to do the same and speak from personal experience and reflection. In the practical examples that follow we ask you to do just this as an active participant in the reading of them. The important issue is to have recognised your own responses, articulated them to yourself. In each section we suggest ways in which this can be done—but these are only suggestions aimed at facilitating the process of self-narration, which can then be offered in the context of a learning or development community.

Fragments for constructing a biography

Our conceptual construction of our past is a vital factor in the way in which we conceive of the parameters of learning and development in schooling, how we relate to those we teach, and how we understand spiritual education. However the concept of biography is neither a universal nor a static one. Rather than explain and illustrate this idea with a detailed and analytical account of the works of other commentators, which can be found elsewhere, we want to demonstrate the pedagogic process that we have explained and will continue to explicate in the classroom practice sections below. Thus we have assembled a collection of fragments in order for you to reflect on your construction of your biography and its relationship with your own childhood and adult experiences.

> Loaded with trepidation, I began that first day with a secret weapon: I believe anybody can write if they have something personal to write about. I took it for granted that if I didn't confuse anyone with literary gobbledegook but tried instead to speak their language, I could help some prisoners to discover that writing could be fun and help them endure their sentences. 'Maybe you just want to learn to write a better letter', I said. But some said that they

wanted to write their life story. It wasn't my objective, but I hoped that I'd find at least one person who had real talent.

'Some journalists and scriptwriters make money writing about prisons and the heroin addiction that is your daily life', I told each group. 'If that's what people want to read about, you lived it, you write it. But only write what you know,' I advised. 'Let the truth tell your story. Start with one memory that stays with you. Something you feel passionate about.

(Hunt 1999:11)

[T]he way in which the teacher too often conducts his school leads one to infer that the intuitive, instinctive side of him—the side that is nearest to practice—has somehow or other held intercourse with the inner meaning of that 'truism' (the necessity of child-centredness) which he repeats so glibly, and has rejected it as antagonistic to the traditional assumptions on which he bases his life. Or perhaps this work of subconscious criticism and rejection has been and is being done for him, either by the spirit of the age or by the genius of the land in which he lives.

(Shute 1998:7)

Down here [in England] they think that they are the same, that boys and the girls are the same . . . but some men who come from India, they don't like girls, they say like do this, do that, use us as their slave and that . . . because you know like a girl, it's not really fair on girls cos they have to do all the housework, why not boys and that? So if you treated them the same that would be better.

(1995 personal interview)

S: We got a baby boy and he be really special.
Q: Why's that?
L: Cos everybody like a baby boy and there should only be one girl in the family cos you need boys.
Q: So what happens if you have more than one girl in the family?
L: It's bad news . . . but like you still get some money . . . they get sad because they got girls, the girls are not as good as boys . . . my mum wishes she had a boy.
S: We're happy now we got a baby boy.

(1995 personal interview)

Every second we live is a new and unique moment of the universe, a moment that never was before and will never be again. And what do we teach our children at school? We teach them that two and two make four and that Paris is the capital of France. We should say to each of them, 'Do you know what you are? You are a marvel. You are unique. In the millions of years that have passed there has never been another child like you'.

(Casals P, conversation with Golda Meir 1969,
quoted in McGuiness 1998:8)

Sold a bill of goods from the time they are infants, many of today's children, I suspect, will never develop the equipment to fight off the system of flattery and propitiation which soothes their insecurities and pumps their egos. By the time they are five or six, they've been pulled into the marketplace. They're on their way to becoming not citizens but consumers. It was not ever thus. Our reality has changed. The media have become three-dimensional, inescapable, omnivorous, and self-referring—a closed system that seems, for many of the kids, to answer all their questions.

(Denby 1996:51)

The constant query of my childhood was 'Where you been?' The answer 'Nowhere'. Neither my stepfather or my mother believed me. But no punishment could discover another answer. The truth was that I did go nowhere—nowhere in particular and everywhere imaginable. I walked and told myself stories. . . . The flush my mama suspected hid an afternoon of shoplifting or vandalism was simple embarrassment. . . . In the world as I remade it, nothing was forbidden; everything was possible.

(Allison 1995:2)

[I]n M. Bernard's class, it fed a hunger in them [the pupils] more basic even to the child than to the man, and that is the hunger for discovery. In other classes, no doubt they were taught many things, but it was somewhat the way geese are stuffed: food was presented to them and they were asked please to swallow it. In M. Bernards class, they felt for the first time they existed and that they were the objects of the highest regard.

(Camus 1996)

Strategies for response

When reading the above extracts you, like us, will have responded in different ways to each one. In fact you could have responded in a number of ways. You could have divided the responses in a typological fashion: by classifying according to type of text, for example child/adult, theme addressed, academic/non-academic style, quality of comment, type of sentiment and so on. This we can regard as a 'distancing', rational response. It is useful in itself and for certain purposes, but it is not a narrative response.

On another level you could have responded with agree/disagree, another form of typology, but a critical and judgemental one. This can be regarded as more personal but justifications for such judgements can either be highly defensive in a 'this is right, that is wrong sense', according to some unquestionable moral rule or imperative; or they can involve distancing again through applying apparently non-personal critical evaluation. Again, we are not saying that such a type of response does not have a function, but it tends to avoid narrative involvement.

Narrative involvement can be identified by the presence of reflexivity, and thinking and expressing ourselves in the first person: 'I . . .' Significantly, we only respond in the first person when we have been, or have allowed ourselves to admit to being, affected by what we have read, heard, seen, touched and so on. By doing so we become vulnerable and need the trust and acceptance of our listeners. This is not to say that responses cannot be critical or introduce difference rather than just accepting. If you apply the idea of narrative response to your reading of the above texts, what happens? Which ones do you want to respond to? Which ones have touched you? What do you want to write or say? What memories of events in your own childhood do you wish to retell, or find yourself retelling as a result? What would happen if we brought together all the readers of this book and listened to what they have to say or have written as responses—what possibilities would that give us and where could it take us in reconsidering our understanding of 'children' and 'spirituality'?

We are aware that positioning the explication of the difference between narrative response and what we have called distanced response after the quotes may seem to privilege us as authors of the activity and belittle the reader. This was not the intention, but intention is difficult to determine unless you already know who you are dealing with (that is, in the classroom, what sort of teacher you have got and what sort of relationships he or she wishes to create). We are also aware that without the process taking place as a communal activity we will all imagine the outcomes in different ways. For example the explanation of the possibilities for learning expressed above could be interpreted in a sentimentalised or idealised fashion (possibly dependent on your own inclinations and the way you responded to the activity), which was not what we sought to convey. Again, the dynamic possibilities of a written text are limited, and can be distortive of the acting situation. Thus we need to remind ourselves of the purposes of pedagogy and the limitations of *commenting* on doing education, which is what we are doing now, as opposed to what this is all about: *doing it*.

8 Concept mapping: a starting point for narration

Jane Erricker

For almost a century, students of educ
ation have suffered under the yoke of the behavioural psychologists, who see
learning as synonymous with a change in behaviour. We reject this view, and
observe instead that learning by humans leads to a change in the meaning
of experience. . . . Furthermore, behavioural psychology, and much of currently popular 'cognitive science', neglects the significance of feelings.
Human experience involves not only thinking and acting but also feeling,
and it is only when all three are considered together that individuals can be
empowered to enrich the meaning of their experience.

(Novak and Gowin 1984:xi)

Concept mapping is a technique developed by Novak and Gowin in *Learning
How to Learn* (1984) and was originally intended for use in concrete curriculum
learning situations, such as science education. We have adapted and extended
the technique for use in spiritual and moral education where the learning does
not involve 'facts' so much as the narrative knowledge described in earlier
chapters. We use concept mapping as a tool to enable learners to reflect on and
interpret their own experience, to construct their own narrative and to determine
its meaning.

Novak and Gowin explain concept mapping as 'intended to represent
meaningful relationships between concepts in the form of propositions'
(ibid.:15). It is a way of expressing an understanding of a particular concept,
which relies on the fact that we understand a concept according to its
relationship with other concepts. When we meet a new concept we place it into
a web of other concepts; in other words we embed a new concept in other
concepts, depending on what we see as the relationship of that new concept to
other concepts that we already know. Concept mapping allows us to express this
understanding by verbalising the propositions that link one concept with another
and placing them on a diagram. The maps thus produced have been used as a
device for assessing cognitive learning, and as a creative device for generating
new connections and expanding a learner's understanding of a particular concept.
It can be used to identify misconceptions and thus to assess learning both before
and after a particular teaching session or a whole course.

However we have found that the technique can also be used to express more affective understanding, depending on the concepts that the learner is asked to map and the way in which the process of mapping is facilitated. Thus using concepts such as loss, friendship, joy or beauty can give us insight into someone's personal experience and her or his interpretation of that experience. The narrating of the links as well as the writing of them is an essential part of the process as the reflection on the experiences allows the construction of meaning.

The activity

There are two ways to begin the teaching of concept mapping. You can either provide the participants with a list of concepts that could be included in the map, or you can give them the topic and ask them to make their own list as they go along. Participants usually need time and practice to develop the skills of concept mapping, and we have found that giving them a list of concepts is the best way to begin. If you do not start with a list then the participant needs some time to consider which concepts might be part of the topic, though more will come to mind as the mapping is carried out. One concept should be chosen as a starting point and written in the middle of a sheet of paper. Another concept should be written close to it, but not too close, and the concepts joined with a line. Their understanding of the connection between the two concepts is written on that line. For example one concept could be *grass* and the other *green*. They could be connected like this:

$$\text{Grass} \xrightarrow{\text{is}} \text{Green}$$

Note that the connection is an arrow in the direction in which the proposition should be read. From this point onwards other concepts can be written around the initial ones and connecting lines drawn wherever necessary:

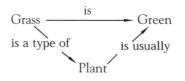

The directional arrows are important. The plant–green connection is factually correct in one direction but not the other. This is even more important when you are not dealing with 'facts' but with experiential issues and emotions. The final map can be quite complicated and difficult to read so explaining the map to someone else allows the participant to clarify his or her thinking and also to make yet more new connections and interpretations. Sometimes redrawing the map can be helpful. If the participants are given the concepts to map, then they should be allowed to cross out any offered concepts they do not feel are relevant, and add any they think should have been included. Everyone, children and adults, get

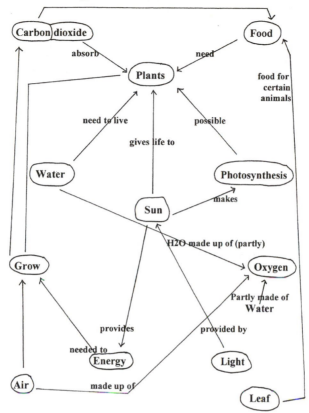

Figure 1 Photosynthesis concept map.

better at concept mapping with practice. Very young children can do maps orally and as a whole class, with or without the teacher scribing at the front.

Interpretation of the maps

If you are just looking for people's factual conceptions and misconceptions then interpreting these maps is very easy. Figure 1 is an example of such a map and you will see that the misconceptions are obvious.

However sometimes when you think you are asking for a 'factual' map you get something more interesting. Figure 2 is a concept map on earth and space constructed by a seven-year-old girl. You can see first of all that she does not have much scientific knowledge of the topic and her ideas imbue the contents of the universe with human feelings and desires. Her propositions are poetic and begin to construct the biographies of the elements she has mapped. Her map is not

Figure 2 Earth and space concept map 1.

continuous, but is separated into discrete sections, leaving loose ends, indicating that she does not understand the connections between all the concepts, but this does not appear to be a problem and she does not try to pull them all together. There are no associations between one group of concepts and another. The very shape of the map tells us something about the way she is thinking. It appears to be thinking that is divergent and not confined by given categories. From this map we can suggest that she does not know much about the traditional science of earth and space, that she is anthropomorphic in her understanding of the concepts and that she has yet to learn the accepted way of writing about scientific topics.

This child was taught about earth and space a few months after constructing this map, and produced a topic book filled with text, diagrams and coloured pictures. Shortly after that she was asked to construct a second map so that her learning could be assessed. Figure 3 is her second map. This map is very different from the first one. The shape is almost a closed circle, with no loose ends, which may be interpreted as

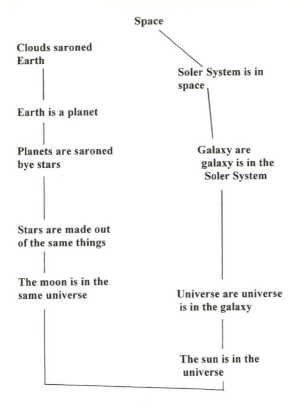

Figure 3 Earth and space concept map 2.

demonstrating convergent thinking. The subject is 'wrapped up', she knows about it now. The map displays more scientific knowledge, but also some misconceptions that she has acquired. The poetic language and the anthropomorphism is gone and it is difficult not to feel that something has been lost in the transition between not knowing and knowing about earth and space. However we must not be too hasty. Maybe she has only learned that a science task is not an appropriate place for poetic language. It would take more investigation to determine exactly what has happened to her thinking.

In interpreting concept maps produced on more affective topics, misconceptions are not an issue. If a participant is mapping a concept such as 'God' then there are no right or wrong answers, simply an individual construction. Giving the participant a list of concepts will restrict her or his thinking, so unless the participant is a child then just a general topic is enough. Again the whole shape of the map can give clues as to the comfort the participant feels with the topic, and the nature of her or his thinking.

Figure 4 is an example of a concept map done by a child aged seven from a list of concepts that included himself and God. This map does not appear to give a great deal of information, but this should not be seen as discouraging. Children

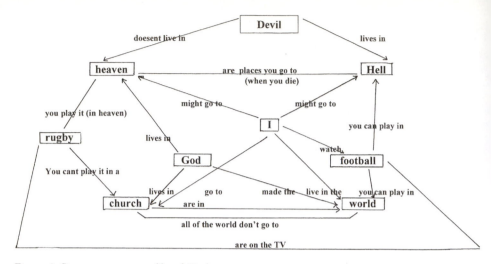

Figure 4 Concept map: myself and God.

often do not make their thinking clear in such an exercise, and the narration of the process is very important in this situation. Talking about the map is just a starting point for narration, particularly since at the age of this child oral skills are likely to be much better than writing skills. When children are given a list of concepts they are likely to assume that these are the only concepts to be used and confine both their maps and their thinking accordingly. In the process of narration other concepts can and will be introduced. Interestingly, in this map, there is no arrow connecting 'I' and 'God'.

Concept mapping is also useful with adults. They usually do not have the problems that children have with determining which concepts to use in a map and can start with just a single concept. Figure 5 is a map on the concept of 'loss', drawn in a session for the development of spiritual and moral sensitivity in teachers. Again you have to be careful about interpreting such maps, but they can be used as starting points for discussion. I have found that getting adults to talk in pairs about their maps is a useful exercise. The discussion can include the shape of the map and the reasons why this shape came about. Often the participant is not aware of those reasons, or the reasons for particular connections being made until the discussion begins, and the self-revelatory nature of this exercise can be emotionally disturbing. The further a participant is distanced from knowledge that can be described as objective, and therefore 'safe' in the sense that the self is not directly and self-consciously involved in the knowing, the more insecure she or he is likely to feel. It is interesting to observe, when a group is involved in concept mapping an affective topic, how some participants attempt to hold on to their objective distance and refuse to participate or resist engagement in the process. Some will produce maps with dead ends, where the topic became too

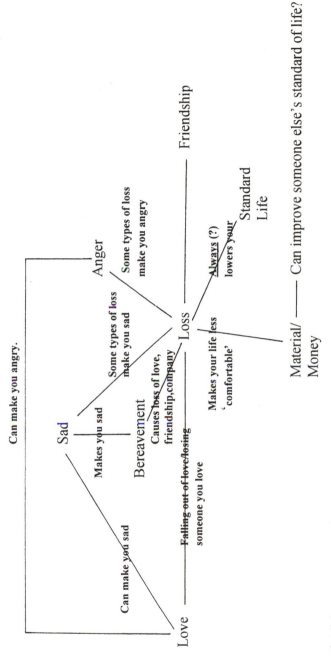

Figure 5 Adult concept map on loss 1.

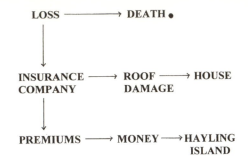

Figure 6 Adult concept map on loss 2.

uncomfortable. Figure 6 is an example of such a dead end, very clearly marked with a large, black full stop. After this point the rest of the map was completed, moving away from the affective and back to the safety of the cognitive.

Concept mapping a tradition

It is also possible to use concept maps to construct a representation of a worldview or tradition/group. This is an interpretive activity that acknowledges and expresses the hermeneutical nature of such a representational task. It can also serve as a way of determining the differences, complexity or simplicity of one's own understanding in relation to that of others. In other words it is a tool for raising issues in relation to representation and reflexivity, one's own cognitive and affective relationship with others.

Activity

The following procedure is a way of structuring this process:

- Write a list of the terms you associate with a particular group or tradition (this might, for example, be as broad as 'Jewish' or 'Christian', or much narrower in scope).
- Connect up these terms and write, as in the concept maps above, the proposition that connects them on each line.
- Take a story or teaching that relates to and conveys one of the concepts on your map, for example the Torah or Shekina in relation to Jewish tradition.
- Take an issue or theme from the story or teaching (for example authority or obedience) and concept map it in relation to your own experience.
- Relate the narrative of your own concept map, that is, tell its story.
- Relate your own story to your understanding of the story in the tradition. What is the relationship between the two narratives? What issues arise?

Response

The point of this activity is, of course, to identify differences in interpretation and representation, and the experiential, affective and attitudinal issues that are involved. This is an activity that needs to be experienced. You may try it on your own, but it is important to compare your experience of doing this with that of others. It is this relational interaction that creates complexity in the process.

9 Developing emotional literacy

Jane Erricker

Since 1995 the Children and Worldviews Project has been investigating children's spirituality, or, as the team prefers to call it, children's *worldviews*. During that time the project team has interviewed approximately 200 children, ranging in age from six to 11. Analysis of the transcripts has revealed particular themes that the children found important, such as relationships, secret places, ethnic identity, religious affiliation, death, separation and the environment. The analysis has also revealed the process that the children go through as they attempt to verbalise what they think and feel. The process involves finding the right words or metaphors to express complex and deeply felt issues, and the verbalisation facilitates the children's self-understanding. As they express themselves their feelings become clearer to themselves and this self-discovery is evident in what they say. Sharing these feelings and the process of discovering them reveals to the children that other people have these feelings too, facilitating the development of empathy and understanding as the children discuss and help each other (Erricker *et al.* 1997).

This process forms the basis of what we understand spiritual and moral education to be. In order to enlarge on our understanding, I would like to use a term that is beginning to be recognised as useful: *emotional literacy*. The exact meaning of this term differs according to the source: in the psychological literature its originator appears to be Daniel Goleman (1996, 1998), whose work on emotional intelligence draws on Howard Gardner's (1984) theory of multiple intelligences. The pressure group Antidote, which campaigns for the recognition of emotional education as a valid part of the curriculum, also uses the term (Parks 1999) but does not clearly define its meaning. At a more mundane level, Southampton City Council uses the term in its Strategic Plan for Education as synonymous with anger management, which restricts its application within the school curriculum.

During the process of accessing children's worldviews explained above, the project team were invited to a junior school to carry out interviews with the pupils. Instead of talking to a small group of pupils, the headteacher wanted the team to take a whole year six assembly, so a slightly different methodology was used. The stimulus for the conversation was a story about a grandmother's death, told by a seven-year-old girl, Victoria, from a different school (see Chapter 10).

The 60 children attending the assembly were asked to write down their personal response to Victoria's story, and were then asked if they wanted to speak, or to be interviewed later. Several children spoke at the assembly, and the main emphasis was their own loss, either the death of a relative or pet, or loss through family breakdown. Although Victoria's story was quite a positive one, several children became upset and had to be comforted by classmates. The members of staff present were disturbed by the level of emotion and wanted to calm down the children by resuming normal school work, but the children wanted to continue the process. However the children were overruled, although the project team arranged to return the following week to speak to those who had asked to be interviewed. Of the 60 children, 48 wanted to be interviewed and the interviews were carried out in small groups. One of the conversations took place with two ten-year-old boys. The conversation was facilitated by the interviewer, but a large amount of the actual discourse was between the boys themselves. They talked in detail about their home lives and the emotional demands that were made upon them. Close analysis of the interview transcript, using a grounded theory approach, allowed identification of the particular skills the boys were using as they affirmed and supported each other. These skills were classified as skills of emotional literacy.

The skills of emotional literacy

- Reflection on one's own emotions.
- Self-knowledge (understanding why one does something).
- Understanding of consequences.
- Self-criticism (according to one's own recognised principles).
- Self-control.
- Reflection on the emotions of others.
- Empathy.
- Criticism of others (according to one's own recognised principles).
- Understanding why others do things.
- Recognition of relationship.
- Recognition of difference.
- Recognition of the complexity of social discourse.
- Generalisation of the principles of behaviour.
- Prophetic statements.

A section of the conversation transcript is reproduced below to demonstrate the nature of the narrative and to show how the boys, Lee and Glen, helped each other to express their feelings.

GLEN: I know for certain my mum's always thinking of me cos she phones up and tells me that . . . so that's a good thing that she's always thinking about me and I'm always thinking about her. It makes me upset though as well . . . like she's always thinking about me but I don't get to see her.

Q: When you come to school does it affect how you behave at school at all or how you feel?

LEE: Yeh.

GLEN: Sometimes.

LEE: A lot.

GLEN: The other day this girl hit someone and I was really messed up about it.

LEE: I just . . . things I never used to do, like messing around and stuff, and like I didn't used to talk a lot . . . it's just things like that, it isn't like crying and stuff like that. I talk a lot cos I want to talk about something, I want to talk about it, but I don't talk about it to my friends.

Q: Would it help when it affects you in school, would it help to be able to talk to somebody?

GLEN: Yeh, who's like in school for about every other week, who's in school and if you have problems you can come up and speak to them.

LEE: If there's someone in your class who's in the same situation, like me and Glen, it's good to talk to each other and comfort each other.

GLEN: Yeh.

LEE: That's what I was thinking about when you first came in and all the girls were crying. I thought like you've really helped them, like it was talking about what had happened to them.

Q: It really helped them by talking? I think that's absolutely right.

GLEN: Talking's the best way to get it off your mind a lot, cos . . . well you get the chance to talk about things, cos this is the first time we've actually got to just discuss it with somebody, but if it was like a group or a class of children about ten people I couldn't say anything then cos I'd be scared cos I would think people might take the mickey out of me.

LEE: Yeh, you just build it up inside don't you? And then it explodes in one go. If you're not talking then something really, really bad's going to happen, if you don't express what you're feeling, just in an instant it happens.

GLEN: But one time I got really . . . I got so sad about it but somebody asked me and I just . . . I told a lot of my friends that what had happened, I told three of them, well, Bradley, Nicky and Drew, what had happened, they understood.

LEE: I talked to Nicky about what had happened to me, he was another person I thought I could talk to because he's . . . his mum and dad were on the verge of splitting up and he felt what I felt then and he . . . he keeps it a secret.

Q: Does he?

GLEN: Bradley was good, Bradley knows what its like to have . . . like another say not have your real mum living with you, cos he's had it all his life so . . . so I talked to him and he knew how I felt cos he's got it with his mum and dad and family and that.

Q: So you've got a whole group of you in the class who you know are in a similar situation?

GLEN: Yeh.

LEE: Yeh.

GLEN: Drew's like in the middle of both really, he doesn't really . . .

LEE: He doesn't really think about us.

GLEN: Cos he always sees them so he can't really hurt so much.

Q: So he sees his dad?

LEE: A lot.

GLEN: Yeh a lot, he like gets a £50 present or goes out all day or goes to MacDonalds or something.

LEE: It isn't what it's about though.

GLEN: No.

LEE: Seeing your parent, it isn't about what they can give you, its . . .

GLEN: You just like to talk to them.

LEE: Yeh, tell them that you love them.

Q: Are you telling me they don't sit down and talk with you?

GLEN: No.

LEE: No, well my dad does sometimes, but I don't . . . I feel I want to speak to him but I don't.

Q: I think you're doing something very, very important, I really do, um, cos the sort of things that you're saying are things that a lot of people don't realise till their a lot older cos they don't go through your experience. You know things about relationships that you only learn this way.

LEE: Yeh.

GLEN: Yeh.

LEE: Most people who've got parents together they might worry about it because they see it on TV and stuff but they don't really know about it, cos my sister's doing a project on—she's 15—she's doing a project on violence and stuff and she knows all about it.

Q: So she would like to talk about that or she wouldn't want to?

LEE: She wouldn't want to.

Q: Not on the project?

LEE: No, but she knows what kind of things to write about though.

GLEN: If it wasn't like we're doing this now . . . like before this I wouldn't even have dreamt of saying anything to my mum about it but now I feel like a lot safer to discuss with my mum, but it's still a bit iffy I feel. I feel more alert to say it because we're all . . . we're discussing it, it feels better.

Q: Sometimes when you talk about things like this, it can be like a rehearsal can't it? You can sort of get things in your mind.

LEE: I don't think of it like that, I think that if you speak to someone, it just helps get things out.

Q: Would it help in school, does it help to talk to teachers or . . . ?

LEE: No.

GLEN: No, not to teachers.

Q: Really?

LEE: You can't talk about anything to teachers.

GLEN: I wouldn't talk to teachers.

LEE: It's too embarrassing.

GLEN: Cos we're afraid . . . like people would take the mickey out of me.

LEE: I'm not afraid of that, I just don't know how to express it to people, teachers, I like to express it to people who will . . . who will listen and take it in. I know the teachers would listen but . . .

GLEN: But in one way they haven't really got much to do about all that, all you see them for is to do with like work or . . . that's all you ever do with them and when you talk to them it's just about work really init? You don't really get to talk about . . . to express your feelings.

Q: Why's that? Cos there's no time or . . . ?

GLEN: Cos they're teaching.

Q: Cos they're teaching?

LEE: No, it's . . . it's just one of those things that you can't do.

GLEN: No.

LEE: It's like anybody in our situation, I don't think . . . if you asked them who's the person who'd they talk to about their parents, they wouldn't speak about that to teachers.

GLEN: No, it's like in class . . . do you know the people who were crying, a lot of them about people who had died . . . yeh, when you came in . . . but one or two, about five of them . . .

LEE: Yeh.

GLEN: Me, Lee and some other people were crying about what happens to families and it feels like my mum . . .

LEE: It feels like they're dead.

GLEN: When I don't see them.

LEE: Yeh.

GLEN: It *feels* like they're dead.

LEE: They're out of your life.

GLEN: Yeh.

Q: It feels like they're dead?

GLEN: Yeh, but they aren't.

Q: Is that a funny feeling?

LEE: Yeh.

GLEN: A horrible feeling.

Q: A horrible feeling?

LEE: Yeh.

Q: Yeh, I understand . . . um, Drew put down to speak . . .

GLEN: Shall we call him? Is he in school today?

This is a powerful piece of transcript, and it is worth noting how little the interviewer says. When she or he does speak, it is usually to repeat what the boy has said, or gently to ask for clarification. The boys affirm and support each other, offering a safe place for personal exposure. They also want to offer the same safety and support to other children in the same class, who have similar problems.

The skills of emotional literacy were identified on the basis of specific statements that the boys made, and these statements are included here.

The evidence for the skills

1. Reflection on one's own emotions:

LEE: The thing that upsets me . . . um . . . is the thought of my dad not thinking about me, I think about him every day, I think of him not thinking about what I'm doing and stuff and it really upsets me and I hope that he does.

2. Self-knowledge (understanding why one does something):

LEE: Cos sometimes I get like my dad and I get really angry and sometimes I hit people too, like my sisters, and I know . . . and I don't do that any more, I take it out on like sports and stuff.

3. Understanding of consequences:

LEE: Yeh, you just build it up inside don't you? And then it explodes in one go. If you're not talking then something really, really bad's going to happen, if you don't express what you're feeling, just in an instant it happens.

4. Self-criticism (according to one's own recognised principles) and
5. Self-control (including managing anger):

Q: A lot of things are kept secret?
LEE: Yeh, it happens all the time. My mum . . . cos sometimes I get like my dad and I get really angry and sometimes I hit people too, like my sisters, and I know . . . and I don't do that any more, I take it out on like sports and stuff.
Q: Does sport help?
LEE: Yeh, a lot.
GLEN: Yeh, a lot.
LEE: You really think that, you're aiming at something, really push it to the limit.
GLEN: It's like kicking a football, you really take it . . . you really kick it really hard, like get your stress out of you and that and just enjoy yourself where you are.

6. Reflection on the emotions of others:

LEE: I talked to Nicky about what had happened to me, he was another person I thought I could talk to because he's . . . his mum and dad were on the verge of splitting up and he felt what I felt then and he . . . he keeps it a secret.
Q: Does he?

GLEN: Bradley was good, Bradley knows what it's like to have . . . like another say not have your real mum living with you, cos he's had it all his life so . . . so I talked to him and he knew how I felt cos he's got it with his mum and dad and family and that.

Q: So you've got a whole group of you in the class who you know are in a similar situation?

GLEN: Yeh.

LEE: Yeh.

7.   Empathy:

LEE: If there's someone in your class who's in the same situation, like me and Glen, it's good to talk to each other and comfort each other.

GLEN: Yeh.

LEE: That's what I was thinking about when you first came in and all the girls were crying. I thought like you've really helped them, like it was talking about what had happened to them.

8.   Criticism of others (according to one's own recognised principles):

Q: And do you have her telephone number now?

GLEN: I'm not sure, I don't know it. My dad might, but I don't.

Q: Right, and you're not sure if your dad does?

GLEN: No.

LEE: A lot of things are kept secret aren't they?

GLEN: Yeh.

Q: A lot of things are kept secret?

LEE: Yeh, it happens all the time.

9.   Understanding why others do things:

GLEN: No, I just go on my own cos my sisters don't like my mum that much and I really love my mum and she . . . when I go there she cries and normally we have to . . . we always go out for like a MacDonalds or go down Gosport because she can't get her mind off it.

LEE: Yeh, it's exactly the same as what I do with my dad, he doesn't cry like cos he doesn't like expressing his feelings, he likes to express his anger a lot cos once I got punched in the eye by him. I had a great big bruise but he didn't get anything done about it.

10.   Recognition of relationship:

GLEN: With my mum for Christmas I woke up and I go . . . it's Christmas and I thought, what's it like with a mum at Christmas? It's totally different with just a dad and I thought, 'oh great' like this, cos I didn't have a mum to wake up with at Christmas, normally like families, they have a mum to stand in their room, but I woke up with just my sisters and my dad in bed still and my mum, she came along ... no she brought this little like car, it's quite a expensive one and I undid it and I thought, it's only a car and I undid it and there was £30 in there to go towards my holiday and everything as well. Jill and that have bought a football and some other stuff like that, the rest probably going for my life savings or towards something for my birthday.

LEE: Christmas day I didn't think of anything, um, happy, when I woke up like with my presents, cos I wasn't around my family, to me, they weren't my family.

Q: Where were you on Christmas day?

LEE: At home with people, just my mum and my sisters and my step-dad and my brother feels part of the family now but I don't really get on with my step-dad cos I don't see him that much cos he goes to work everyday until about 8 o'clock ... so I barely get to see him.

Q: So it didn't feel like a family?

LEE: Well, it almost did.

11.   Recognition of difference:

LEE: Most people who've got parents together they might worry about it because they see it on TV and stuff but they don't really know about it, cos my sister's doing a project on—she's 15—she's doing a project on violence and stuff and she knows all about it.

12.   Recognition of the complexity of social discourse:

GLEN: That's another thing about my mum as well, another reason why she's distressed, she found another man, she had another baby, but where she couldn't cope, where she had no money and everything, that baby had to go into foster care, and I only saw him once, he's my only like step brother.

Q: And you don't see him now?

GLEN: No, cos my mum hardly sees him now ... I don't even know where he is or anything.

Q: And you hardly see her?

GLEN: Yeh.

13.   Generalisation of the principles of behaviour:

GLEN: Yeh a lot, he like gets a £50 present or goes out all day or goes to MacDonalds or something.

LEE: It isn't what its about though.

GLEN: No.

LEE: Seeing your parent, it isn't about what they can give you, it's . . .
GLEN: You just like to talk to them.
LEE: Yeh, tell them that you love them.

14.   Prophetic statements:

Q: So it didn't feel like a family?
LEE: Well, it almost did.
GLEN: That's another thing I had on Christmas . . .
LEE: It's like a key that almost fits the lock but doesn't turn.
Q: What would happen if you could turn the key?
GLEN: You'd see your family back together again.
LEE: It would open the door.
Q: And that key, can you find a way of turning it or do you think it just will never turn?
LEE: It will never turn.
GLEN: It will never turn for me either.

The skills can be divided into four groups: numbers 1–5 being centred around the self, 6–9 with others, 10–12 with society and 13 and 14 are universal statements. It is these skills that the children will be developing as a result of conversation with a facilitating adult and/or other children.

We do not suggest that the terms 'spiritual and moral education' and 'emotional literacy' are necessarily synonymous. Spiritual and moral education could be taken to mean very much more than this. However we would suggest that spiritual and moral education *must* include emotional literacy. This idea of emotional literacy and the skills that make it up is very different from the notion of an imposed moral framework. The 'rules and regulations' are self-determined and self-imposed, there is no conforming to specified values. It is not about knowing, or being told, about how one should be or how one should behave. Instead, recognising and practising the skills should result in recognition of the complexity of social discourse, recognition of one's own agency within it and one's responsibility for its successful functioning (in Aristotle's sense of the maximum happiness).

This is not to deny the possibility of conforming to a set of values or a spirituality derived from a religion, if that is what the individual wants and needs, only that that course of action should be pursued mindfully, in the knowledge that this is a choice and a positive decision that one is free to make. This represents a different position and process from that often found in school PSE or RE lessons, where the values are suggested and then discussion is invited. The discussion takes place within a context that recognises implicitly that no significant change in position is allowed. The value has already been stated. Interestingly, this process was mirrored in the procedures of the 1996 SCAA Forum on Values in Education and the Community. Here discussion was invited, with the suggestion that a consensus was sought, but the agenda had already been decided (Erricker 1998). The issue is one of power; we, the authorities, have decided how you should behave, we will allow you to discuss it but we will give you no power to change it.

If emotional literacy is to be addressed, then it must be done using a pedagogy that gives autonomy and empowerment to the learner and this is difficult to do in a highly prescribed, didactically delivered curriculum. Without protected time and an opportunity to use a process-based teaching method, whatever development occurs will occur in other places, fragmented across the other curriculum areas. However when this happens it will often be a result of discussing situations that are distanced from the children's own lives, such as historical situations, religious stories or fiction. Even if the children make reference to their own autobiographical stories it will only be in passing, because the teacher will need to fulfil curriculum obligations. What is needed for spiritual, moral and emotional development is discussion of children's real life situations, as in the transcript above, with the dimensions of a good relationship—as identified by Rogers (1942, 1951, 1983) and Truax and Carkhuff (1967) and quoted in McGuiness (1998)—present between the teacher and the child, or between the children. The dimensions of a good relationship are:

- Empathy.
- Unconditional positive regard.
- Genuineness.
- Immediacy (McGuiness 1998:34).

When these 'good' conversations are taking place the emphasis for the teacher should not just be on facilitating the discussion of what comes up, but also on constantly trying to help the children to be aware of how they are addressing their own development.

We come back to asking what the best method is for developing skills. Unlike subjects such as PE, science and art, it is quite difficult to practise the skills of emotional literacy. When children are given hypothetical spiritual or moral situations as stories they can distance themselves from these situations because they are not emotionally involved with them. Emotional (spiritual/moral) development only occurs when there is a *personal* emotional connection. You can use whatever you like as a stimulus (moral fables, parables, fairy stories, Bible stories, newspaper stories, art, local events) but these should only be a stepping stone towards children relating and reflecting on their own stories, biographies, narratives. It is in this reflection and discussion that children are given the opportunity to identify and continue to construct and change their moral stances on existential issues. They can work out how they behave, how they should behave, and why they should behave in that way. This can then be extended to how the society they live in should work in order to comply with the moral positions they have defined, and how and why it might or might not work like that—in other words, citizenship.

When children reflect on spiritual, moral and emotional situations they gather a store of practised possible reactions to these situations. These reactions may be determined by their own understanding of their practised skills, the reactions of their peers or reactions determined by tradition. This constitutes 'knowledge' in this field and is used in the development of those skills. To give an example in another field, a child might be practising her football skills. She has developed the skill of kicking the ball and knows where to place it and the consequences of that placement. Similarly a child might have the skill of empathising and know what the result of empathy might be on himself and others.

However, when their spiritual and moral education is restricted to other people's stories and the emotional connection is not there, their spiritual and moral 'knowledge' remains part of the objective, distanced Enlightenment paradigm, where it is possible to look at knowledge as if it has an existence of its own, apart from the 'knower'. I suggest that, especially in respect of the development of emotional skills, this is a nonsense. Emotional, spiritual and moral skills (and/or 'knowledge') are embedded, embodied and subjective. They are part of the being of a person and can only be expressed and developed by reflection on personal narrative.

In order to help teachers to focus on and keep track of what they achieve in these conversations, we have developed a record sheet that lists the skills of emotional literacy, and also gives a little guidance as to the possible content of the conversations. This sheet is only intended to be a starting point for teachers, and is open to development and change so that a particular group of pupils' circumstances can be taken into account.

The Children and Worldviews Project record sheet

Child's name:			
Criterion: Does the child	**Indicate with a ✓ as appropriate**	**Evidence**	**Facilitation**
Talk about her/his experiences			
Describe something as important or significant in her/his life			
Talk about her/his feelings			
Talk about the experiences of others			
Talk about the feelings of others			
Talk about relationships with toys or pets			
Talk about relationships with other people			

Child's name:			
Criterion: does the child	**Indicate with a ✓ as appropriate**	**Evidence**	**Facilitation**
Judge her/his actions against some criteria of her/his own			
Judge others' actions against those criteria			
Generalise those criteria			
Express some sense of connection with something outside her/himself			
Talk about God, Jesus, angels, devils or the equivalent in other traditions			
Talk about relationship with God or Jesus or the equivalent in other traditions			
Talk about the future			
Express awe and wonder			
Does the child show an improvement in her/his ability to:			
Express her/his experiences			
Express her/his feelings			
Reflect on those experiences and feelings			
Listen to others talking about experiences and feelings			
Respond to those expressions by others			
Show empathy			

The record sheet is not intended to be a tool for assessment, but a tracking document that allows the teacher to ascertain what she or he should be looking for in a child's conversation. The development of a child's emotional literacy will occur because of these conversations with other children. As stated above, this does not preclude the use of literature, art or current events for the stimulation of such conversations.

Your response

Give your own response to Lee and Glen as if you were present at the conversation. Note the character of and origins from which your response derives. Try out the record sheet for yourself to determine its usefulness for identifying children's skills.

10 Children's stories and responses

Jane and Clive Erricker

The stories in this chapter were collected from primary school children who were encouraged to talk about their experiences. These are the types of story that children tell when they are given the space and the uncritical, facilitating response suggested in Chapter 9.

In order to allow the children to narrate their experiences the conversations were carried out in small groups, with the emphasis on the children talking to each other rather than to the adult in the group. These conversations were taperecorded, transcribed and analysed in order to help us to understand children's experiences, and what is important to them in their lives. We came to realise that, for children, the process of talking through their experiences is an essential part of making sense of what happens to them, and that they want and need to tell their stories and to be affirmed and respected. We call this process narrative construction.

We have been impressed by the maturity and competence with which children deal with difficult experiences such as family breakdown, death, violence and racism, but even children whose lives have been comparatively calm still need to talk. Children have shown that they can help and support each other and do not necessarily need adult intervention to solve their problems. What they do need is space in a crowded school curriculum to tell their stories and to have them sympathetically and uncritically received. There is often nowhere else to do this and no-one else to listen to them. The children will develop their listening skills as well as their narrating skills as they listen to each other's stories and tell their own.

When children talk they express their spirituality, work out their moral positions and opinions and develop their emotional skills, as explained in Chapter 9. This process can be detected in the stories that follow. There is no need to question children closely for them to demonstrate these things, all that is needed is space, a stimulus to start the process and your interest and encouragement.

When you engage in this process you are not trying to find out things about the children. The process belongs to the children themselves and they must be allowed to construct their stories as they wish. You need not be too concerned with whether they are telling the truth. If the children talk in groups the other children will respond and it is the discussion that is valuable. Of course if a child talks about an experience that appears to be abusive then normal school procedures should be followed.

When the interviews are transcribed the interviewer's contribution can be removed, leaving a continuous piece of prose that we call the child's story. We have used these stories as stimuli to help people to start talking about their own experiences, and the process has been successful for both adults and children. It is interesting that we have found that the age of the person telling the original story is immaterial, and that others respond to the affective message in the story, rather than to the way in which it is told. It is also interesting that the response is not necessarily to the overt message of the story, but to an underlying concept that resonates with the experience of the listener. For example, the discussion about family breakdown between the two ten-year-old boys in Chapter 9 was produced in response to a seven-year-old girl's story about her grandmother dying. The boys were responding to the underlying concept of loss, and interpreting it and responding to its articulation with a resonant story about their loss—the loss of their father or mother as a result of family dislocation, and the loss of their family structure.

The themes of the stories in this chapter vary according to whatever was uppermost in the child's mind at the time of the conversation, and there are stories about death, separation, racism, bullying, religion, pets, family relationships, school and special places. Sometimes the stimulus to share a narrative was not another child's story, but literature, art, a drawing activity, a walk or simply a general inquiry. If you are asking someone to respond to a stimulus it is important for you to act as a facilitator. This means that, as explained in Chapter 9, the dimensions of a good relationship with the narrator are maintained.

In addition, when the children raise an issue they should be allowed to talk freely even if they appear to be moving away from the point, because the most valuable reflections often come unexpectedly. They need to talk about their own experiences and how they feel about them. The facilitator should try not to jump in with judgements about their expressed positions, but allow them to express themselves fully, to explain their positions, and to be challenged by others if possible. Discussion between the members of a group is much better for their development than a conversation between teacher and pupil.

We now come to some of the stories that the children told. The content of their stories was determined partly by the stimulus used to encourage the narration, but also by the children themselves, in that they talked about whatever was most important to them, what was on their minds at the time. As already mentioned, this means that very different stories were produced by a very similar process.

Arthur's story: a story about God, Jesus, heaven and hell

Sometimes, like when I was younger, I used to think Jesus was a man with a long beard and white clothes. Now I think Jesus was like God's messenger really. God's son who

came and told us that God will forgive us cos before people didn't know that . . . before
people were enemies with God, they didn't know God would forgive them.

I believe in God. I think he's kind of like a sort of spirit really that's all around. I can't
really picture God, it's just like there. I think maybe God's in our hearts. If people die,
then they'd still be alive but in your heart. Also they won't be dead, they would just be
like . . . it'll just be the start of a new life.

I wouldn't say like hell was a place where like the devil lives, I'd say it's like an
emptiness, like you're not with God and you'd just be on your own.

If you believe in God I think you should, well, spread the word, be kind and don't
hurt people. It's difficult sometimes cos sometimes like people say 'oh come on, come on,
let's play here' or something.

I think God made us to rule the earth and like look after his animals, he gave them
to us to look after. I dont think we do. If I could ask God three questions I would ask
him am I good enough to go to heaven or do I need to improve? What do you look like?
And can you forgive us because we've done so much wrong? We learn about forgiveness
at school. Like that if we want him to forgive us, if we say sorry for everything then we
will be forgiven.

Calvin's story: a story about friends and enemies, God and family

I like having a gang but I can't tell you who's in my gang, it's a secret. We walk about
the estate and people get scared of me. They try to take us on but there's more of us and
there are big boys. Lee's a big boy and he can't take us on. David's a trouble maker on
the estate. His Dad's name's Sid and he's in prison. When he's in prison we beat David
up. David's big and he tries to get us to do some shoplifting. I beat him up at the disco
and he was bleeding. He felt gutted.

I've got a book with stories about God in it, a kiddies' bible. My Mum and Dad used
to go to church and I believe in God. I think you should and there's a good reason to—he
gives you food and all that and he's the one who made us. You should believe in God and
God the father as well.

If you believe in God you have to be good. But David, he's on the devil's side, he nicks
motorbikes and all that you see. He pushed Jonathan into the river and me, Paul,
Desmond and Jason jumped into the river and saved him. If you talk about a devil the
devil swoops down somewhere in your room and tries to get you to do things. He tries
to get you to hurt the angel in the other ear. The devil sits on my shoulder and he says
things and he flies away and I've killed the devil I have. But he still sometimes whispers
in my ear to tell me naughty things.

When people die I think they go back to God and become an angel. It is true,
I've got a big bible. The angels come at night, they're in the air. They never come
in your house. When my mum dies I'll put some blood in her and she'll stay alive
a bit longer. Cos I don't want her to die. When my Mum dies I might want to go
with her. I'm not too scared to do it you know, I'll do it because I love her, but I'm
not allowed to am I? When she does die she'll become an angel. I'll want to come
and see what she'll be like. I'll wait for her. I'll wait for a long time till I die and
then I'll be the same.

Drew's story: a story about family breakdown, mums and dads

My mum and dad have split up and divorced and I live with my mum. I think they just used to argue a lot and then they didn't get on together. At first they said that they were going to split up for a month or so and if things got better they'd come back together, but things didn't get any better, so they split up.

I think I was only young, about 7, and my mum said we were going away to visit someone, and then after a while, when I got used to it, she said that they had split up. I was really upset and I was crying for about two weeks but I've got used to it cos I go out with my dad every other Saturday, we go out and have a day together and stuff.

I still feel upset about that they've split up. I know that my mum just needs some time on her own and I don't like complaining cos it's not really my mum's fault, it's both their fault together. She decided it would be easier to live on her own and I chose to go with my mum cos I got the choice who to live with. I still love my dad but I just thought I'd find it easier to live with my mum. My dad doesn't like my mum. My mum doesn't like seeing him when he comes to pick me up. She says goodbye in the house, she doesn't come out. She doesn't really want to see him cos it will make her feel really upset for the rest of the day.

I just feel sorry for my mum cos it's not really me that's got the worst of it, it's probably my mum.

I don't really talk about it, I don't really think about it much at home cos now I've just got used to it and it's just a way of life, just living with my mum. When I think about it I get really upset and I don't like it, but I've just learnt not to think about it anymore, cos I really love them both. I still see my dad, I think it helps cos I see him every other weekend. It's quite nice cos I talk to him about what we've done, what I do at home and stuff.

I think that if you speak to someone that hasn't had that happen to them, they don't really know and they just don't really listen cos they don't really know how hurting it can be inside.

For them it was better that they split up, but not for me. I'd like to have them back, but I know it would hurt my mum and dad, cos that's just really thinking about myself.

I'm a bit sad and a bit disappointed, not in them, but I'm just a bit disappointed that my dad's not going to come back and be friends with my mum, cos I wouldn't want him to move in and live with me. Well, I'd like to, but that wouldn't be fair, but I'd still like them to be friends.

My dad used to be a bit sort of strict on my mum, if my mum wanted to buy clothes and like dresses and that, my dad wouldn't like her getting them, he'd get a bit cross if he didn't like them and things, so in a way he was sort of trying to not let her buy anything that he didn't want her to buy, what he didn't like. I think that's wrong because if someone likes something it's not up to the other person, cos it's her own thing, her own life and I don't see you should stop someone living their own life.

That can become a problem when you get married and live together and have children because if you don't agree with each other's way of life, then you just don't get on very well. I think you have to agree to each other's ways to be friends.

I think, before getting married, they should just spend some time with each other, see how they get on, if they like each other and the way they do things. I think they should live together for a bit, not like having children or get married or anything, just live with each other for a bit and then if they didn't like each other's ways they can go, they can split up again before they hurt anyone else, like their children or something. Because the children get really hurt, cos they feel that their mum and dad don't really love each other and the child doesn't know which one to take sides with and they feel really awkward. If they shout back at their mum then they'd hurt their mum's feelings cos their mum would feel that they're on their dad's side and the other way round.

Harpel's story: a story about toys, school and religion

I really care about my teddy at home. Every time my teddy and me cuddle it makes me go to sleep a lot faster than I normally do. I got it from Chessington in these horrid machines. I put 20p in and there is a big kind of hand, a kind of metal hand and I pressed these two buttons and when I'm confident that it can land I press a red button and the hand goes down and grabs the teddy. Nearly everywhere I go to do some betting I take it with me, it brings me good luck.

When my Mum does the cleaning up, Mum puts it away or it'll get lost. When my teddy gets dirty I put it in the washing machine so it comes out nice and clean. I've had it for two years and it is still in good condition. I take my teddy to bed everyday. When I wash it, I wash it in the morning and then put in the boiler and by about when it goes night when I go to bed, it be nice and dry. I wash him when he gets dirty, about every two days. It's important that he's in good condition because if he wasn't, I wouldn't keep him. Now he looks like my brother really.

He helps me go to sleep because I cuddle him and he's nice and furry. Since I had George I've never had a nightmare. I used to get nightmares when I watched like scary films when I was younger. But now I have George and I'm getting a bit older. He brings me luck too, I don't know how really, you just look at him and bet, and it brings you good luck. Like he helps me win money playing cards. If I lost George I'd get another George. If it brings me luck, then I'll be happy. People knows that if they laughs at my teddy, I'll just have to sort them out. My teddy is important because it makes me feel happy. I call him George because of the way he looks—he's kind of browny, with a nose, tie and big ears. He's furry and he makes me happy every time I squeeze his tummy and he makes a noise.

Me and my friends are gangsters, we're the originals, we're original, you can't never mess with us. Some gangsters are outside in the playground, our friends, they go to this school, they're in my class. I'm their boss, they don't mess with me.

I care about this school. Most schools have like Christian people in most schools, only in this school you have like most Indians at this school and Muslims close together. We don't have a uniform, but we're gonna get a uniform, we're voting now so we have to write if we want one.

I like playing music, we practice this kinda Indian, kinda Sikh stuff. I'm Sikh and Asian.

Interjeet's story: a story about family and ambition

I'm eleven, I got only four sisters. I'm the eldest in my family, I have to look after everyone and I have to clean the house and stuff by myself because my other sister is quite naughty and when I say to her 'do the hoovering' she won't listen to me and then I have to do it myself. If you're the eldest you get treated good really because if my dad sees my sister being naughty he doesn't let them be naughty. My dad wants my sisters to listen to me, whatever I say.

We speak English sometimes at home, but my granddad says to me 'speak in Punjabi in the house'. It's important to speak Punjabi cos it's our mother tongue. I care about the adults, I care about like, old people and all that, cos they're quite old and their bones go and sometimes they need care and help, like my granddad.

When I'm older I'd like to be a solicitor, my dad wants me to be a solicitor, he goes 'at the school all your teachers give you a good report and that and I want you to be something', and he goes, 'what do you want to be?' At first I thought I'd be a doctor right, and then I goes, 'no, you have to do all the operations and cut all the tummies up' and then I thought I might be a solicitor.

I don't want to get married because you have to leave your mum and dad and you have to go to another house and you have to try and get mixed up with them, like it's completely starting a new life. I don't know if I could be a solicitor as well, I wish I could though.

Each of the next four stories are followed by the responses made by adults.

Victoria's story: a story about family, death and heaven

I think that in heaven you can ride a white pony and have marshmallows. Before my Nan died she told me lots of things because she knew she was going to die and she told me all about the things she was going to do and she said she was going to send me a postcard.

She said she would be happy and she wanted me to be happy when she died. On that day she got a picture of her and all the family, stuck it on a postcard and wrote on the back, 'I'll see you in your heart'. Now she's always with me. Now I talk to her all the time. I talk to her when I'm lonely. When I've argued with my friends I go and sit on the wall and think about her and talk to her. When I get fed up I sit there and talk to her about my friends. She tells me that she's riding on things. She says she's having a really nice time. She says she's going to ring me up. She says things in my head, she rings up my brain and talks to me. When she went up in heaven she took one of her special secrets. She took it with her and she can just ring me up, it's clever. This special secret makes her able to do that.

I keep on wanting to tell people things but they don't understand. I know everyone's in heaven who has died. Grandma tells me. She works in a cleaners. She washes all the clouds in heaven. She's got lots and lots of friends in heaven. She hopes we'll stay alive a long time but she wants me to go up there to see her. I'd like to go and see her but if you go up there you've got to stay there. You can't go unless you've died. Heaven is high, high in the sky, it's higher than space.

*I've never worried about these things. I just keep it in my heart. It's not a problem.
It makes me quite sad they [people] don't believe. But when God talks to them they will
know. We are very, very lucky that just some people care in this world. Like me and my
friends and everybody in this school. I hope we care. We keep this planet going. I think
heaven is part of this planet.*

*My Nan was burnt when she died, cremated. I think that's better than worms coming
in your coffin.*

Responses to Victoria's story

> I wondered about the first loss
> And what that led to
> At each stage
> I thought of consequences
> And how to live with them
> Truthfully
> Where it might all end up
> And I was grateful

'My Gran was great—annoying and stubborn but a genuine person who led a hard
life. Her main characteristics were her East Bristol accent, her strong tea, her
considerable girth and her memories of past life and of her husband. She did not go
out very much in later years, until eventually she *never* went out, and I visited every
Saturday. She made it clear in her nineties that when her time came, she was under
no circumstances to be taken to hospital and she wanted to remain at home—not
go to the workhouse. She became ill with various worrying aches and pains and after
some dizzy spells and falls she was carted off to hospital before we had a chance to
stop them. When she returned home, we assured her that this would never happen
again and we worked out a way of insuring this. Eventually she became very ill and
was confined to bed. We stayed with her in shifts and gave her morphine when she
needed it. One morning we have a phone call that she was on the way out. We went
over and held her hand. She said my name and then became distant and she died.
I have a photo of her making tea, and I said a poem at her funeral.'

Bradley's story: a story about special places, family and separation

*The estate is fine because there is a playground, trees to climb and thousands of mates
to play with. Not all my friends live on the estate. My brother doesn't, he lives up in
Scotland. I've got a long way to go and see him, I normally see him twice a year in
Scotland.*

*I like playing on the swings in the park. It feels like a rocket going backwards and
forwards up on the air. I like playing on the trees as well. The swings are different if you
shut your eyes. If you shut your eyes on the swing it feels scary. It's black and it looks
like you're in space. Sometimes it feels like I'm going to Scotland on my swing—whoosh!
And then when I get to Scotland I'm going to look for my brother.*

When I'm in a special place I like to think of special people, even though they're not there, like I think of my brother in Scotland, even though he's not there.

I miss my Dad. My Mum married again because he's too busy with someone. I've another Dad called Steve. My Mum and Dad fight. I live with my Mum and Steve cos my Dad chucked my Mum on the floor head first.

Response to Bradley's story

'Though I lived at the seaside I still liked visiting my cousins in Bletchley because there was a 'rec'—no-one used to know what I meant when I said I like the rec —because I didn't know it was short for recreation ground. I loved the swings and the roundabouts. I've always loved movement—though sometimes the big boys would scare me when they made the roundabout go round too fast though it was exciting! Like Bradley I liked playing on the swings; it always soothed me—like when I was very young and used to rock to and fro in bed. When I was swinging I felt everything was possible, and sort of all-right.

I loved climbing trees. Even now when I look at a tree I find myself assessing it for climb-ability! I used to sit at the top of a tree and watch people, and just rest there and think. No-one else I knew seemed to like to be up in a tree as much as I did. Even when I was a student (in my forties) and 'regressed' somewhat, I found a tree leaning over the river, with a mossy branch just inviting me to lie along it, poised over the water—and I did.

I find the stories about Mums and Dads separating very difficult, evokes guilty feelings in me and I wonder what my own children went through. I'm glad they both get on so well with Brian. I feel angry with John my first husband that he doesn't seem to care much about them.'

Dalvinder's story

I had a car accident and I was in a coma, I was in the dark and didn't wake up and you know, I saw God in my dream and he said that you're going to be alright cos you're going to be in that coma for two or three weeks, until you come back. And he goes 'I'm going to be saying things and you're going to remember it for the rest of your life'.

When I recovered I remembered everything and I wrote it down in my book at home. My Mum asked 'what are you doing?' and I told her that when I had that accident I saw God in my dream. My Mum told me to write it down and give it to her so that I can remember it as well. I've got it at home, the things God said. He said that 'you know that in your future, when you're 15 your Mum's going to let you get married and when you're 19, you're going to become a footballer.'

I'm the best in my year. If I become a footballer I'm going to buy a massive, 32-storey company in New York. I'm going to come down here and play my football and when the season's over, I'm going go down and fly out to New York, and control my business there and if I'm not there, I'm going to let my secretary take over, or my wife.

Response to Dalvinder's story

'I had a car accident and I thought I was going to die. Everything went very very slowly. I felt incredibly peaceful and strangely unafraid. I just thought—so that's it. The present moment stretched and then there was a bang. The car, which had been rolling over, stopped, and having automatically and without thought climbed out of it, I was back in the real world and very much alive and aware of the danger. The car was on fire and my sister was in it. I was then suddenly afraid, practical and focused. I didn't wobble until she was out.'

Emma's story

I'm nine years old and I was born in Birmingham. I like living here in Southampton, it's better than Birmingham. I've got a lot of friends here. When we lived in Redditch I had tons of friends but they used to play with knives, that's why my Mum moved, cos it was very violent.

My sister Donna is sixteen and goes to college. I've got two Dads cos the one up in Redditch had an argument with my Mum. He said that she had to go, so my Mum just grabbed any clothes and me and we zoomed down. She took me first and then she had to get Donna. Now I've got this Dad down here and they're married, he's better than my other Dad.

I used to run off, I used to go to my friends a couple of roads back and sleep there for a couple of days. I said to Mum 'I'm going down my friends, if you need me come down, you know which house I'm in', I was only seven! My Mum used to come down and fetch me in about a week when everything was over. My sister used to go to her friends as well to get away from the arguments.

My Dad used to go up in Birmingham to see his Mum cos she lived up there you see, and my Mum used to stay at home. I used to go home when I saw him go, you know for a couple of days. So I went back, so did my sister and when he came back we went back up to our friends and then my Mum would come and fetch us later.

Things were much more different when we got down here, but once or twice my Uncle got drunk. He got drunk once and he smashed a door and he smashed the window. He was going to hit my Mum down the stairs and when he got close up, I put my fist up and went like that and he backed off, he was scared. That was about a week ago I'd say, he gets drunk a lot, every two weeks. When my Dad's there he tells my Uncle to leave the children alone and go to bed and then he pushes him up the stairs. My Uncle is younger than my Dad, he's been my Uncle for a couple of years, he's related to my old Dad, but my old Dad didn't like him. My new Dad down here likes him. When my Dad gets paid he just gets a little bit tipsy and he bangs around upstairs so I can't get to sleep!

My Aunty is twenty-seven and she's my Mum's sister. She picks me up from school cos my Mum's always busy, like she's got to go shopping to do. There's my Aunty and Uncle and me and Donna and my Mum, she's our first Mum you see, we haven't got another Mum.

Donna calls my Dad here, John, she don't call him Dad cos she still thinks of that other one I got as Dad, but I call him Dad. She likes my other Dad but I don't like him. Both my Dads get drunk a lot but my old Dad used to slam the doors and smash the windows and when my Mum was trying to get Donna back, the stupid thing he done, he took an overdose and he got my sister really het up. She doesn't want to live with my old Dad now.

I know the things what I don't enjoy, I don't enjoy sports. I used to but not now cos my legs get tired. I like reading. I go to a majorettes club, it's fun, I enjoy doing that. I can stand on my head, my Dad taught me how to do it, and he taught me cartwheels. I'm going to go into gymnastics cos I can do loads of stuff. I love school. I like writing, reading and PE. It's good cos you do everything, you do something different everyday.

I used to live near Church Street, there was a park down there and you always get all the bullies down there. But there's not really a lot of bullying, not round this area or this school. In the other school I used to go to there was all quite a lot of bullying.

There's a church down there as well. My family go to church, but I don't go, I'm the one who stays at home with the pets. I've got a dog who's an Alsatian, he's quite a good dog actually, and I've got two kittens. We've got seven fish and I've got some stick insects. My Mum and my Dad and my Uncle and my Aunty and my sister go to the church, but I stay at home, it's only down the road. I don't like going like to church, I went once but didn't like it, it was boring. I only went once because I thought it might be good but it weren't. So my Mum and Dad are Christian but I'm not, my Nan didn't want me to be a Christian, I don't know why.

We've got a book where you show your hand and read it. I can read my hand, I'm definitely going to live for quite a long time cos I've got a strong line. I'm going to have four children cos if you look there's four lines going down my hand. I'm not going to get married cos it says there. You can still get a man and have kids you know, I just won't get married. It wouldn't matter to my Mum. Maybe my sister isn't going to get married but I am, it says so in my hand.

My parents don't want me to marry an Indian boy, they want me to marry a white boy, we know which one, Sam . . ., he lives in Church Street. He's strong, when you see him, you wouldn't have fight with him.

Response to Emma's story

'Memories triggered by part of it.

When I was younger my father used to drink heavily—come home drunk at night frequently.

I remember the fear—lying in bed listening to his car coming up the path. Waiting for him to come upstairs and get me to move into my parents bed with my mother, and he'd sleep in my bed.

Feelings of hatred for my dad—wishing he'd die—wanting something to happen so that the problem would go away as I didn't want them to split up—that just didn't happen in our families at that time.'

Your response

We suggest that you, the reader, choose a story, either an original one or one that has been produced as a response, and that you respond with a response of your own. If you wish to you can do this by responding to a story on our website, www.cwvp.cliche.ac.uk. You can also ask children to respond similarly.

11 Reading pictures and telling stories

Clive Erricker

Using visual art is another way of stimulating narrative response. Art involves affective expression and communication in a way that writing often does not. Using pictures and images invites responses based on feelings and emotions. However in order to do this a certain process, with clear strategies, is required. An example is given below. We call this the process of engagement.

This sort of engagement reflects Benjamin's (1970:80–2) idea of translation, and being 'powerfully affected by the foreign tongue' (ibid.:81). It also relates to Hayden White's (1985:4) distinction between dialectical and diatactical. The former interpretative model (dialectical) presumes the outcome to be one of resolving ambiguity in relation to knowledge: we have refined our understanding and can be said to know what we did not know before. The second model (diatactical) seeks to uncover the complexity of interpretation that arises with engagement. Here the work of art does not ask us to resolve interpretative differences about what it means or what it is about. Rather, by engaging with it in a diatactical way (touching and being touched by) the work gains meaning or value for us. The process of engagement can be broken down into the following strategies:

- Observe
- Express
- Enter
- Relate
- Translate
- Re-present
- Comment

We do not wish to spell out what these terms mean in a sense disassociated from the enactment of the process itself. Rather we must try to use the strategies and see what happens. However, what is meant by 'translation' and 're-presentation' may benefit from a brief commentary.

Taking account of Walter Benjamin's observations, here translation means taking what we have understood in one specific context—historical, geographical, artistic—and applying it to our own, using appropriate strategies. Re-

Figure 7 © Italian soldier, Nicosia, 1943 by Robert Capa by arrangement with Magnum Photos.

presentation means understanding how we can represent the feelings or issues that the artist has conveyed in the specifics of his or her work into the relationships and environments of our own life, through the understanding registered in our response. Thus translation and re-presentation work as a means of conversation and re-expression, or counter-expression, between us and the artists with whom we engage, including those within our learning community—a meeting of minds and an exchange of experiences, to use Benjamin's expression. This in turn creates the dynamics of hermeneutical activity in the classroom: the process of poetic interpretation.

Geoff Dyer (1999) gives us an example of this process applied to a photograph by Robert Capa (Figure 7).

Italian Soldier, Nicosia, 1943

Within Robert Capa's photographic oeuvre there is the famous picture of a soldier walking along a rural lane (Figure 7). Close by his side, with her body inclined towards him and her long hair draping her shoulders, is a young woman. She is pushing a man's bike. They are not hurrying and are clearly engrossed in their togetherness. Geoff Dyer comments on his encounter with this photograph in his article 'Hearing is Believing' (Dyer 1998:5). He considers two captions that have been given to it in different sources. The first says 'Italian soldier after end of fighting, Sicily, 1943', the second says 'Near Nicosia, Sicily, July 28, 1943. An Italian soldier straggling behind a column of his captured comrades as they march off to POW camp'. The traditional historical question is 'Which of the two captions is correct?', but the visual truth of the photo pushes the circumstances in which it was taken beyond the edge of the frame, out of sight. Following Dyer's example, we can ' "crop" the narrative [caption] to concentrate on the story contained by the image, to transcribe the caption *inscribed* within it' (ibid.). Dyer goes on to do just this. The questions he asks are to do with how he can engage with the evocations of the image as Capa presented it and how to create the story of the relationship, intentions and concerns of the two figures in a temporal sense that extends beyond the moment of the image itself. He also places himself within the frame of the photo, identifying with the soldier in the circumstance. 'Noticing these things fills me with longing. I want to *be* that soldier' (ibid.). To understand fully the nature of his engagement it is necessary to read the short article, but the point is this: he could have sought to understand the photo as an historical source to be investigated in relation to its captions. Instead he chose to approach it as a work of existential art, pregnant with possible meanings for the viewer that go beyond the specifics of its situation. This is not to suggest that his interpretation is not reliant on some understanding of what the situation meant for the figures captured in the frame and the photographer who framed the shot. However, whilst there is a sense in which the latter is dependent on some historical information, it is required for servicing the aim of existential engagement in the work of art, not for any 'factual' purpose in itself.

We can extend Dyer's reflections to ask, 'If we were to try to find a moment when we have been close to someone in the way the two people in the picture are close and represent it in our life, what would it be? We can then try to re-present this in our own way. Whether or not we are good artists is not the point. However we can be helped to do this by becoming aware of the way in which intimacy is evoked in the photograph: in line, form and composition. These are, if you like, the literal ingredients of intimacy; the way we recognise its presence.

We can now move on to apply our process to another work.

The Raising of Lazarus and the Face of Christ

Figures 8 and 9 show details of a fresco in Chichester Cathedral that dates from the twelfth century and depicts the raising of Lazarus. The size of the individual figures varies in accordance with the importance of their status within the narrative (there is no sense of perspective in the work that can indicate this). As with Dyer's captions above, we can provide our own caption, based on the story of the raising of Lazarus, and read the artwork from acquaintance with the story. This would provide a map of its composition and the characters involved. However, proceeding beyond this and applying our strategies we can observe the scene with greater personal engagement and give expression to what we see in terms of its overall character and detail. This is a more reflexive activity in which we recognise our response as well as what we are responding to. What is it that catches our eye? Where is our gaze led? Where do we find the vitality of the scene? What characters and details are involved in this? What draws our attention and what puzzles us? What do we want to know more about? What are these characters thinking and feeling? What emotions are present and for whom? What feelings, thoughts and emotions arise within us? Expressing these observations amounts to recognising our engagement with the work. Entering takes us one step further. Where am I in this scene? What questions do I want to ask of the characters? What is my understanding of what is happening? What is the artist trying to tell me and where do I find the clues to that? What is my relationship with these characters? Who can I relate to and what do I want to do in this situation? Relating the responses to these questions and others that arise is a retelling of the story with me present. Translating and re-presenting moves me away from the literal event depicted. Where have I found that which I have been confronted with in my reading of the picture in my own life? How can I tell that story and relate it to this one—if at all? What has this story caused me to remember?

It is necessary for us, as teachers, to engage with this process before we can offer it to our pupils. In undertaking it myself I arrived at the following commentary on the picture.

Commentary

The focus is on Christ, especially his facial expression—this is the clue to the

Figure 8 The face of Christ (*detail*). (Reproduced by kind permission of the Dean and Chapter of Chichester. ©Judges Postcards Ltd, Hastings.)

meaning of the whole depiction and to which I am drawn. The value of this piece lies in the skill of the artist and his capacity to relate to the human concern in the story which transcends the strictures of doctrine. He accomplishes this in the way he has crafted the expression on the face, although in other details the message of the church is clear, for example in the doctrinal gesture of Christ's fingers. Thus the depiction of the face of Christ is an image to which I can relate

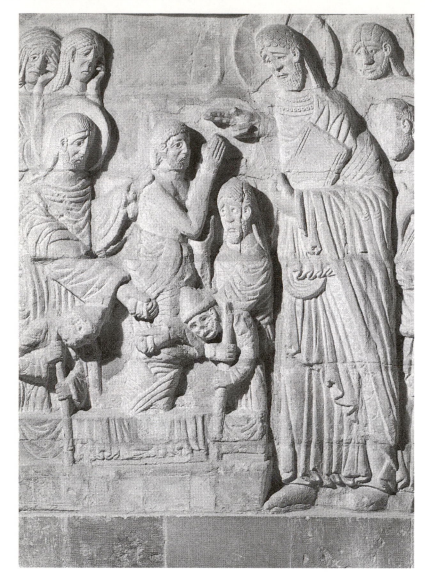

Figure 9 The raising of Lazarus. (Reproduced by kind permission of the Dean and Chapter of Chichester. © Judges Postcards Ltd, Hastings.)

regardless of faith stance; it appeals to my human sensibilities. I want to know what awareness lies behind such profound concern and what has animated the fear on the faces of Martha and Mary, who are also in the scene. This is not to say we have to disregard the gospel narrative, which gives the event a particular significance in a Christian context. But to say that is not a pre-requisite of engagement.

What in my experience has caused me to feel a sense of solidarity and moved me so deeply? I note the way in which lines in the depiction move from the centre down to the bottom corners, and the way in which the face maintains its presence through the solidity of its structure, suggesting resilience and perseverance in the face of suffering. I can enter into, reflect on, translate and re-express the qualities I have found in relation to our own experience—a translation of the spiritual impact of the image. My own translation and re-presentation forces me to reconsider the impact of mortality: it is not just Lazarus who is raised, but also me. The gravitas in Christ's features does not necessarily allow me to overcome death, but at least I will not be spiritually annihilated by it. I can relate the stories of suffering and hope, fear and resolve in my own life and those around me. I wonder what stories the artist had to tell that allowed him to express these feelings with such force.

It seems to me that in the crafting of the facial expression we can locate the 'signature' of the artist. Signature is the term Derrida uses (Ulmer 1985:63–4) to describe the way in which we appropriate the reading of something for ourselves. Derrida refers to this as de-composition. The signature of the artist, we might say, lies in the opportunity he has taken to express his own faith relationship with the event he has crafted in relation to the tradition he is representing. In this he goes beyond ideology, he transcends formal creedal and symbolic expression in order to interpolate his own response and make that available to the reader. This is the point at which I find myself engaging with the story he wishes to record, at an affective level. The spiritual dynamics of the work are released in this signature, by freeing the work from the ideological rhetoric in which it would otherwise be confined. With his eyes downcast and his lips formed into a sensuous but sorrowful curve, Christ expresses pity for our human condition. This expression of sympathy allows us to reflect on the experiences in our own life that have generated the same feeling.

Then this can create a discussion in the reverse direction. Having started with what might produce such an expression, and what we might be looking upon—what situation we might be in, in relation to our own experience—we can end with a consideration of the scene itself and the function it performed for the contemporary viewer. The point is that the context is provided by the caption i.e. by how we frame the visual text. We can provide different readings accordingly. As one rabbi remarked to me when looking at the face without its context 'For a Jew this would be the face of Moses'. There is a sense in which contextualisation is epistemologically everything but spiritually perhaps of less relevance.

This process of engagement does not mitigate against the routine development of knowledge found within the curriculum subjects of RE and art, in this case. But it does severely question what has educational priority. These processes of investigation into values and the spiritual take time. This is precisely because of the emphasis placed on reflection in relation to existential concerns (both of which are significant motivations for faith and art). Yet they impinge only peripherally, if at all, in the curriculum subjects themselves. The excuses for why this is the case range from lack of time, to lack of competence in teachers, to the inappropriateness of raising such issues with children. If such defences are maintained we cannot really claim that we are concerned with spiritual education and values education as aims that underpin the curriculum and institutionalised education itself.

We translate, represent and express in order to create meaning and locate ourselves. It is the creative process of doing this that brings insight and allows us to relate to one another and to ourselves in a deeper and more complex way. This goes beyond any technical judgement on what we produce and ensures that what we do produce is as 'good', skilful, informed and reflective as it can be. It contains our signature; it is not important that our signature may change in the course of enquiry and circumstance.

Your response

Before asking pupils to embark on this sort of activity, try engaging in a narrative way with one of the above images, or with a chosen image of your own, and produce your own commentary.

12 Enactive storytelling

Clive Erricker

This chapter extends the engagement with art in the previous chapter to considering the use of story and ritual for similar narrative purposes. We can regard written or oral texts (stories), ritual, and artistic expression (in the sense of visual art) as part of a common language (though different in form) used for similar purposes: to communicate effectively and affectively. The first example employs ritual as its focus.

Goodbye Joe: practice in narration about death

Helping children come to terms with death is increasingly difficult in a secular and stressful age. The following activity provides a comparatively safe and emotionally secure scenario in which children can explore their feelings about loss. As with all our activities, it is a starting point for the narration of a personal biography, and should be allowed to go in that direction if the children so wish.

It is said that after experiencing the death of someone close to you, you are never the same again; and that a sense of sharing occurs between those who have been through it, even though the experiences have occurred quite separately. There is also often a lingering feeling that you never said goodbye properly and that when the moment occurred you were quite unable, in the sudden impact of the event, to know how to say goodbye. The rite—burial or cremation—is left to the professionals and has no power because it does not engage with the physical fact of the dead person, and the sense of loss is present but not expressed. A friend of mine expressed his frustration in the following way:

> Death should not be a ceremony with the body or coffin as a focal point to say goodbye. It should be made a celebration of the life of the person, including their achievements. Maybe photographs of each stage of the person's life should be enlarged and displayed so that the person is remembered for what he or she was, not a spiritless corpse in a box. Let us enjoy the remembrance of the spirit.

What has this frustration to do with the education of our children? It may seem rather morbid to ask children to consider their own mortality, but—as with all existential issues—it lies at the heart of religious, personal, social, spiritual and moral education. The following activity is a way of starting to explore these issues.

Activity: living and dying

- Go out into the school field and find some things that were living but are now dead, for example a leaf, a piece of wood from a tree, a shrivelled apple, a dead insect.
- Put the objects in the middle of a table and sit round them in groups.
- Decide which object you think is the best thing you have found and write a story about your life as a leaf, an apple or a piece of wood.
- Share your stories about your life as the object. The most important aspect of this part of the activity is the children listening to each other. If each pupil is listened to attentively, they will talk about their story as best they can. If this does not happen they will lapse into the notion that the activity is silly, embarrassing and not serious.
- Create a ceremony that reflects on the qualities of the life of your object as a way of saying goodbye to it.

When this activity was conducted with eight- and nine-year-old children in a school, they made up stories and poems such as the following:

My Life as a Leaf

There I was a leaf in a tree
All snuggled up as warm as could be
I was just sitting there all happy and warm
Then all of a sudden along came a storm.
I was blown and tossed everywhere
I was blown in circles but the wind didn't care
The wind didn't care if I had a cold or the flu
It didn't care but I think it knew.
I was blown into a pool of wet stuff
Then all of a sudden as if this wasn't enough
It started to rain and it started to hail
It tipped it down and the wind started to wail.
I was blown up again into the sky
I was blown on top of the world and I started to fly
I was blown through the air through the cloud, through the fog
Until I was blown right down under a log.
I was sitting under log all happy and warm
Next to my mates all blown here from the storm
I was sitting there as happy as can be
Then the wind blew me into a tree.

(Katy, aged 8)

What follows is one example of the ceremonies that the children performed. This one was for a dead leaf that they called Joe. This is how Lyndsey described it:

> Yesterday my class went outside and found something that was alive but's dead. Emma and Louise found a dead leaf and called it Joe. They had a ceremony for Joe. They put some water in a coffin because he was a sailer then put him in. They took him out a crushed him and put him back in. Then they prayed. They sat in a circle and they said goodbye. Then they buried him. They put mud on top of him and put his family on top and stuck a branch in the middle.

The actual ceremony was performed like this.

- The class sat in a circle. The children in the group carried the leaf round the class in an open box. They did this three times.
- The first time we were asked to blow on it to remind ourselves of the wind of spring blowing and helping it to grow.
- The second time we poured water—which had been blessed by having been blown on—on the leaf.
- Each person poured a little libation.
- The third time we simply said goodbye in whatever way we decided was appropriate for us.
- At the end there was a rocking ceremony to represent the wind blowing and the branches swaying. We passed by the open box with the water and the leaf in it, in turn blowing on the water and leaf as two of the group rocked it to and fro.

After the ceremonies there was discussion about what had been most effective in their ceremonies and what should now be done with the objects. The stories and ceremonies had opened up relationships with the things that had been chosen to represent the passing of living things into death, and the children had tried to develop respect for these once living things. It was agreed that beneath a tree in the grounds was an appropriate place to bury the objects. The children buried them and found that it was important to be able to identify exactly where each object was buried, so they found a means to mark each spot. Afterwards there was a discussion about how they would feel if the place was dug up to make a football pitch or a car park, or if other children trampled on it. It was now a different, more significant space. The children decided to let the rest of the school know, in an assembly, that this place needed to be respected in a new way.

Response

Having read this account the most important task is to recognise what personal associations the issue brings to your mind and the ceremonies associated with them. Reflect on these and perhaps write them down. Then consider how you could introduce, use and adapt the above process.

Temple bells: using an interactive story

As has been expressed previously, our education system has long favoured the idea that learning is a rational activity and that knowing is being informed about a world 'out there', whether in the past or the present. If we try to understand things differently we might say that learning starts and ends with understanding ourselves and others in a relational way and that this is to do with the mind. The mind has two facets that are not entirely distinct from one another: the rational and the emotional (or affective). Therefore we can speak of rational and emotional intelligence. How do we get in touch with these, develop them and bring them together? The answer is that imagination or imaging is the vehicle for doing this. This puts imagination at the centre of educating and, in the sense that we normally use the term, suggests that we must get in touch with our hearts as well as our minds to do this.

We need to encourage reflection on the way in which we all unconsciously use story, symbol and ritual in our own lives, whatever age we are. Once we start to do this we shall begin to understand how others do it in their spiritual and religious life. The process does not change, the elements are the same, only the literal things—the actual stories, things, actions—are different. Put another way, people are not strange because they are different from us, nor are they strange because we do not understand them, they are only strange because we do not understand ourselves and ourselves in relation to others. The aim is to look beyond the literal world of things or appearances as they present themselves to us, and see how these are an expression of making sense of the world.

Activity: the story of The Temple Bells

The following is one example of a method that can be used to achieve what has been described above. The important thing is that the learning is active, by which I mean not just that the listener should be doing things in a literal sense, but also that the telling engages the mind of the listener. It must involve the creation of a story, symbol and ritual in a way that relates to our experience. The aim of the activity is to tell a story in such a way that it moves from the teller (the teacher) to the listeners, so that they can then be the storytellers.

'The Temple Bells' is a story by Anthony de Mello that appears in his book *The Song of the Bird* (1982). This is reproduced below and is followed by my reworking of the story to make it more suitable for the interactive activity.

> *The temple was built on an island and it held a thousand bells. Bells big and small, fashioned by the finest craftsmen in the world. When the wind blew or a storm raged, all the bells would peal out in a symphony that would send the heart of the hearer into raptures.*

But over the centuries the island sank into the sea and, with it, the temple bells. An ancient legend said that the bells continued to peal out, ceaselessly, and could be heard by anyone who would listen. Inspired by this legend, a young man traveled thousands of miles, determined to hear those bells. He sat for days on the shore, facing the vanished island, and listened with all his might. But all he could hear was the sound of the sea. He made every effort to block it out. But to no avail; the sound of the sea seemed to flood the world.

He kept at his task for weeks. Each time he got disheartened he would listen to the village pundits, who spoke with unction of the mysterious legend.
Then his heart would be aflame . . . only to become discouraged again when weeks of further effort yielded no results.

Finally he decided to give up the attempt. Perhaps he was not destined to hear the bells. Perhaps the legend was not true. It was his final day, and he went to the shore to say goodbye to the sea and the sky and the wind and the coconut trees. He lay on the sand, and for the first time, listened to the sound of the sea. Soon he was so lost in the sound that he was barely conscious of himself, so deep was the silence that the sound produced.

In the depth of that silence, he heard it! The tinkle of a tiny bell followed by another, and another and another . . . and soon every one of the thousand temple bells was pealing out in harmony, and his heart was rapt in joyous ecstasy.

Do you wish to hear the temple bells? Listen to the sound of the sea.

Do you wish to catch a glimpse of God? Look intently at creation.

(From *The Song of the Bird* by Anthony de Mello, ©1982 by Anthony de Mello, S.J. Used by permission of Doubleday, a division of Random House, Inc.)

*　　*　　*

When he was young a boy used to be read a bedtime story about a temple, and because it was his favourite story his parents read it to him again and again. The story was about a temple with a thousands bells in a far-off land. When the bells rang they made the most beautiful sound in all the world, and people came from all over the world to hear them. As the boy grew older this story stayed with him. But in the story the temple was destroyed by a huge wave and the ruins were carried to the bottom of the sea. Yet, so it was said, it was still possible to hear the bells if you sat on the shore and listened patiently and silently enough. When he grew up the boy set off to hear these bells. He travelled a long distance to the island, where he sat quietly on the beach to hear this most beautiful of sounds. For a whole year he sat there every day, but all he heard was the sound of the gulls in the air, the wind in the trees and the waves on the shore. After a year he decided to go home, disappointed. But before he did he went to the beach to sit for one last time and listen to the sounds with which he had become so familiar and had come to love: the gulls, the wind and the waves. As he did so, sitting silently and still, he heard the most beautiful sound he had ever heard.

After telling the story ask the listeners to do the following:

- Close your eyes and go back through the story in your mind.
- Choose your favourite moment.
- Put your hands out, palms up, next to one another.
- Transfer your favourite moment from your mind into your hands and close them together.
- Turn to the person next to you and tell them what you have in your hands, and why.
- Discuss your conversations with the whole class, if you wish, and explain why you chose the moment you did.

When telling the story, you can introduce moments when everyone can close their eyes and silently imagine the sounds and images; in other words, use the story as a form of meditation. The purpose of the ritual and sharing, at the end, is to transfer the story to the listeners and encourage them to link it to their own experiences and reflections. This can then lead into further expressive and creative activities.

At the end of the story and activity that follows it I sometimes distribute a shell to each of the listeners and say that they can now tell the story to someone else by using the shell. Thus the story can start from the object, which has become a symbol or image by virtue of embodying a story.

Sometimes I do not tell the ending, but ask the listeners to imagine their own ending. Did they hear the bells? Over time and with many tellings the story has come to incorporate embellishments, for example a cafe/inn where the boy stayed when he first arrived on the island, people in the cafe whom the boy asked if they had ever heard the bells and so on. This has involved the listeners role-playing these people. The responses then become incorporated into the next telling of the story and so on. The important thing, of course, is not the particular story, nor the specific activities, but the process employed, and adapting the content and the telling to the age of the group and their responses. The above is just a beginning. If you can relate to the story, give it a try and see what happens. Start by taking yourself through the process and noting the associations that the story brings to mind from your own experience.

The Prodigal Son: a purposive use of parable

This story is well known for its catechetical use in Christian nurture and for its value as an instructive moral tale. I wish to use it to neither of these effects.

Following the principles of the process employed above it can become a striking literary and dramatic device. The purpose of parable, of which this story is an example, is to subvert myth. It makes us reconsider the story in which we live and creates moral tensions and questions (Crossan 1975:11–13, quoted in Cockett 1997:8).

The question is how we can use this parable to that effect when it has already been historically appropriated for religious and moral catechetical service. We need to consider the characters, the events, the plot and the changing emotions as the story progresses, as well as the interlinear (what is not stated but must be presented or raised for discussion as the story unfolds).

The tale of the Prodigal Son may be familiar to us (Luke 15:11–32), but perhaps only as a moral and theological teaching. It tells of the reckless and profligate younger son who demands his inheritance early and then absents himself before returning penniless; the father who accedes to the demand and celebrates his return, repentance and reconciliation; the obedient elder son who is resentful about the younger's return; the absent mother; and the unstated metaphor of God's unconditional acceptance of the penitent sinner.

How is this to be dealt with? If we enact the tale we can ask: 'where are the tensions within it?' Who feels what towards whom, and why? This needs to be discussed and explored, not just in relation to the characters presented, of whom we have but a thumbnail sketch, but in relation to ourselves. The experiences of resentment, forgiveness, the assertion of rights and shame, the feeling of absence (in gender terms) in the story as presented—these constitute powerful emotions that we can only voice according to our experience of them. Such emotions are the substance of the story and in the telling of our experience of them the story gains an existential vitality—it becomes real and germane. This is not a story about what you should feel or do, but of the difficulties or frictions involved in the feeling and doing. The parable does not resolve these tensions but throws them at us to consider. How can we deal with the emotional messiness of this and still arrive at reconciliation? Act and talk it out and see. There is no simple answer, and possibly no answer at all, but in raising the issues we address the conflicts. That is progress in learning, but not an acceptance *per se* of a cautionary tale. The difference is that which exists between narrative exposition and ideological circumscription. This means that we have to regard the story as a literary and pedagogical tool rather than as canonical or moral advice.

We can use the strategies used for the Temple Bells story as a way of entering this one—we can travel through the story, the characters and their emotions. But here we are asking which characters and moments we identified with most in order to provoke discussion about moral issues and relational tensions, rather than relive times in which we felt secure, affirmed or empowered by events, or the simple rightness of certain qualities and values.

If we take a common Christian interpretation of the parable—that we are presented with God as the forgiving father—we must investigate the implications of this. If we understand this to mean the need to confess our errors and emulate the capacity for forgiveness, then it must be applied to our own experiences. It is a hard teaching in practice—what do we find to be its merits and our difficulties? For Christians, this can act as guidance in discipleship and offer a way of coming closer to God, but beyond the knowledge of what the Christian understanding(s) of the merits of the parable are, given its scriptural status, we must ask what merits it has as a narrative on which to reflect, deserving of a place in a 'non-denominational' spiritual and moral education that gives no particular status to narratives and teachings because they are 'religious'.

Your response

Take another parable or use the one above and apply the suggested learning strategies and process to yourself. Write down the outcomes and reflect on how this might affect your classroom practice, including issues it raises about which you are not entirely (personally or professionally) confident.

Postscript

When we sat down to write this postscript we intended to consider where this book was meant to take you, the reader, and where it was meant *not* to take you. We thought we should make some grand statement about hoping that we had achieved our aim of making you see education in a different light and participate in education as teacher or learner in a different way. However, in keeping with our vision of the process of learning, we realise that we cannot write this postscript. The only person who can is you, the reader. You have had the experience of reading this book, you have had the experiences leading to your reading of the book. What you make of it is your own individual construct, and what will follow depends on the way you relate your construct to others.

References

Introduction

Erricker, C., Erricker, J., Ota, C., Sullivan, D., and Fletcher M. (1997) *The Education of the Whole Child*. London: Cassell.

1 True stories and other dreams

Allison, D. (1995) *Two or Three Things I Know for Sure*. New York: Plume.

Barnard, H. C. (1961) *A History of English Education from 1760*. London: University of London Press.

Coles, R. (1992) *The Spiritual Life of Children*. London: HarperCollins.

Erricker, C., Erricker, J., Ota, C., Sullivan, D., and Fletcher, M. (1997) *The Education of the Whole Child*. London: Cassell.

Geaves, R. (1998) 'The Borders Between Religions: A Challenge to the World Religions' Approach to Religious Education', *British Journal of Religious Education*, 21(1) pp. 20–31.

Griffiths, J. (1999) 'The Word', *Guardian Saturday Review*, 28 August, p. 9.

Gugliemo, C. and Chartier, R. (eds) (1999) *A History of Reading in the West*. Cambridge: Polity Press.

Hattenstone, S. (1997) 'Kitchen Sink Drama: an Interview with Ken Loach', *Guardian Weekend*, 31 October, pp. 36–40.

Helms, R. (1988) *Gospel Fictions*. Amherst, NY: Prometheus.

Hilton, M. (1997) *Potent Fictions*. London: Routledge.

Holmes, E. (1911) *What is and What Might Be*. London: Constable.

Jung, A. (1987) *Unveiling India: A Woman's Journey*. Harmondsworth: Penguin.

MacIntyre, A. (1988) *Whose Justice? Which Rationality?* London: Duckworth.

SCAA (1994a) *Model Syllabuses for Religious Education: Model 1: Living Faiths Today*. London: School Curriculum and Assessment Authority.

SCAA (1994b) *Model Syllabuses for Religious Education: Model 2: Questions and Teachings*. London: School Curriculum and Assessment Authority.

Schute, C. (1998) *Edmond Holmes and 'The Tragedy of Education'*. Nottingham: Educational Heretics Press.

Smart, N. (1982) 'Foreword' in R. Jackson (ed.), *Approaching World Religions*. London: John Murray.

Thatcher, A. (1996) 'Policing the Sublime: a wholly (holy?) ironic approach to the spiritual development of children', in J. Astley and L. J. Francis (eds), *Christian Theology and Religious Education: Connections and Contradictions*. London: SPCK.

2   A critical review of religious education

Barth, F. (1994) 'A Personal View of Present Tasks and Priorities in Cultural and Social Anthropology', in R. Borofsky (ed.), *Assessing Cultural Anthropology*. New York: McGraw Hill.

Bauman, Z. (1998) 'Postmodern Religion', in P. Heelas (ed.), *Religion, Modernity and Postmodernity*. Oxford: Blackwell.

Bauman, Z. (1999) *Culture as Praxis*. London: Sage.

Bess, M. (1988) 'Interview with Michel Foucault', *History of the Present*. Spring 1988, p. 13.

Bowker, J. (1987) *Licensed Insanities: Religions and belief in God in the contemporary world*. London: Darton, Longman and Todd.

Bowker, J. (1996) 'World Religions: The Boundaries of Belief and Unbelief', in B. Gates (ed.), *Freedom and Authority in Religions and Religious Education*. London: Cassell.

Carrithers, M. (1992) *Why Humans Have Cultures*. Oxford: Oxford University Press.

Clifford, James (1988) *The Predicament of Culture*. Cambridge, Mass.: Harvard University Press.

Copley, T. (1997) *Teaching Religion: Fifty years of religious education in England and Wales*. Exeter: University of Exeter Press.

Cox, E. (1983) *Problems and Possibilities for Religious Education*. London: Hodder and Stoughton.

Erricker, C. (1998) 'Phenomenological Approaches to the Study of Religion', in P. Connolly (ed.), *Approaches to the Study of Religion*. London: Cassell.

Geertz, C. (1973) *The Interpretation of Cultures*. New York: Basic Books.

Geertz, C. (1983) *Local Knowledge*. New York: Basic Books.

Geertz, C. (1988) *Works and Lives: The Anthropologist as Author*. Cambridge: Polity Press.

Hull, J. (1998) *Utopian Whispers*. Norwich: RMEP.

Jackson, R. (1997) *Religious Education: an interpretive approach*. London: Hodder and Stoughton.

Jacobson, J. (1997) 'Religion and ethnicity: dual and alternative sources of identity among young British Pakistanis', *Ethnic and Racial Studies*, 20, pp. 238–56.

Jung, A. (1987) *Unveiling India: A Woman's Journey*. Harmondsworth: Penguin.

McIntyre, J. (1978) *Multi-culture and Multifaith Societies: Some Examinable Assumptions*, Occasional Paper. Oxford: Farmington Institute for Christian Studies.

Nesbitt, E. (1998) 'British, Asian and Hindu: identity, self-narration and the ethnographic interview', *Journal of Beliefs and Values*, 19(2), pp. 189–200.

Oakeshott, M. (1962) *Rationalism in Politics and other essays*. London: Methuen.

Ota, C. (1998) 'The Place of Religious Education in the Development of Children's Worldviews', unpublished PhD thesis, University of Southampton.

Otto, R. (1959) *The Idea of the Holy*. Harmondsworth: Pelican.

Said, E. (1978) *Orientalism*. London: Routledge and Kegan Paul.

Said, E. (1993) *Culture and Imperialism*. London: Chatto and Windus.

SCAA (1994a) *Model Syllabuses for Religious Education: Model 1: Living Faiths Today*. London: School Curriculum and Assessment Authority.

SCAA (1994b) *Model Syllabuses for Religious Education: Model 2: Questions and Teachings*. London: School Curriculum and Assessment Authority.

SCAA (1994c) *Model Syllabuses for Religious Education: Faith Communities' Working Group Reports*. London: School Curriculum and Assessment Authority.

Schools Council (1971) *Religious Education in Secondary Schools*, Schools Council Working Paper 36. London: Evans/Methuen.

Smart, N. (1968) *Secular Education and the Logic of Religion*. London: Faber and Faber.

Smart, N. (1971) *The Religious Experience of Mankind*. London: Fontana.

Smart, N. (1973) *The Science of Religion and the Sociology of Knowledge*. Princeton, NJ: Princeton University Press.

Smart, N. (1983) *Worldviews—Crosscultural Explorations of Human Beliefs*. New York: Charles Scribner's Sons.

Smart, N. (1989) *The World's Religions*. Cambridge: Cambridge University Press.

Smart, N. (1998) 'Foreword', in P. Connolly (ed.), *Approaches to the Study of Religion*. London: Cassell.

Smith, W. C. (1978) *The Meaning and End of Religion*. London: SPCK.

Waardenburg, J. (1978) *Reflections on the Study of Religion*. The Hague: Mouton.

Watson, B. (1993) *The Effective Teaching of Religious Education*. London: Longman.

3   A critical review of spiritual education

Chadwick, P. (1997) *Shifting Alliances: Church and State in English Education*. London: Cassell.

Coles, R. (1990) *The Spiritual Life of Children*. Glasgow: HarperCollins.

Cooling, T. (1992) 'Christianity in the Primary School', *Resource*, 14(3), pp. 1–3.

Cooling, T. (1993) 'The Use of Christianity in the Primary School Curriculum', *British Journal of Religious Education*, 15(3), pp. 14–22.

Cooling, T. (1994) *Concept Cracking: exploring Christian beliefs in school*. Nottingham: Stapleford House.

DFEE (1989) Circular 3/89. London: HMSO.

DFEE (1994) Circular 1/94. London: HMSO.

Gadamer, H.-G. (1979) *Truth and Method*. London: Sheed and Ward.

Habermas, J. (1991) *The Theory of Communicative Action. Vol. 1: Reason and the Rationalisation of Society*. Cambridge: Polity Press.

Hardy, A. (1966) *The Divine Flame: An Essay Towards a Natural History of Religion*. London: Collins.

Hay, D. (1982) *Exploring Inner Space: Scientists and Religious Experience*. London: Penguin.

Hay, D. (1985) 'Suspicion of the Spiritual: Teaching Religion in a World of Secular Experience', *British Journal of Religious Education*, 7(3), pp. 140–7.

Hay, D. and Nye, R. (1996) 'Investigating Children's Spirituality: The Need for a Fruitful Hypothesis', *International Journal of Children's Spirituality*, 1(1), pp. 6–16.

Hay, D. with Nye, R. (1998) *The Spirit of the Child*. London: HarperCollins.

Henson, H. H. (1939) *The Church of England*. Cambridge: Cambridge University Press.

Hull, J. (1993) *The Place of Christianity in the Curriculum: The Theology of the Department for Education*. Frinton-on-Sea: Hockerill Educational Foundation.

Hull, J. (1998) *Utopian Whispers*. Norwich: RMEP.

Hume, D. (1757) *The Natural History of Religion*, in *Principal Writings on Religion including Dialogues Concerning Natural Religion and The Natural History of Religion*, edited with an introduction by G. C. A. Gaskin (1993), Oxford: Oxford University Press.

Jackson, R. (1997) *Religious Education: an interpretive approach*. London: Hodder and Stoughton.

James, William (1902) *The Varieties of Religious Experience: A Study in Human Nature*. New York: Longman.

Lyotard, J.-F. (1984) *The Postmodern Condition: A Report on Knowledge*. Manchester: Manchester University Press.

MacIntyre, A. (1985) *After Virtue: a study in moral theory*. London: Duckworth.

Ofsted (1994) *Framework for Inspection*. London, DfEE.

Priestley, J. (1996) *Spirituality in the Curriculum*. Frinton-on-Sea: Hockerill Educational Foundation.

Priestley, J. (1997) 'Spirituality, Curriculum and Education', *International Journal of Children's Spirituality*, 2(1), pp. 23–34.

Rahner, K. (1974) *Theological Investigations XI*, trans. David Bourke. London: Darton, Longman and Todd.

Rizzuto, A.-M. (1979) *The Birth of the Living God: A Psychoanalytic Study*. Chicago, Ill.: University of Chicago Press.

Robinson, E. (1983) *The Original Vision*. New York: Seabury Press.

SCAA (1994a) *Model Syllabuses for Religious Education: Model 1: Living Faiths Today*. London: School Curriculum and Assessment Authority.

SCAA (1994b) *Model Syllabuses for Religious Education: Model 2: Questions and Teachings*. London: School Curriculum and Assessment Authority.

SCAA (1994c) *Model Syllabuses for Religious Education: Faith Communities' Working Group Reports*. London: School Curriculum and Assessment Authority.

SCAA (1995) *Spiritual and Moral Development*, Discussion Paper 3. London: School Curriculum and Assessment Authority.

SCAA (1996a) *Education for Adult Life: the spiritual and moral development of young people*, Discussion Paper 6. London: School Curriculum and Assessment Authority.

SCAA (1996b) *Findings of the Consultation on Values in Education and the Community*. London: School Curriculum and Assessment Authority.

Starkings, D. (ed.) (1993) *Religion and the Arts in Education: Dimensions of Spirituality*. Sevenoaks: Hodder and Stoughton.

Tate, N. (1996) Address to the SCAA conference on 'Education for Adult Life: Spiritual and Moral Aspects of the Curriculum', London. January 1996.

Thatcher, A. (1990) 'The Recovery of Christian Education', in L. Francis and A. Thatcher (eds), *Christian Perspectives for Education*. Leominster: Gracewing.

Thatcher, A. (1996) 'Policing the Sublime: a wholly (holy?) ironic approach to the spiritual development of children', in J. Astley and L. J. Francis (eds), *Christian Theology and Religious Education: Connections and Contradictions*. London: SPCK.

Thatcher, A. (1997) 'Theology of education and church schools', in W. K. Kay and L. J. Francis (eds), *Religion in Education: volume 1*. Leominster: Gracewing.

Warnke, G. (1987) *Gadamer: hermeneutics, tradition and reason*. London: Polity Press.

Winnicott, D. W. (1971) *Playing and Reality*. London: Tavistock.

Wright, A. (1997a) 'Embodied Spirituality: the place of culture and tradition in contemporary educational discourse on spirituality', *International Journal of Children's Spirituality*, 1(2), pp. 8–20.

Wright, A. (1997b) 'Hermeneutics and Religious Understanding. Part one: the hermeneutics of modern religious education', *Journal of Beliefs and Values*, 18(2), pp. 203–16.

Wright, A. (1998a) 'Hermeneutics and Religious Understanding. Part two: towards a critical theory for religious education', *Journal of Beliefs and Values*, 19(1), pp. 59–70.

Wright, A. (1998b) *Spiritual Pedagogy: A survey, critique and reconstruction of contemporary spiritual education in England and Wales*. Abingdon: Culham College Institute.

4   Relativism and the spirit of educational enquiry

Benjamin, W. (1970) *Illuminations*. London: Jonathan Cape.

Carroll, D. (1987) 'Narrative, Heterogeneity, and the Question of the Political: Bakhtin and Lyotard', in M. Krieger (ed.), *The Aims of Representation: Subject, Text, History*. New York: Columbia University Press.

Cioran, E. M. (1975) *A Short History of Decay*. Oxford: Basil Blackwell.

Cumming, R. D. (1968) *The Philosophy of Jean-Paul Sartre*. London: Methuen.

Cupitt, D. (1998) *After God*. London: SCM.

Derrida, J. (1977) *Of Grammatology*. Baltimore, MD: Johns Hopkins University Press.

Eisenstein, G. (1989) 'The Privilege of Sharing: Dead ends and the Life of Language', in D. Michelfeder and R. Palmer (eds), *Dialogue and Deconstruction*. Albany, NY: State University of New York Press, pp. 267–83.

Erricker, C. (forthcoming) 'Surviving the Guilotine: Past Hopes, Past Fears, Prospects for the Future; the Aporia of Faith', in D. Tombs (ed.), *Faith in the Millennium*. Sheffield: Sheffield University Press.

Erricker, C., Erricker, J., Ota, C., Sullivan, D., and Fletcher, M. (1997) *The Education of the Whole Child*. London: Cassell.

Foucault, M. (1971) *The Order of Things: An Introduction to the Archaeology of the Human Sciences*. New York: Pantheon.

Gaidenko, P. (1966) 'Existentialism and the Individual', in G. Novak (ed.), *Existentialism Versus Marxism*. New York: Delta, pp. 259–76.

Hazelrigg, L. (1995) *Cultures of Nature*. Tallahasee, Fl: Florida State University Press.

Kermode, F. (1979) 'What Precisely are the Facts?' in *The Genesis of Secrecy: on the interpretation of narrative*. Cambridge, Mass.: Harvard University Press.

Kierkegaard, S. (1962) *Philosophical Fragments*, trans. David F. Swenson. Princeton, NJ: Princeton University Press.

Lyotard, J.-F. (1984) *The Postmodern Condition: A Report on Knowledge*. Manchester: Manchester University Press.

Marx, K. (1973) 'Theses on Feuerbach', in K. Marx and F. Engels, *The German Ideology*. New York: International Publishers.

Newman, F. and Holzman, L. (1997) *The End of Knowing: a new developmental way of learning*. London and New York: Routledge.

Norris, C. (1982) *Deconstruction: Theory and Practice*. New York: Methuen.

Novak, G. (1966) *Existentialism versus Marxism: Conflicting Views on Humanism*. New York: Delta.

Sartre, J.-P. (1948) *Existentialism and Humanism*, trans. P. Mairet. London: Methuen.

Sartre, J.-P. (1957) *Being and Nothingness*, trans. Hazel Barnes. London: Methuen.

Sartre, J.-P. (1964) *The Problem of Method*, trans. Hazel Barnes. London: Methuen.

SCAA (1995) *Spiritual and Moral Development*. Discussion Paper 3. London: School Curriculum and Assessment Authority.

SCAA (1996) *Education for Adult Life: the spiritual and moral development of young people*, Discussion Paper 6. London: School Curriculum and Assessment Authority.

Schwandt, T. (1996) 'Farewell to criteriology', *Qualitative Inquiry*, 1, pp. 1–9.

Shotter, J. (1993a) *Conversational Realities: Constructing Life through Language*. London: Sage.

Shotter, J. (1993b) *Cultural Politics of Everyday Life: Social Constructionism, Rhetoric and Knowing of the Third Kind*. Toronto: Toronto University Press.

Smith, J. (1998) 'Learning to Live with Relativism', in P. Hodkinson (ed.), *The Nature of Educational Research: Realism, Relativism or Post-Modernism*. Crewe: Manchester Metropolitan University, pp. 25–36.

Smith, J. (1999) 'The Problem of Criteria in the Age of Relativism', Paper delivered at the British Educational Research Association Annual Conference, 4 September 1999, University of Sussex, UK.

Swift, A. (1997) *Children for Social Change: education for citizenship of street and working children in Brazil*. Nottingham: Educational Heretics Press.

Tate, N. (1996) Address to the SCAA Conference on 'Education for Adult Life: Spiritual and Moral Aspects of the Curriculum'.

Vygotsky, L. S. (1987) *The Collected Works of L. S. Vygotsky*, vol. 1. New York: Plenum.

White, H. (1985) *The Tropics of Discourse: Essays in Cultural Criticism*. Baltimore, MD: Johns Hopkins University Press.

Wittgenstein, L. (1967) *Philosophical Investigations*. Oxford: Blackwell.

Wright, A. (1997) 'Embodied Spirituality: the place of culture and tradition in contemporary educational discourse on spirituality', *International Journal of Children's Spirituality*, 1(2).

Wright, A. (1998) *Spiritual Pedagogy: A survey, critique and reconstruction of contemporary spiritual education in England and Wales*. Abingdon: Culham College Institute.

5   Moral education as relationship in community

Arendt, H. (1958) *The Human Condition*. Chicago, Ill.: University of Chicago Press.

Baldwin, G. (1996) 'Modern Spirituality, moral education and the history curriculum', in R. Best (ed.), *Education Spirituality and the Whole Child*. London: Cassell.

Benhabib, S. (1992) *Situating the Self*. Cambridge: Polity Press.

Chodorow, N. (1978) *The Reproduction of Mothering*. Berkeley, Los Angeles and London: University of California Press.

Chodorow, N. (1987) 'Feminism and difference: gender, relation, and difference in psychoanalytic perspective', in Mary Walsh (ed.), *The Psychology of Women*. New Haven, CT: Yale University Press.

Cooper, H. (1992) 'Young children's thinking in History', *Teaching History*, October, pp. 8–13.

Duska, R. and Whelan, M. (1977) *Moral Development: a guide to Piaget and Kohlberg*. Dublin: Gill and Macmillan.

Giddens, A. (1999) *The Fourth Reith Lecture: The Family*, BBC Radio 4, April.

Gilligan, C. (1982) *In A Different Voice*. Cambridge, Mass.: Harvard University Press.

Hampshire County Council, Portsmouth City Council, Southampton City Council (1998) *Vision and Insight*. Winchester: Hampshire County Council.

Hekman, S. (1995) *Moral Voices, Moral Selves*. Cambridge: Polity Press.

Hyman, H. H. (1967) 'The Value Systems of Different Classes', in Bendix and Lipset, *Class, Status and Power*. London: RKP.

Kohlberg, L. (1984) *The Psychology of Moral Development: essays on moral development 2*. San Francisco, CA: Harper and Row.

Mitchell, S. (1988) *Relational Concepts in Psychoanalysis: an integration*. Cambridge, Mass.: Harvard University Press.

Oakeshott, M. (1977) *The Rationalism of Politics*. London: Methuen.

Osler, A. (1999) Paper given at the Conference on Citizenship, London Institute of Education.

Piaget, J. (1932) *The Moral Judgement of the Child*. London: Routledge and Kegan Paul.

Poole, R. (1991) *Morality and Modernity*. London: Routledge.

SCAA (1995) *Discussion Paper 3: Spiritual and Moral Development*. London: SCAA.

SCAA (1996) *Discussion Paper 6: Education for Adult Life*. London: SCAA.

6   Narrative constructions towards community

Barnard, H. C. (1961) *A History of English Education from 1760*. London: University of London Press.

Benjamin, W. (1970) *Illuminations*. London: Jonathan Cape.

Benjamin, W. (1979) *One Way Street and Other Writings*. London: NLB.

Carroll, D. (1987) 'Narrative, Heterogeneity, and the Question of the Political: Bakhtin and Lyotard', in M. Kreiger (ed.), *The Aims of Representation: Subject/ Text/History*. New York: Columbia University Press.

Chodorow, N. (1978) *The Reproduction of Mothering*. Berkeley, Los Angeles and London: University of California Press.

Code, L. (1991) *What Can She Know? Feminist theory and the construction of knowledge*. Ithaca, NY: Cornell University Press.

Copley, T. (1997) *Teaching Religion: Fifty years of religious education in England and Wales*. Exeter: University of Exeter Press, p. 113.

Duska, R. and Whelan, M. (1977) *Moral Development: a guide to Piaget and Kohlberg*. London: Gill and Macmillan.

Frazer, I. (1975) *The Fire Runs*. London: SCM.

Freeman, M. (1983) *The Rights and Wrongs of Children*. London: Frances Pinter.

Gilligan, C. (1982) *In A Different Voice*. Cambridge, Mass.: Harvard University Press.

Gilligan, C. (1997) Keynote speech, Association of Moral Education Conference, Atlanta, USA.

Grimmitt, M. (1978) *What Can I Do in RE?*, 2nd edn. Great Wakering, Essex: Mayhew-McCrimmon.

Grimmitt, M. (1987) *Religious Education and Human Development*. Great Wakering, Essex: McCrimmon.

Grimmitt, M. (1994) 'Religious Education and the Ideology of Pluralism', *British Journal of Religious Education*, 16(3), pp. 133–47.

Hekman, S. (1995) *Moral Voices, Moral Selves*. Cambridge: Polity Press.

Hendrick, H. (1990) 'Constructions and Reconstructions of British Childhood: An Interpretative Survey, 1800 to the Present', in A. James and A. Prout (eds), *Constructing and Reconstructing Childhood*. London: Falmer Press.

Higonnet, A. (1998) *Pictures of Innocence: The History and Crisis of Ideal Childhood*. London: Thames and Hudson.

Hudson, L. (1976) *The Cult of the Fact*. London: Jonathan Cape.

Jackson, R. (1997) *Religious Education: an interpretive approach*. London: Hodder and Stoughton.

James, A. and Prout, A. (eds) (1990) *Constructing and Reconstructing Childhood*. London: Falmer Press.

Jordan, J. (1991) 'The meaning of mutuality', in Jordan *et al.* (eds), *Women's Growth in Connection*. New York: Guilford Press, pp. 81–96.

Jung, A. (1987) *Unveiling India*. New Delhi, Penguin.

Lyotard, J. (1984) *The Postmodern Condition: A Report on Knowledge*. Manchester: Manchester University Press.

Mantin, R. (forthcoming) 'Feminist Theology Making a Difference to Religious Education', *Resource*.

Mitchell, S. (1988) *Relational Concepts in Psychoanalysis: an integration*. Cambridge, Mass.: Harvard University Press.

Newman, F. and Holzman, L. (1997) *The End of Knowing: A new developmental way of learning*. London: Routledge.

Oakeshott, M. (1962) *Rationalism in Politics and other essays*. London: Methuen.

Piaget, J. (1932) *The Moral Judgement of the Child*. London: Routledge and Kegan Paul.

QCA (1998) *Education for Citizenship and the teaching of Democracy in Schools*. London: QCA.

Ricoeur, P. (1984) *Time and Narrative Volume 1*. Chicago, Ill.: University of Chicago Press.

Robertson, P. (1976) 'Home as a Nest: Middle Class Childhood in Nineteenth Century Europe', in L. De Mausse (ed.), *The History of Childhood*. London: Souvenir Press.

Sontag, S. (1979) 'Introduction' in W. Benjamin, *One Way Street and Other Writings*. London: NLB.

Steinberg, L. (1996) *The Sexuality of Christ in Renaissance Art and Modern Oblivion*. London: Heinemann.

Tappan, M. (1991) 'Narrative, language and moral experience', *Journal of Moral Education*, 20(3).

Ulmer, G. (1985) *Applied Grammatology*. Baltimore, MD: Johns Hopkins University Press, p. 162

West, M. (1965) *The Ambassador*. London, NEL.

Wren, B. (1977) *Education for Justice*. London: SCM.

Zipes, J. (1997) *Happily Ever After: Fairy Tales, Children and the Culture Industry*. London and New York: Routledge.

7 Principles of pedagogical practice

Allison, D. (1995) *Two or Three Things I Know for Sure*. New York: Plume.

Benjamin, W. (1970) *Illuminations*. London: Jonathan Cape.

Benjamin, W. (1979) *One Way Street and Other Writings*, trans. E. Jephcott and K. Shorter. London: NLB.

Camus, A. (1996) *The First Man*. London: Penguin.

Casals, P. (1969) Conversation with Golda Meir at the performance of his oratorio *El Pesebre* in Israel, BBC.

Denby, (1996) *New Yorker*, 72, p. 51.

Holmes, E. (1911) *What is and What Might Be*. London: Constable.

Holmes, E. (1921) *The Tragedy of Education*. London: Constable.

Hunt, M. (1999) *The Junk Yard*. London and Edinburgh: Mainstream Publishing.

Lang, P. (1996) 'Towards an understanding of affective education in a European context', in P. Lang with Yaacov Katz and Isabel Menezes (eds), *Affective Education, A Comparative View*. London: Cassell.

McGuiness, J. (1998) *Counselling in Schools*. London: Cassell.

Shute, C. (1998) *Edmond Holmes and the Tragedy of Education*. Nottingham: Educational Heretics Press.

8   Concept mapping: a starting point for narration

Novak, J. and Gowin, B. (1984) *Learning How to Learn*. Cambridge: Cambridge University Press.

9   Developing emotional literacy

Erricker, C., Erricker, J., Ota, C., Sullivan, D. and Fletcher, M. (1997) *The Education of the Whole Child*. London: Cassell.

Erricker, C. (1998) 'Spiritual Confusion: a critique of current educational policy in England and Wales', *International Journal of Children's Spirituality*, 3(1), pp. 51–64.

Gardner, H. (1984) *Frames of Mind: the theory of multiple intelligences*. London: Heinemann.

Goleman, Daniel (1996) *Emotional intelligence: why it can matter more than IQ*. London: Bloomsbury.

Goleman, Daniel (1998) *Working With Emotional Intelligence*. London: Bloomsbury.

McGuiness, J. (1998) *Counselling in Schools*. London: Cassell.

Parks, J. (1999) 'Emotional Literacy: Education for Meaning', *The International Journal of Children's Spirituality*, 4, p. 1

Rogers, C. (1942) *Counselling and Psychotherapy*. Boston, Mass.: Houghton Mifflin.

Rogers, C. (1951) *Client Centred Therapy*. London: Constable.

Rogers, C. (1983) *Freedom to Learn for the Eighties*. Columbus, Ohio: Merrill.

Truax, C. B. and Carkhuff, R. R. (1967) *Towards Effective Counselling and Psychotherapy*. Chicago, Ill.: Aldine.

10   Children's stories and responses

Erricker, C. (1998) 'Spiritual Confusion: a critique of current educational policy in England and Wales', *International Journal of Children's Spirituality*, 3(1), pp. 51–64.

11   Reading pictures and telling stories

Benjamin, W. (1970) *Illuminations*. London: Jonathan Cape.

Dyer, G. (1999) *Anglo-English Attitudes*. London: Abacus, pp. 48–51.

Ulmer, G. L. (1985) *Applied Grammatology: Post(e)-Pedagogy from Jacques Derrida to Joseph Beuys*. Baltimore, MD: Johns Hopkins University Press.

White, Hayden (1985) *The Tropics of Discourse: Essays in Cultural Criticism*. Baltimore, MD: Johns Hopkins University Press.

12   Enactive storytelling

Cockett, S. (1997) 'Drama, Myth and Parable: problem solving and problem knowing', *Research in Drama Education*, 2(1), pp. 11–13.

Crossan, J. D. (1975) *The Dark Interval: towards a theology of story*. Nils, Ill.: Argos Communications.

De Mello, A. (1982) *The Song of the Bird*. New York: Random House.

Bibliography

Allison, D. (1995) *Two or Three Things I Know for Sure*. New York: Plume.

Arendt, H. (1958) *The Human Condition*. Chicago, Ill.: University of Chicago Press.

Astley, J. and Francis, L. (1996) *Christian Theology and Religious Education: Connections and Contradictions*. London: SPCK.

Baldwin, G. (1996) 'Modern Spirituality, moral education and the history curriculum', in R. Best (ed.), *Education Spirituality and the Whole Child*. London: Cassell.

Barnard, H. C. (1961) *A History of English Education from 1760*. London: University of London Press.

Barth, F. (1994) 'A Personal View of Present Tasks and Priorities in Cultural and Social Anthropology', in R. Borofsky (ed.), *Assessing Cultural Anthropology*. New York: McGraw Hill.

Bauman, Z. (1998) 'Postmodern Religion', in P. Heelas (ed.), *Religion, Modernity and Postmodernity*. Oxford: Blackwell.

Bauman, Z. (1999) *Culture as Praxis*. London: Sage.

Benhabib, S. (1992) *Situating the Self*. Cambridge: Polity Press.

Benjamin, W. (1970) *Illuminations*. London: Jonathan Cape.

Benjamin, W. (1970) 'The Storyteller', in H. Arendt (ed.), *Illuminations: essays and reflections/Walter Benjamin*. London: Jonathan Cape.

Benjamin, W. (1970) 'Theses on the Philosophy of History', in H. Arendt (ed.), *Illuminations: essays and reflections/Walter Benjamin*. London: Jonathan Cape.

Benjamin, W. (1979) *One Way Street and Other Writings*. London: NLB.

Bess, M. (1988) 'Interview with Michel Foucault', *History of the Present*, Spring, p. 13.

Bowker, J. (1987) *Licensed Insanities: Religions and belief in God in the contemporary world*. London: Darton, Longman and Todd.

Bowker, J. (1996) 'World Religions: The Boundaries of Belief and Unbelief', in B. Gates (ed.), *Freedom and Authority in Religions and Religious Education*. London: Cassell.

Camus, A. (1996) *The First Man*. London: Penguin.

Carrithers, M. (1992) *Why Humans Have Cultures*. Oxford: Oxford University Press.

Carroll, D. (1987) 'Narrative, Heterogeneity, and the Question of the Political: Bakhtin and Lyotard', in M. Krieger (ed.), *The Aims of Representation: Subject, Text, History*. New York: Columbia University Press.

Casals, P. (1969) Conversation with Golda Meir, at the performance of his oratorio *El Pesebre* in Israel, BBC.

Chadwick, P. (1997) *Shifting Alliances: Church and State in English Education*. London: Cassell.

Chodorow, N. (1978) *The Reproduction of Mothering*. Berkeley, Los Angeles and London: University of California Press.

Chodorow, N. (1987) 'Feminism and difference: gender, relation, and difference in psychoanalytic perspective', in Mary Walsh (ed.), *The Psychology of Women*. New Haven, CT: Yale University Press.

Cioran, E. M. (1975) *A Short History of Decay*. Oxford: Basil Blackwell.

Clifford, James (1988) *The Predicament of Culture*. Cambridge, Mass.: Harvard University Press.

Cockett, S. (1997) 'Drama, Myth and Parable: problem solving and problem knowing', *Research in Drama Education*, 2, p. 1.

Code, L. (1991) *What Can She Know? Feminist theory and the construction of knowledge*. Ithaca, NY: Cornell University Press.

Coles, R. (1990) *The Spiritual Life of Children*. London: HarperCollins.

Cooling, T. (1992) 'Christianity in the Primary School', *Resource*, 14(3), pp. 1–3.

Cooling, T. (1993) 'The Use of Christianity in the Primary School Curriculum', *British Journal of Religious Education*, 15(3), pp. 14–22.

Cooling, T. (1994) *Concept Cracking: exploring Christian beliefs in school*. Nottingham: Stapleford House.

Cooper, H. (1992) *Young children's thinking in History, Teaching History*, October.

Copley, T. (1997) *Teaching Religion: Fifty Years of religious education in England and Wales*. Exeter: University of Exeter Press.

Cox, E. (1983) *Problems and Possibilities for Religious Education*. London: Hodder and Stoughton.

Crossan, J.D. (1975) *The Dark Interval: towards a theology of story*. Nils, Ill.: Argos Communications.

Cumming, R. D. (1968) *The Philosophy of Jean-Paul Sartre*. London: Methuen.

Cupitt, D. (1998) *After God*. London: SCM.

De Mello, A. (1982) *The Song of the Bird*. New York: Random House.

Denby, (1996) *New Yorker*, 72, pp. 51.

Derrida, J. (1977) *Of Grammatology*, Baltimore, MD: Johns Hopkins University Press.

DFEE (1989) Circular 3/89. London: HMSO.

DFEE (1994) Circular 1/94. London: HMSO.

Duska, R. and Whelan, M. (1977) *Moral Development: a guide to Piaget and Kohlberg*. Dublin: Gill and Macmillan.

Dyer, G. (1999) *Anglo-English Attitudes*. London: Abacus.

Eisenstein, G. (1989) 'The Privilege of Sharing: Dead ends and the Life of Language', in D. Michelfeder and R. Palmer (eds), *Dialogue and Deconstruction*. Albany, NY: State University of New York Press.

Erricker, C. (1998) 'Spiritual Confusion: a critique of current educational policy in England and Wales', *International Journal of Children's Spirituality*, 3(1), pp. 51–64.

Erricker, C. (1998) 'Phenomenological Approaches to the Study of Religion', in P. Connolly (ed.), *Approaches to the Study of Religion*. London: Cassell.

Erricker, C. (forthcoming) 'Surviving the Guilotine: Past Hopes, Past Fears, Prospects for the Future; the Aporia of Faith', in D. Tombs (ed.), *Faith in the Millennium*. Sheffield: Sheffield University Press.

Erricker, C., Erricker, J., Ota, C., Sullivan, D., and Fletcher, M. (1997) *The Education of the Whole Child*. London: Cassell.

Foucault, M. (1971) *The Order of Things: An Introduction to the Archaeology of the Human Sciences*. New York: Pantheon.

Frazer, I. (1975) *The Fire Runs*. London: SCM.

Freeman, M. (1983) *The Rights and Wrongs of Children*. London: Frances Pinter.

Gadamer, H.-G. (1979) *Truth and Method*. London: Sheed and Ward.

Gaidenko, P. (1966) 'Existentialism and the Individual', in G. Novak (ed.), *Existentialism Versus Marxism*. New York: Delta.

Gardner, Howard (1984) *Frames of mind: the theory of multiple intelligences*. London: Heinemann.

Geertz, C. (1973) *The Interpretation of Cultures*. New York: Basic Books.

Geertz, C. (1983) *Local Knowledge*. New York: Basic Books.

Geertz, C. (1988) *Works and Lives: The Anthropologist as Author*. Cambridge: Polity Press.

Giddens, A. (1999) *The Fourth Reith Lecture: The Family*, BBC Radio 4, April.

Gilligan, C. (1982) *In A Different Voice*. Cambridge Mass.: Harvard University Press.

Goleman, Daniel (1996) *Emotional intelligence: why it can matter more than IQ*. London: Bloomsbury.

Goleman, Daniel (1998) *Working With Emotional Intelligence*. London: Bloomsbury.

Griffiths, J. (1999) 'The Word', *Guardian Saturday Review*, 28 August.

Grimmitt, M. (1978) *What Can I Do in RE?*, 2nd edn. Great Wakering, Essex: Mayhew-McCrimmon.

Grimmitt, M. (1987) *Religious Education and Human Development*. Great Wakering, Essex: McCrimmon.

Grimmitt, M. (1994) 'Religious Education and the Ideology of Pluralism', *British Journal of Religious Education*, 16(3).

Guevara, Che (1969) *Guerrilla Warfare*. Harmondsworth: Penguin.

Gugliemo, C. and Chartier, R. (eds) (1999) *A History of Reading in the West*. Cambridge: Polity Press.

Habermas, J. (1991) *The Theory of Communicative Action. Vol. 1: Reason and the Rationalisation of Society*. Cambridge: Polity Press.

Hampshire County Council, Portsmouth City Council, Southampton City Council (1998) *Vision and Insight*. Winchester: Hampshire County Council.

Hardy, A. (1966) *The Divine Flame: An Essay Towards a Natural History of Religion*. London: Collins.

Hattenstone, S. (1997) 'Kitchen Sink Drama: an Interview with Ken Loach', *Guardian Weekend*, 31 October.

Hay, D. (1982) *Exploring Inner Space: Scientists and Religious Experience*. London: Penguin.

Hay, D. (1985) 'Suspicion of the Spiritual: Teaching Religion in a World of Secular Experience', *British Journal of Religious Education*, 7(3), pp. 140–7.

Hay, D. and Nye, R. (1996) 'Investigating Children's Spirituality: The Need for a Fruitful Hypothesis', *International Journal of Children's Spirituality*, 1(1).

Hay, D. with Nye, R. (1998) *The Spirit of the Child*. London: HarperCollins.

Hazelrigg, L. (1995) *Cultures of Nature*. Tallahassee, Fl.: Florida State University Press.

Hekman, S. (1995) *Moral Voices, Moral Selves*. Cambridge: Polity Press.

Helms, H. (1988) *Gospel Fictions*. Amherst, NY: Prometheus.

Hendrick, H. (1990) 'Constructions and Reconstructions of British Childhood: An Interpretative Survey, 1800 to the Present', in A. James and A. Prout (eds), *Constructing and Reconstructing Childhood*. London: Falmer Press.

Henson, H. H. (1939) *The Church of England*. Cambridge: Cambridge University Press.

Higonnet, A. (1998) *Pictures of Innocence: The History and Crisis of Ideal Childhood*. London: Thames and Hudson.

Hilton, M. (1997) *Potent Fictions*. London: Routledge.

Holmes, E. (1911) *What is and What Might Be*. London: Constable.

Holmes, E. (1921) *The Tragedy of Education*. London: Constable.

Hudson, L. (1976) *The Cult of the Fact*. London: Jonathan Cape.

Hull, J. (1993) *The Place of Christianity in the Curriculum: The Theology of the Department for Education*. Frinton-on-Sea: Hockerill Educational Foundation.

Hull, J. (1998) *Utopian Whispers*. Norwich: RMEP.

Hume, D. (1757) *The Natural History of Religion*, in *Principal Writings on Religion including Dialogues Concerning Natural Religion*, edited with an introduction by G. C. A. Gaskin (1993), Oxford: Oxford University Press.

Hunt, M. (1999) *The Junk Yard*. London and Edinburgh: Mainstream Publishing.

Hyman, H. H. (1967) 'The Value Systems of Different Classes', in Bendix and Lipset, *Class, Status and Power*. London: RKP.

Jackson, R. (1997) *Religious Education: an interpretive approach*. London: Hodder and Stoughton.

Jacobson, J. (1997) 'Religion and ethnicity: dual and alternative sources of identity among young British Pakistanis', *Ethnic and Racial Studies*, 20.

James, A. and Prout, A. (eds) (1990) *Constructing and Reconstructing Childhood*. London: Falmer Press.

James, William (1902) *The Varieties of Religious Experience: A Study in Human Nature*. New York: Longman.

Jung, A. (1987) *Unveiling India: A Woman's Journey*. New Delhi and Harmondsworth: Penguin.

Kermode, F. (1979) 'What Precisely are the Facts?', in *The Genesis of Secrecy: on the interpretation of narrative*. Cambridge, Mass.: Harvard University Press.

Kierkegaard, S. (1962) *Philosophical Fragments*, trans. David F. Swenson. Princeton, NJ: Princeton University Press.

Kohlberg, L. (1984) *The Psychology of Moral Development: essays on moral development 2*. San Francisco: Harper and Row.

Lang, P. (1996) 'Towards an understanding of affective education in a European context', in P. Lang with Yaacov Katz and Isabel Menezes (eds) *Affective Education, A Comparative View*. London: Cassell.

Lyotard, J.-F. (1984) *The Postmodern Condition: A Report on Knowledge*. Manchester: Manchester University Press.

MacIntyre, A. (1985) *After Virtue: a study in moral theory*. London: Duckworth.

MacIntyre, A. (1988) *Whose Justice? Which Rationality*. London: Duckworth.

Mantin, R. (forthcoming) 'Feminist Theology Making a Difference to Religious Education', *Resource*.

Marx, K. (1973) 'Theses on Feuerbach', in K. Marx and F. Engels, *The German Ideology*. New York: International Publishers.

McGuiness, J. (1998) *Counselling in Schools*. London: Cassell.

McIntyre, J. (1978) *Multi-culture and Multifaith Societies: Some Examinable Assumptions*, Occasional Paper, Oxford: Farmington Institute for Christian Studies.

Merleau Ponty, M. (1962) *Phenomenology of Perception*. London: Routledge and Kegan Paul.

Mitchell, S. (1988) *Relational Concepts in Psychoanalysis: an integration*. Cambridge, Mass.: Harvard University Press.

Nesbitt, E. (1998) 'British, Asian and Hindu: identity, self-narration and the ethnographic interview', *Journal of Beliefs and Values*, 19(2).

Newman, F. and Holzman, L. (1997) *The End of Knowing: a new developmental way of learning*. London and New York: Routledge.

Norris, C. (1982) *Deconstruction: Theory and Practice*. New York: Methuen.

Novak, G. (1966) *Existentialism versus Marxism: Conflicting Views on Humanism*. New York: Delta.

Novak, J. and Gowin, B. (1984) *Learning How to Learn*. Cambridge: Cambridge University Press.

Oakeshott, M. (1962) *Rationalism in Politics and other essays*. London: Methuen.

Ofsted (1994) *Framework for Inspection*. London: DfEE.

Osler, A. (1999) Paper given at the Conference on Citizenship, London Institute of Education.

Ota, C. (1998) 'The Place of Religious Education in the Development of Children's Worldviews', unpublished PhD thesis, University of Southampton.

Otto, R. (1959) *The Idea of the Holy*. Harmondsworth: Pelican.

Parks, J. (1999) 'Emotional Literacy: Education for Meaning', *The International Journal of Children's Spirituality*, 4(1).

Piaget, J. (1932) *The Moral Judgement of the Child*. London: Routledge and Kegan Paul.

Poole, R. (1991) *Morality and Modernity*. London: Routledge.

Priestley, J. (1996) *Spirituality in the Curriculum*. Frinton-on-Sea: Hockerill Educational Foundation.

Priestley, J. (1997) 'Spirituality, Curriculum and Education', *International Journal of Children's Spirituality*, 2(1).

Rahner, K. (1974) *Theological Investigations XI*, trans. David Bourke. London: Darton, Longman and Todd.

Randel, H. (1988) *Gospel Fictions*. Amherst, NY: Prometheus.

Ricoeur, P. (1984) *Time and Narrative Volume 1*. Chicago, Ill.: University of Chicago Press.

Rizzuto, A.-M. (1979) *The Birth of the Living God: A Psychoanalytic Study*. Chicago, Ill.: University of Chicago Press.

Robertson, P. (1976) 'Home as a Nest: Middle Class Childhood in Nineteenth Century Europe', in L. De Mausse (ed.), *The History of Childhood*. London: Souvenir Press.

Robinson, E. (1983) *The Original Vision*. New York: Seabury Press.

Rogers, C. (1942) *Counselling and Psychotherapy*. Boston, Mass.: Houghton Mifflin.

Rogers, C. (1951) *Client Centred Therapy*. London: Constable.

Rogers, C. (1983) *Freedom to Learn for the Eighties*. Columbus, Ohio: Merrill.

Said, E. (1978) *Orientalism*. London: Routledge and Kegan Paul.

Said, E. (1993) *Culture and Imperialism*. London: Chatto and Windus.

Sartre, J.-P. (1948) *Existentialism and Humanism*, trans. P. Mairet. London: Methuen.

Sartre J.-P. (1957) *Being and Nothingness*, trans. Hazel Barnes. London: Methuen.

Sartre, J.-P. (1964) *The Problem of Method*, trans. Hazel Barnes. London: Methuen.

SCAA (1994a) *Model Syllabuses for Religious Education: Model 1: Living Faiths Today*. London: School Curriculum and Assessment Authority.

SCAA (1994b) *Model Syllabuses for Religious Education: Model 2: Questions and Teachings*. London: School Curriculum and Assessment Authority.

SCAA (1994c) *Model Syllabuses for Religious Education: Faith Communities' Working Group Reports*. London: School Curriculum and Assessment Authority.

SCAA (1995) *Spiritual and Moral Development*, Discussion Paper 3. London: School Curriculum and Assessment Authority.

SCAA (1996a) *Education for Adult Life: the spiritual and moral development of young people*,

Discussion Paper 6. London: School Curriculum and Assessment Authority.

SCAA (1996b) *Findings of the Consultation on Values in Education and the Community*. London: School Curriculum and Assessment Authority.

SCAA (1997a) 'Work on Values Gets Go Ahead', press release. London: School Curriculum and Assessment Authority.

SCAA (1997b) *Developing the Primary School Curriculum: The Next Steps*. London: School Curriculum and Assessment Authority.

Schools Council (1971) *Religious Education in Secondary Schools*, Schools Council Working Paper 36. London: Evans/Methuen.

Schute, C. (1998) *Edmond Holmes and 'The Tragedy of Education'*. Nottingham: Educational Heretics Press.

Schwandt, T. (1996) 'Farewell to criteriology', *Qualitative Inquiry*, 1.

Shotter, J. (1993a) *Conversational Realities: Constructing Life through Language*. London: Sage.

Shotter, J. (1993b) *Cultural Politics of Everyday Life: Social Constructionism, Rhetoric and Knowing of the Third Kind*. Toronto: Toronto University Press.

Smart, N. (1968) *Secular Education and the Logic of Religion*. London: Faber and Faber.

Smart, N. (1971) *The Religious Experience of Mankind*. London: Fontana.

Smart, N. (1973) *The Science of Religion and the Sociology of Knowledge*. Princeton, NJ: Princeton University Press.

Smart, N. (1982) 'Foreword', in R. Jackson (ed.), *Approaching World Religions*. London: John Murray.

Smart, N. (1983) *Worldviews—Crosscultural Explorations of Human Beliefs*. New York: Charles Scribner's Sons.

Smart, N. (1989) *The World's Religions*. Cambridge: Cambridge University Press.

Smart, N. (1999) 'Foreword', in P. Connolly (ed.), *Approaches to the Study of Religion*. London: Cassell.

Smith, J. (1998) 'Learning to Live with Relativism', in P. Hodkinson (ed.), *The Nature of Educational Research: Realism, Relativism or Post-Modernism*. Crewe: Manchester Metropolitan University.

Smith, J. (1999) 'The Problem of Criteria in the Age of Relativism', Paper delivered at the British Educational Research Association Annual Conference, 4th September 1999, University of Sussex, UK.

Smith, W. C. (1978) *The Meaning and End of Religion*. London: SPCK.

Sontag, S. (1979) 'Introduction', in W. Benjamin, *One Way Street and Other Writings*. London: NLB.

Starkings, D. (ed.) (1993) *Religion and the Arts in Education: Dimensions of Spirituality*. Sevenoaks: Hodder and Stoughton.

Steinberg, L. (1996) *The Sexuality of Christ in Renaissance Art and Modern Oblivion*. London: Heinemann.

Swift, A. (1997) *Children for Social Change: education for citizenship of street and working children in Brazil*. Nottingham: Educational Heretics Press.

Tate, N. (1996) Address to the SCAA conference on 'Education for Adult Life: Spiritual and Moral Aspects of the Curriculum'. London, January 1996.

Thatcher, A. (1990) 'The Recovery of Christian Education' in L. Francis and A. Thatcher (eds), *Christian Perspectives for Education*. Leominster: Gracewing.

Thatcher, A. (1996) 'Policing the Sublime: a wholly (holy?) ironic approach to the spiritual and moral development of children', in J. Astley and L. Francis (eds), *Christian Theology and Religious Education*. London: SPCK.

Thatcher, A. (1997) 'Theology of education and church schools', in W. K. Kay and L. J. Francis (eds), *Religion in Education: volume 1*. Leominster: Gracewing.

Truax, C. B. and Carkhuff, R. R. (1967) *Towards Effective Counselling and Psychotherapy*. Chicago, Ill.: Aldine Publishing.

Ulmer, G. (1985) *Applied Grammatology*. Baltimore, MD: Johns Hopkins University Press.

Vygotsky, L. S. (1987) *The Collected Works of L. S. Vygotsky*, vol. 1. New York: Plenum.

Waardenburg, J. (1978) *Reflections on the Study of Religion*. The Hague: Mouton.

Warnke, G. (1987) *Gadamer: hermeneutics, tradition and reason*. London: Polity Press.

Watson, B. (1993) *The Effective Teaching of Religious Education*. London: Longman.

West, M. (1965) *The Ambassador*. London: NEL.

White, H. (1985) *The Tropics of Discourse: Essays in Cultural Criticism*. Baltimore, MD: Johns Hopkins University Press.

Winnicott, D. W. (1971) *Playing and Reality*. London: Tavistock.

Wittgenstein, L. (1967) *Philosophical Investigations*. Oxford: Blackwell.

Wren, B. (1977) *Education for Justice*. London: SCM.

Wright, A. (1997a) 'Embodied Spirituality: the place of culture and tradition in contemporary educational discourse on spirituality', *International Journal of Children's Spirituality*, 1(2).

Wright, A. (1997b) 'Hermeneutics and Religious Understanding. Part one: the hermeneutics of modern religious education', *Journal of Beliefs and Values*, 18(2).

Wright, A. (1998a) *Spiritual Pedagogy: A survey, critique and reconstruction of contemporary spiritual education in England and Wales*. Abingdon: Culham College Institute.

Wright, A. (1998b) 'Hermeneutics and Religious Understanding. Part two: towards a critical theory for religious education', *Journal of Beliefs and Values*, 19(1).

Wright, A. (1998c) *Spiritual Pedagogy: A survey, critique and reconstruction of contemporary spiritual education in England and Wales*. Abingdon: Culham College Institute.

Zipes, J. (1997) *Happily Ever After: Fairy Tales, Children and the Culture Industry*. London and New York: Routledge.

Index

A History of English Education from 1760
    121
A History of Reading in the West 10
Age of Innocence 118
agreed syllabus for religious education 82,
    83
'Alice Liddell as the Beggar Maid' 118
Allison, D. 8, 9, 139
Anglican Church 16
Antidote 150
Archbishop of Canterbury 42–4
Arendt, H. 102
Asian identity 28

bad faith 76
Baldwin, G. 97, 98
Balint, A. and M. 110
Bardige, B. 81
Barnard, H. C. 4, 121
Barth, K. 32, 65
Barthes, R. 65
Bauman, Z. 21, 26, 27, 32–4, 58, 73
Bell, A. 121
Benhabib, S. 103, 115
Benjamin, W. 66, 128, 129, 135, 173
Berlin Chronicle 128
Bernard, Sir Thomas 121
Bess, M. 34
Bihar 7
Bishop of London 17
Bowker, J. 21, 22, 29, 31, 35
Bowlby, J. 110
Brede Kristensen, W. 20
British culture 124
British Journal of Religious Education 38
Bruegel 1
Buddha 75
Buddhist tradition 75

Camus, A. 139
Capa, R. 175
Carrithers, M. 26
Carroll, D. 66, 108, 109
Carroll, L. 118
Casals, P. 138
Chadwick, P. 36
Chantepie de la Saussaye 20
charity 72
Cherry Ripe 118
Children and Worldviews Project 92–8,
    150, 160
chilman 122
Chodorow, N. 110, 111
Cioran, E.M. 72
Circular 3/89 38
Citizenship 41, 102–6, 159
Cleveland Report on Sexual Abuse 121
Cockett, S. 187
Code, L. 109
Coles, R. 6, 56
collective worship 40, 85
Compte A. 52
concentration camp 81
connaissance 108
Constructing and Reconstructing Childhood
    119
constructing childhood and adulthood
    116–23
convergent thinking 145
Cooling, T. 46
Cooper, H. 97
Copley, T. 16–18, 26, 53
Cox, E. 18
Crick, B. 103, 105, 106
Crossan, J. D. 187
cultural absolutism 124
Culture and Imperialism 24
Culture as Praxis 32

Cumming, R. D. 76
curiosity 84
Curriculum 11–16 (DES) 37

de Mello, A. 184, 185
De Quincy 9
Dearing, R. 53, 85
Denby 139
Department for Education and Science 36, 37
Derrida, J. 59, 60, 66, 130, 179
Derridean undecidables 113
Descartes, R. 111
Desert Fathers 74
development community 72
DFEE 37
dialogic self 113
Dionysian conceptions 118
discursive subject 112
Dodgson, C. 118
Durkheim E. 52
Duska, R. 114
Dyer, G. 175, 176

Education Act 1902 4
Education Act 1944 36
Education for Adult Life 41, 54, 55
Education for Adult Life (SCAA conference) 53
Education Reform Act 1988 2, 4, 17, 23, 26, 37
Eisenstein, G. 59
emotional intelligence 184
emotional literacy 150, 159, 161; the skills of 151, 155–8
Enlightenment, the 1, 37, 82, 160
Erricker *et al.* 150
Erricker, C. 19, 20, 60, 159
Erricker, C. and J. 76
Escher 1
ethnic cleansing 81
Evangelicals 120
existentialism 75
existentialist 76
existentialist humanism 74
existentialist philosophy 70
Exploring Inner Space 51

Factory Act 1802 120
faith and religion 21
Forum on Education for Adult Life 60
Forum on Values in Education and the Community 158

Foucault, M. 34, 68, 71
Frazer, I. 124
Freeman, M. 121
French Revolution 120
Freud, S. 52, 110, 111

Gadamer H.-G. 45, 46, 49, 59
Gaidenko, P. 76
Gardner, H. 150
Geaves, R. 8
Geertz, C. 21, 27, 32
George Villiers 118
Giddens, A. 104
Gilligan, C. 81, 85, 102, 111, 112, 115
Goldman R. 45, 55
Goleman, D. 150
Gowin, B. 141
Griffiths, J. 10
Grimmitt, M. 124–7
Gugliemo, C. and Chartier, R. 10

Habermas J. 45, 49
habits of conduct 102, 108
Hall, Canon J. 36
Hampshire County Council 83
Hardy, A. 51, 52, 56
Hattenstone, S. 3
Hay, D. 37, 51–6, 57, 58, 126
Hazlrigg, L. 60
Heidegger, M. 76
Hekman, S. 110–12
Helms, R. 9
Hendrick, H. 120–1
Henson H. H. 36, 58
hermeneuts 127
heterogeneity 108
Higonnet, A. 117–20
Hilton, Mary 2
Hindu 7, 28
Hinduism 28
Hockerill Lecture 38
Holmes, E. 9, 10
Holy Spirit 48
Holzman, L. 60, 69, 70, 71, 72, 73
Hopi 6
Hudson, L. 126, 127
Hull, J. 31, 34, 38
Hume, D. 52, 110
Hunt, M. 138
Husserl 20

industrial revolution 120
Islam 28

Jackson, R. 18, 19, 20, 23, 25–7, 32–4, 54–5, 57, 58, 76, 124
Jacobson, J. 28
James, W. 51
James, A. 119
Jaspers, K. 76
Jordan, J. 111
Jung, A. 7, 8, 24, 122, 123

Kant 110
Kantian theories 85
Kermode, F. 66, 67
Kierkegaard, S. 64, 65, 67, 70
knowing of the third kind 72
knowledge and method 69–73
Kohlberg L. 55, 85, 102, 103, 111, 114–15
Kohlbergian theories 85, 87, 89

Lancaster, J. 121
Lawrence, P. 44
Lazarus 176, 179
leap of faith 65
learning from religion 124
Learning How to Learn 141
Leonard, G. 17
liberation theology 31
Licensed Insanities 29
Loach, Ken 2, 3
Lord Chancellor, the 105
Loukes H. 45
Luxenburg, R. 72
Lyotard, J.–F. 48, 62, 64, 66, 67, 68, 70, 73, 108, 109, 130, 131

McGuiness, J. 138, 159
MacIntyre, A. 8, 45
McIntyre, J. 26
Madhyamika philosophy 74
Manic Street Preachers 116
Mantin, R. 126
Marx, K. 52, 69, 70, 76, 111
Marxism 22
meditation 186
Meir, Golda. 138
metanarrative 108
Millais, Sir John Everett 117
mimesis 127
mimetics 128, 130
Mirbeau, O. 116
Mitchell, S. 112

Model Syllabuses 24
Model Syllabuses for Religious Education 40
moral absolutes 87
moral ideals 101, 108
More, H. 120
multiple intelligences 150
Muslim 7, 28

narrative and metanarrative 66–9
narrative construction 136
narrative involvment 139
narrative pedagogy 130
narrative pragmatics 66, 69
National Curriculum Council (NCC) 40, 41, 85
National Forum for Values in Education 88
National Society, the 36
Nesbitt, E. 28
Newman, F. 60, 69–73
Nietszche, F. 64, 65, 68
non–epistemological education 73–7
normative morality 77
Novak, J. 76, 141
Nye, R. 51, 54–6

Oakeshott, M. 35, 84, 98–102, 108
Ofsted 4, 37, 38, 39, 101
open–mindedness 84
Orientalism 24
Orthodox Jews 25
Osler, A. 105
Ota, C. 28
Otto, R. 20
Owen, R. 121

parable 186, 187
Parks, J. 150
Pestalozzi, J. H. 121
phenomenology 18–21
Philosophical Fragments 64
Piaget J. 55, 85, 114–15
Piagetian theories 85, 87
Picture of Innocence 117
Plato 110
poetic language 145
poetics 68, 69, 130
Poole, R. 97
Portsmouth City Council 83
predictive assimilation 127
Priestley, J. 36, 37, 54–8

Protestant Evangelicalism 120
Prout, A. 119
PSE 4, 17, 104, 158
PSHE 41

Quakers 31
Qualifications and Curriculum Authority
  (QCA) 26, 37, 40, 82, 103

radical alterity 60
Rahner K. 52
Rape of Europa 118
Raphael 118
Rees–Mogg, Lord 44
relational consciousness 56
religion and culture 26–9
religion and secularity 15
Religious Education in Secondary Schools 21
Rénan, E . 52
Reynolds, Sir Joshua 117, 118
Ricoeur, P. 127, 128
Rizzuto A.–M. 56
Robertson, P. 120
Robinson, E. 56
Rogers, C. 159
Roman Catholics 25
root metaphor 126
Rousseau, J. 39, 120, 121

Said, E. 25, 32
Sartre, J.–P. 70, 74–7
Sathya Sai Baba 28
savoir 108, 130
SCAA 4, 24, 37, 40, 41, 44, 45, 50,
  53–5, 66, 82, 83, 158
*SCAA Discussion Paper 3: Spiritual and
  Moral Development* 85–8
Schools Council Project 21
Schwandt, T. 62
SCMS 83, 92
*Second Duke of Buckingham and Lord
  Francis Villier* 118
Second World War 16
secular indoctrination 16
secularisation 52
secularity 15, 53
self–understanding 84
serial unity 75
seriousness 76
Sharpe, E. 20
Shia 7
Shotter, J. 72, 73
Shute, C. 9, 138

Siddhartha 75
sincerity 76
Sistine Madonna 118
Situating the Self 115
skills of ideological criticism 124
Smart, N. 4, 19, 21–3
Smith, A. 121
Smith, J. 59, 60, 61, 62, 63
Smith, W. C. 19, 21– 5, 32
SMSC 55, 88
Socrates 110
Sontag, S. 128, 129
Southampton City Council 83, 150
Spiritual Pedagogy 45, 46
spiritual essence 125, 127
Starkings D. 50, 51
statement of values, The 90
Steinberg, L. 118
story telling 128
Sufi mysticism 74
Sunday schools 121
Swift, A. 60

Tate, N. 26, 41–5, 50, 53, 54, 59, 60
Teacher Training Authority 41
Temple W. 36
Thatcher, A. 8, 39, 44, 45, 49, 50, 53, 57
The Aims of Representation 66
The Cult of the Fact 126
*The End of Knowing: a new developmental
  way of learning* 69
The History and Crisis of Ideal Childhood
  117
The Holy Bible 116
The Idea of the Holy 20
The Moral Judgement of the Child 114
The Prodigal Son 186, 187
The Rationalism of Politics 98
*The SCAA guidance for schools on their
  promotions of SMSC development* 88–92
The Song of the Bird 184, 185
The Spirit of the Child 51
The Task of the Translator 129
The Temple Bells 184, 185, 187
The Torture Garden 116
Theses on Feuerbach 69
Thody, P. 65
Titian 118
tradition 29
Truax, C. V. and Carkhuff, R. R. 159
Two or Three Things I Know for Sure 8

Ulmer, G. 130, 179
Unveiling India 24, 122

van der Leeuw, G. 20
Van Dyck 118
Varieties of Religious Experience 51
Vision and Insight 83
Vygotsky, L. 69, 71

Waardenberg, J. 20, 21
Warnke, G. 49
Watson, B. 18
Wealth of Nations 121

West, M. 107
Whelan, M. 114
White, H 64, 66, 69, 131, 173
Whitehead, A. N. 54
Winchester College 26
Winnicott, D. W. 56, 110
Wittgenstein, L. 54, 67, 69, 70, 74
Wren, B. 125, 126
Wright, A. 39, 45–51, 53, 54, 57, 59, 76

Zipes, J. 121